Home for Christmas

HOME *for* CHRISTMAS

Stories for Young and Old

Compiled by Miriam LeBlanc
Illustrated by David G. Klein

ORBIS BOOKS

Maryknoll, New York 10545

Founded in 1970, Orbis Books endeavors to publish works that enlighten the mind, nourish the spirit, and challenge the conscience. The publishing arm of the Maryknoll Fathers and Brothers, Orbis seeks to explore the global dimensions of the Christian faith and mission, to invite dialogue with diverse cultures and religious traditions, and to serve the cause of reconciliation and peace. The books published reflect the views of their authors and do not represent the official position of the Maryknoll Society. To learn more about Maryknoll and Orbis Books, please visit our website at www.maryknoll.org.

ORBIS/ISBN 1-57075-558-2

The Library of Congress has catalogued the original edition as follows:

Home for Christmas : stories for young and old / compiled by Miriam LeBlanc ; illustrated by David Klein
     p. cm.
   ISBN 0-89486-924-2
1. Christmas—Literary collections. I. LeBlanc, Miriam.
   PN6071.C6 H585 2002
   808.8'0334—dc21

                                                    2002009677

EVEN THOUGH CHRISTMAS is exploited for profit, even though its meaning is often corrupted, it is still the time of year that we feel the impulse to think of others. It is still the season of anticipation and joy. The brightness and fragrance of a Christmas tree under which gifts are laid – here is light and warmth; here is life and love.

Emmy Arnold

Contents

Brother Robber

Helene Christaller

THE HUT HUNG like a swallow's nest on the southern slope of the Apennines. Built of the same stone as the rock on which it stood, it appeared a part of nature, not a work of man. A small window opening was stopped with straw to keep out the cold wind that blew over the mountains.

The inside looked wretched, even though Brother Angelo was trying to clean and decorate the hermitage for Christmas. His brown habit was tucked up to his knees, and he was sweeping together a big pile of rubbish with a homemade broom – pieces of wood and bark, ashes and brushwood. At last the dirty red of the rough brick floor became visible, and the young Franciscan put the broom in the corner. Satisfied, he looked around the bare, gloomy room. Through the half-open door came the faint light of day, together with a moist, chilly draft.

The monk broke a dry branch into pieces and threw them into the fire burning in a crooked brick stove. He hung a rusty kettle filled with water over the flame, and, shivering, closed the door. The flickering flame of the stove gave a dim light to the room.

"It ought to be warm when the brothers come home, and festive," he murmured. Proudly he examined the rough wooden cross on the wall, which he had decorated with fresh ivy. Two white candles were fastened to the beams of the cross. They were to burn for the Christmas Eve celebration.

The water began to boil, puffing out big clouds of steam. The fire flickered and crackled, showering the monk with sparks as he clumsily threw handfuls of meal into the pot for soup. The small room was warming up, except for the draft from the window, and for the north wind, blowing in through the chimney, filling the hut with smoke.

Brother Angelo sat down on the floor close to the fire, folded his delicate brown fingers across his thin knees, and listened for something outside. His soft, fair hair hung down to his shoulders. The well cut features with the aquiline nose and fine mouth were those of a young Knight of the Cross rather than of a brown-clad penitent monk.

Suddenly the door opened and a small, gaunt man came in, barefoot and carrying a coarse, half-filled sack on his back and a little pitcher of wine in his hand. Brother Angelo started up devotedly and relieved him of his burden.

"Come to the fire and warm yourself, Brother Francis," he said eagerly. "It is cold outside, but the soup is simmering already, and the brothers will be here soon."

The dark-haired man with the emaciated face, in which great eyes shone, looked around the little hut. "You have been quite busy, Brother Angelo. The Holy Child may well visit our hut. Would that our hearts, too, be well prepared!"

"Yes, Brother Francis." The youth's reply sounded slightly embarrassed. The older man raised his eyes in question.

The younger kept silence and bowed his head.

"You were alone this morning?"

"Not the whole time. I had a great fright. Three robbers from the mountains – they are known here, I think – came and asked me for food."

"And you?"

"I sent them away and scolded them well for their bad ways. I told them God would damn them eternally."

"You said that and sent them away?"

"Their hands were red with blood."

"They stretched them out for help and you left them unfilled?"

"They were robbers, Brother Francis."

"They were brothers, Brother Angelo."

"Brothers? The robbers?"

Francis looked at him severely and his great eyes blazed. "Yes, the robbers," he said emphatically.

The young man blushed and did not answer.

"They wander in cold and hunger," Francis continued, "and you make yourself comfortable in the warm house. Oh, Brother Angelo, your heart is not so well prepared for Christmas as this hut is."

Tears sprang to the youth's eyes. "Be not angry with me, my brother; I will make good where I failed!"

A mild light began to glow in the monk's serious face. "If you want to make it good, take this sack of bread and the pitcher of wine, and go out into the mountain to seek the robbers. Take the food to them and ask their forgiveness for your hardness. Then return, so that we may celebrate Christmas together with pure hearts."

"And if they kill me in anger?"

Francis smiled, serene and unworried, and remained silent.

Thereupon the young man bowed his head obediently, threw the sack over his shoulder, and walked out of the house without a word of contradiction.

A thin blanket of snow covered the mountains. Mighty old oaks stood out boldly in dark masses from the dazzling white; here and there stood a gnarled olive tree rooted in the stony soil, still with a few ripe olives on it. Snow covered the branches, and when the wind blew on them, fell to the ground with a soft rustling.

Brother Angelo kept his eyes turned to the ground looking for footprints. There were deer and fox tracks coming from the nearby forest. And there, that was a mule, with a driver who wore heavy wooden sandals. But here – these were naked feet; they went criss-cross in confusion, rather as if several people had walked one behind the other. Blood marked one of the footprints again and again.

The monk followed these footprints. They were leading into the mountains. The sun was no longer high – he must hurry if he wanted to find the robbers before nightfall. A snow flurry had started and whirled a few handfuls of white flakes into his face. Soon gaps were torn in the clouds and the sun smiled through, only to be swallowed up again by gray monsters chased by the strong wind. His brown habit whipped about him and his long fair hair tossed while he patiently battled the gale, his eyes turned to the ground, all the time taking care not to spill the wine in the pitcher.

The landscape was growing wild and desolate. He came across a ruined hut, but it was abandoned. Big boulders with caps of snow were scattered over the mountain slope. In the distant plain a dense sea of fog was swelling, hiding the church towers and pinnacles, the winding river and the houses. Not a sound penetrated to him, no ringing of bells, not a voice could be heard. Silence of death, stones, defiant rocks, ice, snow, howling storm. A flock of crows flew cawing over the wanderer's head toward the plain, disappearing in the billowing gray masses of fog.

The monk stood still. He wiped the sweat from his brow and looked back. How long had he been walking in this wintry silence, in dull obedience, toward an adventurous goal? Just in this way had he left wealth and family upon a word of the friar who was now sending him to the robbers. His face lit up as he thought of Brother Francis. "No, not dully and lifelessly like a corpse," he cried aloud. "I go in joyful obedience on the way you send me, Brother Francis!"

With new zeal he climbed over the rocks. Here on the summit the wind had blown away the snow and blotted out the footprints. The fog was creeping up on him from the valley, dampening his hair and the hem of his robe so that it flapped heavily against his legs.

"You robbers, where are you?" he cried aloud in his perplexity. But only the echo answered and another flock of crows flew hurrying over him. Dark caves and clefts yawned in the rocks here, not a tree gave life to the wilderness, no water rushed over the stones. Everything was white and gray, the last blue patch had vanished from the sky, and the sun was hanging, pale as the disc of the moon, behind dark veils.

Suddenly a black, disheveled head appeared behind a rock, staring at the approaching friar with sinister, burning eyes. The young man's step faltered. Horror gripped his heart. He turned pale.

"Ho there," the robber shouted, rising to his feet in anger. Slowly another figure rose and threatened the frightened monk with his hairy fist. Then a third man came into view; he was standing over a small, smoldering fire, plucking a crow in order to roast it.

"It seems you want to share our Christmas treat, pious brother?" he mocked. "I can't promise you more than a leg."

"What do you want, monk?" the first one bellowed at him, making Brother Angelo tremble. "To give us a penitential sermon as you did this morning? It's hard preaching to empty stomachs. Look out!"

"No," said Brother Angelo humbly, stepping close. He laid down the sack of bread and placed the pitcher of wine carefully on a ledge. Then he knelt in the snow and said pleadingly, "Dear robbers, forgive me for sending you away from the threshold today with such hard words. I have come now to bring you some bread and wine and to ask your forgiveness for my sin." He remained on his knees with head bowed. The wild men looked at the delicate, aristocratic figure, the youthful, sensitive face. The oldest of them turned pale, bit his lip, and stubbornly turned away. As for the second, the hot blood rose to the black tufts of hair above his brow. He covered his eyes with his hands like an ashamed child. But the third, the youngest, laughed a little, embarrassed, and said, "We'll gladly forgive you, because you are a good man. We felt very hungry today…"

"Why don't you get up?" asked the pale one.

"Stay and eat with us," said the other.

Brother Angelo stood up and shook the snow from his habit. "I cannot stay and eat with you," he said timorously. "Brother Francis expects me for Midnight Mass down at the monastery. And I must hurry, for it will soon be night. But perhaps you can visit us in the monastery some time when you are in need of something."

"And Brother Francis? Will he not scold us?"

The face of the young man lit up. "He calls you brothers."

"Brothers!" said all three as with one voice, and then kept an uneasy silence.

"Farewell, brother robbers," said Brother Angelo, extending his delicate fingers to take their rough, stained ones. "Good-bye." Without answering a word, the three wild men stared after the youth as he disappeared rapidly from their sight. Nor did any one of them reach for the wine or bread, and each avoided the glance of his companions. Now the fog had swallowed up the figure of the young man and the desolate countryside lay silent and white. Then clear notes could be heard in the distance, sounding now like the deep ringing of bells, now like the chanting of a priest at the altar, and then again like the jubilant song of a skylark. And so the old Christmas carol was carried up to the three lost men: "Adeste fideles, laeti triumphantes, Venite, venite ad Bethlehem."

There is a legend that at a later time the three robbers came down and joined the Brotherhood of Franciscans and led a blessed life until their peaceful end.

Three Young Kings

George Sumner Albee

THE TOWN OF CÁRDENAS, a hundred miles to the east of Havana on the north coast of Cuba, is an old dog – a small, taffy-colored dog that is learning new tricks. Three times a week, nowadays, a ferry from Key West brings Cárdenas a boatload of American tourists, and these Americans, all of whom have such white faces that they appear to have been sick, seem strange and wondrous to the people of the town. Small boys follow them on the sidewalks and, when they speak, race around in front in order to watch their lips form the mysterious, incomprehensible foreign words.

As for the small girls, they clap their hands over their mouths and giggle, for the American women often wear hats, and, as everybody knows, a hat is a garment worn solely by men. But the little girls' mothers shriek at them and snatch them indoors, for the Americans are bringing money into Cárdenas and so they must be treated with the courtesy money deserves.

But this is the story of something that took place in

Cárdenas in the days before there were tourists or a ferry. At that time the young men sat all day on the iron rocking chairs in the park under the royal palms, talking excitedly about the day when they would go to work and make vast fortunes and buy fast automobiles. The shopkeepers opened at ten in the morning, strolled home at noon for heavy dinners of rice and black beans, took two-hour siestas and returned to their stores to play dominoes until suppertime, setting their prices sky-high so that would-be customers would not interrupt them. The women mopped their white tile floors, cooked, gossiped and, at dusk, locked themselves into the houses behind their heavy hardwood doors. And the children, when they had fathers who could pay the tuition, went to school. The boys, in white shirts and neckties of the soft blue that is the Virgin's own color, attended the Escuela Pia. The girls, in blue pinafores with white stripes around the hems of the skirts, went to the Escuela de las Madres Escolapias.

Which brings us to three boys of the Escuela Pia: Eduardo, Ramoncito, and Lazaro.

Eduardo was sixteen, while Ramoncito and Lazaro were a few months younger. They were the oldest boys at the *colegio,* and the biggest. In fact, Eduardo amounted to a giant in Cuba, where the horses are the size of large dogs and the dogs are not much larger than rabbits; his nickname was Elephant. He had a flat, snub-nosed face and a cubical skull on which his hair looked like a coat of glossy black lacquer because he soaked it daily in scented brilliantine. Ramoncito was finely made, with a headful of tight little curls and eyelashes half an inch long over eyes the color of clear green sea water. Lazaro was the shortest of the three, but that did not keep him from being the heaviest. He was so fat that he exploded his clothes two and three times a day, popping shirt buttons and the seams of his knickerbockers or the buckles that fastened them at his plump knock-knees. Lazaro ate three huge meals a day, treated himself to custard éclairs on the way to school and fresh coconut macaroons on the way home, and devoted the recess periods to eating candy. Ramoncito's nickname was Monkey. Lazaro's was Macaroon.

The fact that they happened to be the three oldest students laid quite a few responsibilities on Eduardo, Ramoncito, and Lazaro. When the school's forty-seven boys scrambled into the bus for the annual picnic at St. Michael of the Baths it was Eduardo, Ramoncito, and Lazaro who served as monitors – umpiring ball games, arbitrating quarrels, seeing to it that appearances and decorum were maintained in general. And at Christmas time, because they were the oldest, it was their duty to play the parts of the Three Kings of Orient.

Jesus' birthday in Cuba is a day to go to church, not a day for gifts. Gifts are distributed later, on the sixth of January, not by Santa Claus but by the Three Kings who carried gifts to the newborn Christ-child in the manger at Bethlehem. On the second of January, therefore, Father Miguel called Eduardo, Ramoncito, and Lazaro into his office.

"Seat yourselves," he directed them.

Father Miguel, who was eighty-two, was so frail that his white linen cassock appeared more often than not to be unoccupied. There was very little of him still in residence on earth. He had a small, poetically modeled head and a voice, and that was about all. His voice, after all the years away from home, still had the lisp of his native Asturian mountains, and it too was fragile – a faint, musical buzz,

like that made by a small but energetic fly in the schoolroom on a hot afternoon.

"Children," he said, for he was so aged that he could no
longer perceive the difference between sixteen and six. "I
have done this many times, but it is new to you, so I must
explain the procedure of the Three Kings. All the gifts
your schoolmates will receive from their families and
friends are upstairs in the janitor's room. The gifts for the
girls are here as well; Mother Superior brought them over
to me from Madres Escolapias. I want you here two hours
before dusk on Day Five to load the mules, saddle the
horses, and disguise yourselves in your robes and turbans.
The robes will fit; they always do. Do you ride well?"

"Yes, Father," murmured the boys. All Cuban boys ride
well, using neither saddle nor bridle but only a length of
rope looped at one end around the horse's muzzle.

"*Bueno;* you will be handsomely mounted. Don Alfredo
de la Torre is sending me three cream-colored mares from
his farm, with silver-mounted Mexican saddles and packsaddles for the mules. You will set out at dusk. It will take
you three hours or so to deliver the presents; then you will
return here and hand back the animals to Don Alfredo's
foreman and hang away your robes. Understood?"

"Understood, Father," replied Eduardo when neither
Ramoncito nor Lazaro spoke. He did not ask for leadership.
It annoyed him, actually. But it was always thrust on him.

"Now go along to your homes," concluded the old
priest, "and do not reveal to anyone that you are the Three
Kings. We would not wish to sadden the hearts of any of
the little ones."

During the next couple of days, as they discussed the
roles they were to play, Ramoncito grew somewhat bitter

about the "little ones." "What do we care if they find out the Kings aren't real?" he exclaimed resentfully. "We found out."

"That's no way to talk," replied Eduardo brusquely in his deep voice. "Before we knew the Kings did not exist, we thought they were marvels. We nearly went out of our heads waiting for them to come to our houses and bang the knockers. True?"

Fat little Lazaro offered no opinion one way or the other. Instead, he made a street map and planned the route they would take, so that they would be able to visit the houses on their list with the least possible amount of back-tracking. Lazaro was efficient. Either that or he was lazy. Or it may be that efficiency and laziness are merely different names for the same thing.

WITH THE SCHOOL empty for the holidays, the playground seemed strange to the boys when they met there late on the afternoon of the fifth, a lonely square of red, grainy earth over which dry leaves skated. Land crabs had dug comfortable homes for themselves in the basketball court.

They loaded the four pack mules one at a time, with Eduardo carrying out the heavier toys – the tricycles and the miniature automobiles – because he was the strongest, Lazaro arranging the boxes and parcels in accordance with his map, and Ramoncito, who was a passionate fisherman and good at tying knots, filling the large burlap sacks that would serve as their saddlebags and lashing them to the mahogany packsaddles. The mules, more intelligent than the horses, understood at once that they were being invited to join in some kind of game. They behaved well, neither balking nor biting. With the mules loaded, the boys saddled the three small, beautiful mares, who would have looked to an American as if they had pranced right off a merry-go-round. Then the boys put on their costumes.

The school had had the costumes for so many years that nobody remembered any longer who had made them originally – somebody's mother, probably. Whoever she was, she had used the same rich materials she would have used in embroidering an altar cloth for the church. Eduardo's robe was of turquoise satin belted with a gold cord, and on his head he wore a multicolored turban. Lazaro's robe was of heavy silver brocade, and his turban was of purple velvet. Ramoncito wore a mandarinlike coat of blue silk, ornately embroidered, and a wine-colored turban. They wore their ordinary shoes, because the belled Mexican stirrups would hide them when they were on horseback and the long robes would cover them when they got down to enter the houses. Last of all, they attached their long white beards with liquid adhesive, and, using an eyebrow pencil, drew the wrinkles of old age on their brown young faces.

Then, the horses ready, the mules waiting eagerly in single file on their lead ropes, the boys watched the sun go down behind the palm groves to the west. It sank, a giant illuminated peach sending up a spray of golden searchlights through the massed clouds. After it was below the horizon, the sky was filled with dazzling lime-green light, and then, with no interval, it was dusk. It had been a fruit punch of a sunset, complete with maraschino cherries and lemon sherbet, but the boys had seen it every night of their lives, and they supposed that the sun behaved as extravagantly in all countries. To them it was merely a signal that the time had come for them to start.

"Mount," ordered Eduardo, and they swung themselves into the high-backed, embossed saddles. The lead mule brayed gaily in a spirit of adventure. Off they trotted.

"The top end of Princess Street," directed Lazaro. "The Montoros live there at Number 17."

"I believe thee," replied Ramoncito, whose secret intention it was one day to marry the middle Montoro girl, Gladys.

The houses of Cárdenas, like the houses in most Latin cities, are invisible. That is, you see nothing of them from the street except the front wall, which joins the front walls of the residences on either side and is plastered over with the same golden stucco. Inside the wall, from front to back, each house is divided into two long, narrow strips, side by side. One of these strips, which has no roof over it, is a tiled garden with a fountain, stone flower boxes, lime and mango and papaya trees, and an array of outdoor furniture. Here the family lives three hundred days in the year. The long strip on the other side, roofed over with faded vermilion tiles, contains the formal living room with its crystal chandelier and cumbersome mahogany furniture; the bedrooms, each of which has its own door opening into the garden; the dining room, with another chandelier and a big electric refrigerator from the United States standing in a corner; and the kitchen, where the food is cooked over square, cast-iron baskets of fragrant, glowing charcoal. Behind the kitchen live the servants and all their relatives who are able to think up convincing hard-luck stories.

But there is something about the houses of Cárdenas that is stranger still, and this is that the richest man in the block may live next door to the poorest. There are poor neighborhoods and rich neighborhoods, but often a banker lives in the poor one and a shrimp peddler in the rich one. For this reason, as the boys dismounted at the Montoro house they could not help seeing the nine barefoot children of Emilio, the shoemaker, dressed in ragged shirts and nothing else, who stared at them hopefully as they took down the saddlebag containing the Montoro youngsters' gifts. Eduardo, whose voice was already so much deeper than many a man's, thudded on the door with the brass knocker and bellowed, "Do the good young ones of the Señores Montoro live here?"

Señor Montoro swung open the tall door, elegant in his starched white jacket of pleated linen. "Yes, sir, we have good young ones in this house," he replied. "May I ask who you are, gentlemen?"

"We are the Three Kings of Orient," boomed Eduardo.

"Enter, then. This is thy house."

The Montoro children, jabbering with excitement, accepted the presents that had their names on them as Eduardo and Ramoncito took them from the opened burlap sack. Hasty good-bys were said, the Kings explaining that they had a great distance to travel before morning, and they mounted and rode on.

"The shoemaker's kids are all crying," said Lazaro over the clip-clop of the hoofs. "I can hear them. They thought we'd leave something for them when we came out of the Montoros'."

"Maybe Jaime Montoro will give them his express wagon after he smashes it," said Ramoncito. "I'll bet there won't be a wheel left by noon tomorrow."

At the Cabrera house on Shell Street they delivered a fifty-dollar French doll to Myriam Cabrera, along with a dozen other packages. Mounting again, they turned into Anglona Street. By now it was dark, the only light on the street falling from unshaded bulbs at the intersections. They were conscious as they rode along, of people, grownups as well as children, watching them from the sidewalks. Everybody was out for an evening stroll in the cool bay breeze. Now and again somebody called out, "Look, the Three Kings!" and each time the voice was thrilled and reverent. There was mystery in the night. The mules felt it, pricking up their ears, and the horses, catching the murmurs of admiration, tossed their manes and lifted their forefeet higher than they really needed to, showing off. A group of men around the white pushcart of a *tamalero* cheered and waved. One of them, a farmer in high-laced boots with his sugar-cane knife at his belt, ran into the street and tried to feed his tamale to Eduardo's horse.

On Saint John of God Street the horses shied at the peanut seller who was chanting, "Peanuts, a little hot, peanuts, a little hot," and again there were watchers in the darkness under the rustling palms. Distinctly the boys heard a little girl ask in a trembling voice, "Mamma, will they come to us?" And they heard the mother's patient, desperate answer: "Who knows, soul of my soul? But if they do not come tonight, you must be valiant, for surely they will come next year."

On the lead mare, Eduardo, who knew a number of words which did not meet with Father Miguel's approval, muttered a particularly bad one.

"Now she's crying," exclaimed Lazaro, "because we've passed her house."

"If you think this is bad," said Ramoncito, "wait till we

get down by the market. My brother Pepe told me when he was a King he rode through four blocks of bawling beggar kids there."

"The poor are always with us," replied Eduardo gruffly. "Jesus says so in the Bible."

"He means they are always with us to remind us to do something about them, Elephant," said Lazaro. "That's what he means."

"What do you want?" Eduardo shouted back. "Am I to blame because there are families that can't earn a living? The cane crop is poor this year."

Eduardo's anger was something to be quenched promptly, it was well known. "No, Elephant, dear, you are not to blame," said Ramoncito. "We don't say you are."

"Then shut up, the two of you!"

"I just think," said Lazaro in the clear, sweet voice that permitted him, at fifteen, still to sing in the choir, "it's a shame to take gifts to rich kids like us when it's the poor kids that need them."

"Me too. My father is giving me a bicycle," added Ramoncito. "What do I want with a domino set and a silly card game that's supposed to teach me how to spell?"

"Father Miguel told us what to do," said Eduardo grimly, "and we're going to do it."

But not a hundred yards farther on a small boy of seven or eight, in a shirt made of second-hand cheesecloth washed white for the holiday, ran hysterically into the street crying: "Oh, Kings, Kings! We live here, señores, at Number 22!"

Eduardo reined in so sharply that he hurt his mare's dainty mouth. Leaning down from his saddle, he bellowed in a voice that frightened the boy nearly out of his senses. "What's your name? Is there light in your house, so we can see? Then take us there. Monkey, gallop back and get that girl that was howling!"

In the one-room house at Number 22, where an entire family slept on the clay floor and the only light was that from the candle blinking in its ruby cup at the feet of the Virgin, they handed out half a dozen packages, Eduardo glowering, Ramoncito scared but resolute, and Lazaro struggling to control the giggle that always assailed him at the wrong moment. The gratitude of the little boy and girl embarrassed them so terribly that they got away quickly, shutting the rickety door behind them with a slam. They gathered around the horses.

"Well, anyhow," said Eduardo, "those two won't bawl all night. But now what? You know we ought to obey the father."

"*Tú eres jefe,*" answered Ramoncito with a shrug. "You're the boss."

"I'm not the boss," roared Eduardo. "You always make me the boss, and then I get into trouble. Do you realize the scandal it will be if we go down to the market and give all this stuff to the beggar kids?"

"Clearly it will be a scandal," responded Ramoncito. "It has never been done."

"We're wearing eleven-yard shirts now," protested Eduardo, as we might say, "We're in hot water now." He turned to Lazaro. "What do you say, Macaroon?"

When a person of Spanish blood does not know what other answer to give, he answers with a proverb. "That which does not kill us," quoted Lazaro, "will make us fat." The saying did not fit the situation especially well, but it conveyed his meaning.

"All right," said Eduardo, "but you're both in this with me. Don't you forget it, either!"

"For an elephant," said Ramoncito, "you do a lot of talking."

Dramatically Lazaro crumpled his map and flung it into the gutter. They turned the horses' heads and trotted toward the market. In the street approaching it, Colonel Hangman Street, with its reek of fish heads and rotten cabbage, they drew rein. Somebody had smashed the street light with a cabbage or a pebble from a slingshot, but there was light enough from the stars to see by; the stars hung just over the rooftops like green and red Christmas tree ornaments lowered from heaven on wires. Eduardo stood erect in his stirrups. "Hear me," he shouted. "Is this the town of Cárdenas, in Cuba?" That was a fine imaginative touch. "Are there good young ones on this street who have behaved well this year? If there are, come you all to the market!"

The market, a maze of heavy stone archways, was brilliantly lighted. Curious, laughing butchers and vegetable sellers at once gathered around the Three Kings as they entered, dragging their bulky saddlebags. Even as the crowd formed a ring, dirty, barefoot children with uncombed hair and noses that badly needed wiping were pushing and wriggling and, where it was necessary, kicking their way to its center. Recklessly Eduardo, Ramoncito, and Lazaro tore away tissue paper and ribbons, so that they could see what the gifts were, and passed them out. Arguments broke out in the crowd, but not among the children. They snatched their dolls and painting sets, their toy fire engines and scooters, and raced away shrieking, carrying the greatest news of their lives to brothers, sisters, and deserving friends.

In twenty minutes the saddlebags were empty. Not an all-day sucker was left. Even Ramoncito's white beard was gone, for it had fallen to the concrete floor and a youngster had snatched it in the belief that it was a toy. Streaming perspiration, and as hoarse as crows, the three boys thrust their way through the chattering, mystified, admiring crowd that jammed the sidewalk for a block, mounted and trotted back to the school under the late moon. The moon could not manage anything quite as spectacular as the sun, but it was doing its best. It turned the massed clouds over the sea into great clusters of white camellias, wrapping each cluster in shining aluminum foil.

SCIENTISTS SAY nothing travels more swiftly than light. This is not true; in a small town good news, bad news, any kind of news at all, travels faster. By the time the boys had hung up their costumes and turned over the animals to Don Alfredo's foreman, furious, gesticulating parents were already haranguing the boys' fathers. And by morning the anger had solidified into a demand that all three of them be expelled at once from school. The movement was headed by Triunfo Anilina, who had made a large fortune out of a small drugstore by selling medicines for much more than they were worth to people too sick to argue over price.

The druggist, sending around notes to everybody's house by messenger, demanded that all parents of boys attending the *colegio* meet there and put the matter to a vote at four o'clock.

At four that afternoon the outraged parents were at the school – not two hours late, nor even one hour late, as was the custom, but on the dot. Plump fathers with cigars, plump mothers with small, exquisite feet in high-heeled, patent leather shoes, they followed Triunfo Anilina into the large, cool room in which arithmetic was taught. There they squeezed themselves into the seats behind the students' small desks while the burly druggist arrogantly preempted the mathematics teacher's desk on the dais. As for the boys themselves, without anybody's ordering them to do so, Eduardo, Ramoncito, and Lazaro ranged themselves before the blackboard, standing with their backs to it. In their own minds they were guilty, convicted and ready for the firing squad.

"We are here," stated Triunfo Anilina curtly. "Let us begin."

He presented a detailed account of the crime that had been committed, using a number of large and impressive words he had picked up from his brother, a lawyer. It took him half an hour.

After this the fathers of the culprits spoke for the defense, Eduardo's father offering to repay the cost of all the gifts, Ramoncito's father pleading that boys would be boys, and Lazaro's father volunteering to pitch Triunfo and all the other male members of the Anilina family, to whom he referred as cockroaches, through the window.

But Triunfo Anilina shouted down the defense, pounding the desk with his hairy fist and upsetting the inkwell.

"The thieves must be punished!" he cried.

"Then the truth of the matter," said Eduardo's handsome father, getting once more to his feet, "is that nothing will satisfy you – not honorable apology, not repayment, nothing. What you want is revenge."

"Yes, revenge!" gasped Triunfo Anilina, his linen jacket dark with perspiration. "What a scandal! It is the first time in the history of our *colegio* that this thing has happened!"

"Ah, Anilina," came a faint, musical buzz of a voice from the rear of the room, "you have a point there."

Every head turned as Father Miguel, pausing several times to gather strength along the way, came up the aisle in his long, tallow-colored gown. All the mothers and fathers had forgotten him.

Triunfo Anilina scrambled clumsily to his feet: "Take my seat, Father," he said.

"It is not your seat," replied Father Miguel. Standing on the dais, steadying himself with one small, dry hand on the edge of the desk, his bald skull reflecting the white light from the windows, he faced the parents. "Dear friends," he whispered, "it is so. For fifty years I have sent into the town, on the eve of Three Kings' Day, the three oldest boys of the school. And always they have distributed the gifts as I bade them, because they were good boys. Not until last night have they ever disobeyed me."

Behind the desk Triunfo Anilina jerked his head sharply in agreement.

"But these three boys are good boys also, since all boys are good boys," continued Father Miguel, "so, in fairness to them, we must examine their misdeed very closely. Exactly what, we must ask ourselves, did they do? They took rich gifts, provided by the bounty of our beloved island, and carried them to babes who sleep on straw pallets, if they are lucky enough to find any straw in the streets around the market. Does the straw remind you of anything, señores and señoras? It reminds me of another Babe, swaddled in coarse cloth, who slept on straw in a manger because there was no room for him in an inn. And with this in mind it becomes clear beyond doubt that these are not good boys. No, they are something more than ordinary good boys. In the generosity of their hearts, the sweetness of their spirit, the courage of their will they are, indeed, Three Young Kings."

At the blackboard, arms stiff at his sides, Eduardo spoke out of the corner of his mouth to fat little Lazaro. "Giggle one time," he said, "and I advise thee that it will be thy last giggle."

In the schoolroom there was silence. Then Ramoncito's mother began to cry and Lazaro's father burst into boisterous laughter.

Father Miguel raised a hand.

"Now," he said, "if you will kindly help me to my house next door, a delegation from the neighborhood of the market is waiting. They wish to thank you for your sympathy and kindliness, which have so deeply touched them. They wish also to know the identities of the Three Noble Kings, in order that they may kiss their hands."

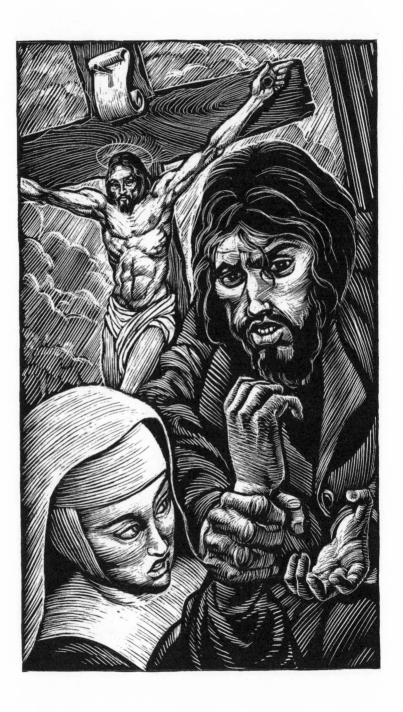

Transfiguration

Madeleine L'Engle

SISTER EGG LEFT the convent with the shopping cart. Over her simple habit she wore a heavy, hooded woolen cape. Even so, she shivered as the convent door shut behind her and she headed into the northeast wind. There was a smell of snow in the air, and while it would be pleasant to have a white Christmas, she dreaded the inevitable filthy drifts and slush that would follow a city snow. She dreaded putting on galoshes. But she would enjoy doing her share of shoveling the snow off the sidewalk.

The twenty-five pound turkey was waiting in the pantry, but she needed to get cranberries and oranges for relish, and maybe even some olives to go with the celery sticks. There's only one Christmas a year, and it needs to be enjoyed and celebrated. She pulled her cape more closely about her. In her mind she started counting the weeks till August. The first two weeks of August were her rest time, when she went to her brother's seaside cottage and swam in the ocean, and for her that time was always transfigured and gave her strength to come back to the Upper West Side of New York City.

"Hi, Sister Egg!" It was the small child of the Taiwanese shopkeeper from whom she always bought garlic because he had the best garlic in the city. The child rushed at her and leaped into her arms, pushing the empty market cart aside. Sister Egg caught the little boy, barely managing not to fall over backward, and gave him a big hug. "Whatcha doing?" the little boy asked.

"Christmas shopping."

"Presents?"

"No. Food. Goodies." And she reached into her pocket and drew out some of the rather crumbly cookies she kept there for emergencies such as this. The little boy stuffed the cookie into his mouth, thereby rendering himself speechless, and Sister Egg walked on. The vegetable stand she was heading toward was across Broadway, so she turned at the corner and crossed the first half of the street; then the light turned red, so she stopped at the island. In Sister Egg's neighborhood islands ran down the center of Broadway, islands that were radiant with magnolia blossoms in the spring, followed by tulips, and delicately leafing trees. By August the green was dull and drooping from the heat. In December all the branches were bare and bleak.

She stood on the island, waiting for the light to change. She, too, felt bare and bleak. She felt in need of hope, but of hope for what she was not sure. She had long since come to terms with the fact that faith is not a steady, ever-flowing stream but that it runs over rock beds, is sometimes dry, sometimes overflows to the point of drowning. Right now it was dry, dryer than the cold wind that promised snow.

"Hi, Sister Egg." She turned to see a bundle of clothes on one of the benches reveal itself to be an old woman with her small brown dog on her lap, only the dog's head showing, so wrapped were woman and dog in an old brown blanket.

"Hello, Mrs. Brown." Sister Egg tried to smile. It was Christmas Eve, and no one should spend it wrapped in an inadequate blanket, sitting on a bare island on upper Broadway. But she had learned long ago that she could not bring every waif and stray she saw out in the streets back to the convent. It was not that anybody thought it was a bad idea; it was just that the Sisters were not equipped to handle what would likely be hundreds of people hungry in body and spirit. They had taken pains to learn of every available shelter and hostel, and the hours of all the soup kitchens.

Sister Egg had tried to get this particular old woman into a home for the elderly with no success. Mrs. Brown had her share of a room in a Single Room Occupancy building. She had her dog and her independence and she was going to keep both.

From the opposite bench came a male voice, and another bundle of clothes revealed itself to be a man whose age was anybody's guess. "Sister *what?*"

"Oh – " Sister Egg looked at him, flustered.

"Sister Egg," the old woman announced triumphantly.

"Sister Egg! Whoever heard of a Sister named Egg? What are you, some kind of nut?" The scowl took over the man's body in the ancient threadbare coat as well as his face, which was partly concealed by a dark woolen cap.

Sister Egg's cheeks were pink. "My real name is Sister Frideswide. People found it hard to pronounce, so I used to say that it was pronounced 'fried,' as in fried egg. So people got to using Egg as a nickname."

"What idiot kind of a name is Frideswide?" The man's scowl seemed to take up the entire bench.

"She was an abbess in Oxford, in England, in the eighth century."

"What's an abbess?" The man sounded as though he would leap up and bite her if her answer didn't satisfy him.

"She's – she's someone who runs – runs a religious order," Sister Egg stammered.

"So what else about her?"

Did he really want to know? And how many times had the light already turned to green? And she was cold. "She was a princess, at least that's what I was told, and she ran away rather than be coerced into a marriage she didn't want."

"So she married God instead?"

"Well. Yes, I guess you could put it that way." What an odd man.

"And Merry Christmas to you," he said.

She looked up just as the light changed from green to yellow to red. Wishing him Merry Christmas in return was obviously not the right thing to do. She hesitated.

"And give me one reason why it should be merry. For me. For her." He jerked his chin in the direction of the old woman.

Why, indeed, should it be merry? Sister Egg wondered. There were thousands homeless and hungry in the city. Even though soup kitchens would be open for the holidays, and although volunteers would make an attempt at serving a festive meal, the atmosphere of a soup kitchen, usually in a church basement, was bleak. A basement is a basement is a basement, even with banners and Christmas decorations.

"Well?" the man demanded.

"I'm not sure it's supposed to be merry," Sister Egg said. "I'm not sure when 'merry' came into it. It's a time to remember that God came to live with us."

"That was pretty stupid," the man said. "Look where it got him."

Mrs. Brown's face peered out of the old blanket. "You hadn't ought to talk like that."

A young man on a bicycle rode through the red light. He carried a large transistor radio which blared out, "Joy to the world! The Lord is come."

"Joy, joy, joy." The man spat the words out. "What good did it do, this Lord coming? People were bad then, and they aren't any better now. Fighting. Bombing. Terrorism."

"You're upsetting Sister," Mrs. Brown said.

Sister Egg watched the light change yet again from green to yellow to red. "It's all right," she told Mrs. Brown. "Really, it's all right."

"What's all right?" the man demanded.

"It's all right to say what you feel. Only – "

"Only what?"

"I don't have any answers for you."

"Thank God," the man said.

Sister Egg smiled. "Do you?"

"Well...no. Thank *you*."

Sister Egg shivered. "I really have to make the next light."

"You're not warmly enough dressed," Mrs. Brown chided.

"Oh, I'm fine, as long as I keep moving."

The man stood up, and Mrs. Brown's little dog barked. "Shut up, mutt. What're you doing tonight, Sister?"

If she heard the suggestiveness in his voice, Sister Egg gave no sign. "We always go to the cathedral for midnight mass. Are you coming, Mrs. Brown?"

"Sure," the old woman said. "I been coming since you first told me it was okay. Beautiful. All those candles. And the music. And people smiling and being nice."

"Yeah, and they come around with silver plates and expect you to put all your money in."

"Sister Egg puts in something for me," Mrs. Brown said. "Anyhow, you don't have to pay God."

"Yeah? And who pays for all those candles? You got to pay somebody."

The light changed to green. Sister Egg fumbled in her deep pocket. It would never do to give the man one of the crumbled cookies. Then her fingers touched something more solid, and her fingers pulled out a silver-foil-wrapped chocolate kiss. She dropped it in his lap, then started across the street, feeling herself flush as she heard him making smacking kissing noises after her.

I should have had some answers for him, she thought. *I should have known what to say.*

A flake of snow brushed her cheek. She hurried to her favorite vegetable store and bought cranberries and oranges and some good celery for celery sticks, and a bunch of celery that had been marked down and a bag of onions for the turkey stuffing.

"Merry Christmas, Si'r Egg." The Korean man at the cash register greeted her, and charged her half price for the oranges.

She would have to hurry. Christmas Eve Vespers and the blessing of the crib was at five, and the chapel would be full of children from the school, and parents, too, and there would be hot, spiced cider afterward, and cookies.

It was always a special time for the children. They sat through the singing of Vespers, restless, but then there was the procession to the crèche, with the shepherds adoring, and the wise men still far off, because they couldn't arrive till Twelfth Night. And food! In half an hour the cookie plates would be empty, and the Sisters had been baking for weeks.

What did the children think? Was it all cookies and fruitcake and presents? Did they think at all about God coming to live with human beings as a human being, or was it only a baby in a manger? Did they see the shadow of the cross, and failure, thrown darkly across the golden singing of the angels?

Hearts were hard two thousand years ago. Hearts were still hard.

She started to cross Broadway again, but the light had already been green when she started so, again, she was stopped at the island.

Mrs. Brown was gone. That was all right. She would see her after the midnight mass.

But the man was there.

And she still had no words of comfort. For him. For herself.

"Take me there," the man said.

Startled, she nearly dropped the bag of onions. "Where?"

"To the church. The cathedral."

It was not far. One block south, one block east. But

there was no time. "Mother Cat won't like it if I'm late," she started.

"Mother *what?*" he roared.

"Oh – Mother Catherine of Siena."

"Is there a Sister Hen and a Mother Dog? Do you all have idiot nicknames?"

"Oh, no, and we don't *call* her Mother Cat, you know, it's Mother Catherine of – "

"But she calls you Egg?"

"Sometimes it's Frideswide."

He snorted. Rose. "Let's go."

"But – "

"Here. I'll carry your bags." He took the heaviest one, which contained the cranberries and oranges.

She could leave him. She was quite capable of saying, "I'm sorry, I can't be late for Vespers." She could direct him to the cathedral, she –

"Hi, Sister Egg." It was Topaze, one of the children who was in the school. His father was in and out of jail. His mother looked as though if she spat, nails could come out of her mouth. Topaze looked like an angel. "Can I carry your bags?"

"You know I can't pay you anything, Topaze," she said. The child picked up quarters and occasionally a dollar by doing errands.

"Hey, Sister Egg, Merry Christmas!" And he took the bags out of her arms, leaving her empty handed. "Where're we going?"

"To the cathedral," she said. "Mr., uh – I don't know your name."

"Joe," the man said.

"Mr. Joe wants to go to the cathedral. If you'll carry the bags to the convent and give it to one of the Sisters, you won't be late for Vespers."

"What about you?" Topaze asked.

"I guess I'll be late. Tell them not to worry about me, Topaze. I'll come as soon as I can."

"Unh unh, Sister Egg. I'm staying with you and Joe. Merry Christmas, Joe."

"Merry yourself." Once again Joe's scowl seemed larger than his body. "Let's go."

Sister Egg knew that Topaze didn't want to miss Vespers. Nevertheless she was glad to have him accompanying her, especially when they turned off brightly lit Broadway to the much darker east-bound street.

The cathedral loomed at the far end, the large and handsome lamps in front of it brightly lit. Another flake brushed Sister Egg's face, but the snow had not really begun yet; there was just an occasional flake drifting down from the low clouds.

People were already starting up the steps in small groups, to be sure of finding seats, even though they would have to wait for hours. A few greeted Sister Egg. Topaze walked on her left, holding her hand. Joe walked on her right, his threadbare coat hanging loosely. But his feet did not shuffle and his scowl was fierce.

They walked up the steps, an odd trio, Sister Egg thought, and she felt a wave of compassion flow out of her and over the man whose coat had once seen very much better days. The boy squeezed her hand.

Once they were in the vast nave of the cathedral, they stopped and looked around. The clusters of people hurrying forward to claim seats seemed small and few in that enormous space. Both sides of the nave were lined with bays, small chapels in themselves. There was a bay for St. Francis, a bay for education, a bay where a long-dead bishop was buried. Joe stopped at the bay of the Transfiguration, where there was an enormous painting that had been given the cathedral, of Jesus, James, John, and Peter on the Mount of Transfiguration. Jesus' face and garments were brilliant even in the semi-darkness of the cathedral, but through and behind him was the shadow of a cross. Depending on the angle at which one looked at the picture, Jesus was transfigured with light, or his outstretched arms were on the cross. It was a stunning painting, and the bay was one of Sister Egg's favorites.

Joe put his hand against his chest, and his scowl became a grimace. "Water," he choked. "I need water."

"Topaze." Sister Egg pushed the boy in her urgency. "You know where to go. Hurry to the choir rooms and get a glass of water, quickly." Perhaps Joe needed food, too. His face was not gray. She did not think he was having a heart attack.

As soon as Topaze had put the bags of groceries down at Sister Egg's feet and vanished into the shadows, Joe braced himself against one of the stone columns of the bay, then reached out and grabbed Sister Egg's wrist. "Don't scream. Don't try to run. Give it to me."

"What?" She tried to pull away from his grasp, not understanding.

"Your money. I know you have some. You didn't spend it all on two bags of groceries."

For this she was going to be late for Christmas Eve Vespers. Even if Mother Cat – Mother Catherine of Siena –

was not angry with her, the other Sisters would be. Sister Egg was always late, always stopping to speak to people.

"Come on, Egg," Joe said.

She was angry. "Couldn't you even call me a good egg?" She demanded. "Couldn't you just have asked me for it? 'Sister, I need money.' That's all you'd have needed to say."

"I don't ask for things."

"I only have a couple of dollars left. You're welcome to them." With her free hand she reached into her pocket. Pulled out a handful of crumbling cookies. "Here." Three more chocolate kisses.

"Come off it." He let her wrist go but reached for her pocket, putting his hand in and turning the pocket inside out. A small wooden cross fell to the stone floor. Some knotted woolen prayer beads. A can opener. A dog biscuit. A tiny sewing kit. "Holy – What are you, a walking dime-store?"

She looked past his head to the painting of Jesus, and now all she saw was the man on the cross. The body of the dying Christ was richly muscled. It was a strong man who hung there. Joe moved toward her impatiently, and his face came between Sister Egg and Jesus, and by some trick of the dim lighting in the nave, Joe's face looked like that of the man on the cross.

"Well, there you are," she said.

He pulled two dollars and a few coins out of her turned-out pocket. "It's not enough."

"Oh, yes it is," she said. "It's more than enough." She gestured toward the painting. "God cared enough to come and be one of us, and just once during his life on earth he revealed his glory. We matter to God. We matter that much."

"Don't shout," Joe growled.

"That's why it's Merry Christmas." She hardly heard him. "Not that he died. But that he cared enough to be born. That's the whole point of it all. Not the Crucifixion and the Resurrection but that God cared enough to be born. That was the real sacrifice. All the power and glory of all the galaxies – " Again she waved her arm toward the painting, and now she could not see the cross, only the glory.

She stopped for breath as Topaze hurried up with a glass of water.

Joe said, "Give it to Sister Fried Egg. She needs it more than I do."

Topaze looked at them suspiciously.

"We matter that much," Sister Egg repeated wonderingly.

Joe said, "She spilled some stuff. Help her pick it up." Two dollar bills floated to the floor. Coins dropped.

Topaze squatted and picked up Sister Egg's assorted treasures, then slipped them, one by one, into her pocket.

Joe handed him the remains of the cookies. "Here, kid, these are for you. I'll keep these." His open hand held three silver-foil-wrapped chocolate kisses. Light from somewhere in the cathedral touched them so that the silver was bright.

Sister Egg found that she was holding a glass of water.

When she turned to Joe, he was gone. She saw only the back of a man in a worn coat walking away.

"You all right?" Topaze asked anxiously. "You want the water?"

She took a sip. She could shout, "Thief!" and someone would stop Joe. Her wrist was sore where he had grabbed her. He was not a nice man.

She looked again at the painting. The face on the cross was Joe's. She turned so that the light shifted, and she saw the transfigured Christ.

"If we hurry," she said to Topaze, "we may miss Vespers, but we'll get there for the blessing of the crèche and the baby in the stable."

Willibald's Trip to Heaven
Reimmichl

WILLIBALD KRAUTMANN and Christmas – these two things belonged together like a door and its hinges, like a clock and its face, like a bell and its tower. The whole year round he dreamed of and prepared for Christmas. In his lifetime he had carved more than a thousand figurines; he had built sixty manger scenes, and never once had he missed the annual crèche-makers' conference in Innsbruck.

Willibald had a round, stocky figure that was much too small for his ambitious soul. Often his ego would inflate itself, rise up, and whisper in his ear, "Willibald, don't forget that you are the greatest artist in the land; there is no other worthy of comparison. And this is common knowledge in heaven too: there is hardly another craftsman there as highly esteemed as you. When you die, the gates of Paradise shall be flung wide in welcome, and you shall enter in triumph. And just wait till you see the mansion that has been prepared for you!" Such little murmurings fell often into Willibald's ear, and he was always a ready listener.

Now it happened that just on the night before Christmas Eve, Willibald passed away peacefully, and found himself trotting up a steep road toward heaven, and talking to himself.

"Do you see, my dear old Willibald, how the Christ Child honors those whom he loves? He has fetched you home on Christmas Eve, just in time for the most beautiful feast day in heaven. Perhaps he wants you to set up the heavenly manger scene. But it couldn't be – it's such short notice. Indeed, he's running very late, if that's the plan! Well, well, we will see…"

As Willibald thought about setting up a manger scene in heaven, excitement came over him like a fever, and his progress seemed to him much too slow. The climb was steep, he wasn't the youngest, and – being winter – it was bitterly cold. Often he stumbled or slipped backward several steps, which annoyed him, and he soon began to grumble.

"If they really wanted me in heaven, they could at least send a coach. That wouldn't be asking too much, would it? And it wouldn't have to be a coach-and-twelve; I'd be just as satisfied with a coach-and-four. And where are all the angels – what are they up to? Won't even *one* come out to meet me, Willibald Krautmann? Certainly I didn't expect a whole legion, but a few dozen archangels would have made a nice escort; indeed, it would only be proper. I'm no mere journeyman, after all; they ought to know *that* by now."

But in spite of all his muttering and grumbling, no angelic escort, nor any heavenly coach-and-twelve (or even four) appeared. There was nothing Willibald Krautmann could do but walk wearily onward. And so he continued in silence for a long time.

Darkness fell, the moon rose, and soon his strength began to ebb. He sat down on a large rock. Suddenly he noticed in the distance a wonderful city – the heavenly Jerusalem. It stood on a silver hill, and the walls, houses, and towers gleamed with gold. The city was illuminated with a light that was brighter than the sun, yet not half as blinding – it was mysteriously mild and soft. The windows and facades shimmered with reds and purples. Willibald gaped. Soon, however, the cold got to him, and he began to grumble again.

"Isn't *anyone* coming? Perhaps they are not quite finished preparing my reception – or they think I'm still far off. Well, I'll let them know they are mistaken!"

So Willibald stepped onto a nearby star, raised himself to his full height, waved his big hat and shouted with all his might, "Hey you, up there!"

There was no response. Not even an echo. He waited.

Suddenly a little angel in a white gown fluttered up over the city walls, glanced down at him, and disappeared again.

"Ah," he thought. "Now it's going to begin. Now all the bells are going to ring at once, and they'll set off the cannons."

But a quarter of an hour passed, and then half an hour, and still nothing happened. At one point he was sure he heard the ringing of chimes, as sweet as the bells of the cathedral in Salzburg. He heard singing too, but it was far away. Willibald shook his head in disbelief. What did it mean?

Suddenly it dawned on him: they wanted to surprise

him. He was supposed to go right up to the gate, and once he was there, the gates would open, and the heavenly hosts would stream out in all their splendor, and the angelic choirs would receive him with singing. "Yes," he thought, "that's the only way they would welcome a person like me. To be sure, I've never been one for surprises, but if they really take pleasure in such nonsense up here, then in the name of goodness I won't spoil their joy."

In good spirits once more, Willibald marched confidently up the last silvery rise, and stood expectantly right before the gate of heaven. Nothing happened. The gate did not spring open, no music broke forth, and no host streamed from within – nor even a single cherub. There was nothing but eerie silence. It was as if heaven were completely abandoned.

By now, Willibald was getting hot under the collar. A surprise is a surprise – that he could understand; and if the Heavenly Father wanted to greet him with a host of little rascals, fine. He'd play hide-and-seek with them, if he had to. After all, he had often carved amusing little cherubs; he had had his fun too. But this was going a little too far – and if it went on, it would no longer be a joke.

"What do they really want me to do?" he wondered. "Stand here like a beggar, and ask for shelter? What do they think I am? A wayward tramp?" No, he really didn't need that – he, Willibald Krautmann, who had given his very life to Christmas and the Christ Child. "Oh well," he sighed. "If they can wait, so can I. We'll see who runs out of patience first!"

And so he sat down on a stone near the gate, his chin in his hands. He began to feel rather sorry for himself. Then it happened: suddenly, from behind the arch of the closed gate, he heard hundreds of jubilant, high-pitched voices growing louder and louder. Then the gates of heaven opened, and a great crowd of cherubs pressed forward and spilled out. And who was standing at the threshold, but St. Peter himself, speaking in a deep voice and directing the multitude. "I knew it!" thought Willibald, overcome with relief.

Strangely, no one noticed him, and after a few moments, his joy turned to bewilderment. He coughed purposefully, and coughed again, trying to draw the angels' attention to him. It didn't work. Not a single angel so much as glanced in his direction. By now he was really at a loss.

Was it someone else they had come out to meet? Had they forgotten him altogether? Perhaps God, in all the flurry of holiday activities, had forgotten to announce that he, Willibald Krautmann, was due to arrive. "Well, then," he decided, "I'll have to announce the news myself."

Seeing a bell-pull to one side of the gate, he grasped it and threw his whole weight on the rope. It worked. A gong sounded, and a head popped out from the window above him. It was St. Peter himself.

"What on earth do you think you're doing, yanking on the bell-pull like that?" he asked. "And who are you, anyway?"

"It is I, Willibald Krautmann, well-known Tyrolean artist, carver of manger scenes."

"Willibald Krautmann," repeated St. Peter, bemused. "What an odd name! Never heard it before. I suppose you were looking for a place to stay?"

"Well, this is heaven, isn't it?" Willibald threw back at him. "And I've been waiting out here for an hour already. Of course I'd like a place to stay."

"Of course? It is not a matter of course at all. Let's see what is written about you in the Book."

St. Peter disappeared from the window, leaving Willibald open-mouthed. "Well, *that* was a friendly welcome! They don't even know me up here? They have to look for my name in some stupid registry? The world pays with ingratitude; everyone knows that. But I wouldn't have thought it was like that in heaven!"

Now St. Peter was back at the window, thumbing the pages of a large, black book. He took his time. "All right, here we are," he said evenly, looking up. "But it says that you cannot enter."

"What? *I* cannot enter! I'd just like to ask you for one good reason."

"Of course. Just listen. You have been arrogant and vain, and proud of your own work. You have considered the art of others worthless in comparison to your own; you have acted as if no one else was as gifted as you."

"Mr. Heavenly Gatekeeper, you're making mountains out of molehills. You used to be a fisherman, so I'm not surprised – but you just have no idea what an artist feels. And what about all the *good* I have done? In my lifetime I have carved more than half a hundred nativity scenes. I have awakened many dull hearts with my artistry, and brought much joy into the world; it has even been said that people could take an example from the integrity of my figures."

"I'm sure that's all true," said St. Peter dryly. "But there is more – about your arrogance – that I can't just scratch out."

"Read on, then. I know I'm not the humblest. Everyone has his faults, and I'm not so conceited as to think that I'm an exception. But really, you're making quite a fuss over nothing."

"My good Mr. Krautmann, I'm only just getting started. There are other things recorded here. You have been impatient and irritable. When a piece of work wasn't going smoothly, you flared up in such anger – "

"That was *holy* anger," Willibald interrupted. "The Evil One could not stand my work, and often hid my tools or knocked over a scene, so that all the figures toppled onto the floor, and several broke. And then – why, certainly a righteous indignation would come over me."

"The things you said were anything but quick prayers."

"For goodness sake, Mr. Gatekeeper! Who thinks about what he says in the heat of the moment? You can't weigh that sort of thing on a golden scale. Besides, I never did anything violent in my anger, like...like other people I know. I never struck off anyone's ear."

"So we're trying to start a lawsuit?" asked Peter sharply, "Then you ought to find yourself an advocate."

"Just let me in, and I'll find one in a hurry."

"No one impure can enter. You'll have to find someone on earth to speak on your behalf."

"On *earth?* That's a fine to-do. It's unfortunate, I know, but I really don't know anyone that well down there. I was a busy man in my day; I had very little time for other people."

"There you have it, exactly," agreed St. Peter. "But now I'm going to read you the heaviest debt on your account: In the course of an entire lifetime you were so self-centered that you were unable to make even one friend through performing a work of mercy – not even one advocate to speak for you in heaven."

"Now listen here!" Willibald retorted. "I spent my time and my money on the Christmas work I did."

"No expense is so great as a gift from the heart, especially to someone in need."

"Of course; but you can't throw away money unless you've got extra. And I always gave *something*."

"Always? Last year, on Christmas Eve, you turned away a widow with three hungry children from your door."

"Well, that's not hard to explain: I was working overtime on a late order, one that required a new design. And I had an entire nativity scene to re-gild. Such things cost money – and everything is sinfully expensive these days."

"You still had enough left over to go out for a drink on Christmas Eve – and you did more than just quench your thirst."

"Goodness, that was just a little celebration, a very small one – and that, because it was Christmas. Besides, the wines they sell nowadays are so cheap that you only have to drink one glass, and it goes to your head."

"What? You drank two bottles of the most expensive vintage! You won't get far with lying, Mr. Krautmann; that's something I really detest."

"Dear St. Peter, don't take it ill!" begged Willibald. "Little white lies like that come over the best people. I once read about someone who lied his way out of a tight spot *three times* in one night."

"And wept for it the rest of his life, while you cover up and explain away your sins," thundered St. Peter. "I've had it; that's the end of my patience. Now get out of here!" And he slammed the window shut.

For the first time Willibald realized that he was really in a fix, and he decided to try another tack. Trembling, he reached up to knock on the window, and when he found he wasn't tall enough, hung his head and begged and whined like a little boy. St. Peter ignored him. Next he tried the bell-pull again, though this time he didn't yank at the rope, but pulled on it gently. Still no response.

What should he do now, he wondered? Hopeless – and dead tired – he stumbled along the wall, looking for a place to lie down and sleep. He had not gone far when he came to a small window that bathed the ground below it in a golden light. Curious, he peered in, and – dear God! What a celebration was going on inside! It was absolutely heavenly: hundreds of angels were dancing in a sea of light and joy.

Ecstatic, Willibald drank in the scene, and as he did the scales fell from his eyes: he saw that the source of all that light and joy was love, the unending delight of the soul. And to think that he was seeing only a fraction of it all! Perhaps only a thousandth part of it!

Then a rush of heavenly music rose and swept over him – the voices of at least a million angels chanting and singing in praise of God. "No one on earth would believe me if I described this," thought Willibald to himself. "No one on earth has even *imagined* such music!"

Ecstatic, he began to sway with the music. Suddenly his chest tightened. He felt hot and breathless. Grasping at his heart, he panicked. His breast burned with such longing to be part of the heavenly scene in front of him that he was sure he was going to die. He wanted to cry out, but couldn't; he wanted to sing, but his mouth was dry. And so he wept, from the depths of his heart. "Forgive my sins!" he sobbed piteously. "Never again will I be haughty or cruel! Forgive me! *Please* forgive me!"

Willibald wept softly at first, then louder, and then very loudly, yelling and howling. He pressed his head against the windowpane so hard that the glass shone with his tears.

Crack! Suddenly the window shattered and gave way, and he lost his balance, and found himself falling. Down, down, and farther down he fell, into what seemed a bottomless pit...And now he heard a familiar voice: "For God's sake, stop your yelling; what on earth is going on?" He opened his eyes. There he was, lying in his warm bed, and beside him his bleary-eyed wife, who was shaking him by the shoulder.

"What's the matter with you, you silly fool?" cried his wife. "You've been howling and carrying on like a hog at the butcher's!"

"Oh – I have been in heaven!" he replied.

"In heaven? A fine heaven, where you have to whimper and yelp like that."

"Quiet, woman, and I'll tell you all about it."

Willibald Krautmann did not tell his wife everything; but he did became more thoughtful. During the Christmas holidays he lost a big sum of money – at least his wife believed he had lost it. In fact, he gave it to the widow he had turned away the year before. He softened in other ways, too, and was no longer rude or impatient or unkind.

To his next-door neighbor, who asked why, Willibald explained very simply that this year he had finally begun to understand what Christmas was really about. But he also told this neighbor, who was his best friend, the whole story of his trip to heaven.

The Guest

Nikolai S. Lesskov

Many years ago, in Czarist Russia, a man was traveling through Siberia. While he was staying with a family in a remote village, his host told him this story:

OUR DISTRICT IS ONE of the places in Siberia to which exiles are sent as a punishment for political offenses, or for other reasons. But in spite of this it is not a bad place to live in, with a life of its own and plenty of trade. My father settled here as a young man in the days when serfdom was still the rule in Russia – so you can see how long ago that was! I myself was born here. We have always been fairly well off, and even now we are not poor. We belong to the Mother Church of Russia and we hold firmly to the simple faith of our fathers. My father was a great reader, and he taught me to love books and knowledge. So it came about that all my friends were people who had the same taste. In my youth I had a very true friend, Timofai Ossipovitch, and it is his story I want to tell you.

When he came to us, Timofai was still a young man. I was eighteen at the time, and he was a little older. He was a young man of excellent character, and you may wonder why he had been banished to Siberia. In a village like ours we never asked an exile why he was there. It might be too embarrassing. But so far as we could understand this is what had happened: Timofai was an orphan, and had been brought up by his uncle, who was his legal guardian. When Timofai was about seventeen he found that nearly all his fortune had been either wasted or simply used selfishly by his uncle. When he discovered this, he was so angry that in a quarrel he fired at his uncle. Fortunately he only wounded him in the hand. The judge treated Timofai leniently on account of his youth, so he was exiled to Siberia, and indeed to my own village.

Now although Timofai had lost nine-tenths of his inheritance, the tenth was enough to keep him in some comfort. He built a small house close to us, and settled down. But the injustice he had suffered still affected him very deeply. He was so angry and resentful that he could not lead a normal life. For a long time he lived like a recluse; he refused to make any contact with his neighbors. He shut himself up in his house; the only people he saw were the couple who looked after him. He spent his time reading book after book, most of them on serious subjects, and especially on religion. At last there came a day when I was able to talk with him over the fence; then later, he asked me to come to his house. From that time I often went to see him, and we became very good friends.

At first my parents were not very pleased with me for making friends with Timofai. "We don't know who he is or why he hides himself from everybody. We do hope he won't do you any harm." But when I told my parents the kind of man he was, how we read religious books together, and talked about the Faith, they were satisfied that there could not be anything seriously wrong with him. Then my father visited him, and invited Timofai to come to see us. At once my parents saw that he was a good fellow and they began to like him. Indeed, they were very sorry for him, because he was always brooding over the wrong that had been done to him; if anyone happened to mention the uncle, Timofai would go as white as a sheet, and looked as though he were about to faint. He was a very honorable man, and had a good mind; but owing to this bitterness of spirit he could not settle to any useful work.

However, when he fell in love with my sister this extreme bitterness passed away. He married her, gave up his melancholy brooding, and began to live and prosper; he went into business and became wealthy. After ten years everyone in the district knew and respected him. He built a new house with large rooms. He had everything he needed, his wife was very capable, and he had healthy, delightful children. What more could he want? It seemed as though all the troubles of his youth were over and forgotten. But one day when we were out driving in his pony cart I suddenly asked him: "Brother Timofai, are you now quite happy in your mind?"

"What do you mean?" he said, looking at me with a strange look on his face.

"Have you recovered everything you lost in your youth?"

He went very white, and said nothing; but he went on driving through the forest. After some moments of silence I said, "Forgive me, brother, for asking this question. I

thought all that trouble was over long ago...over and forgotten?"

"That's not the point," he answered, "it makes no difference that it happened so long ago. It is over, yes, but I still
keep thinking about it."

I felt very sorry for him, for I now saw that although
Timofai knew the Scriptures so well, and could talk elo-
quently about religion, he still nursed the memory of this
injustice in his heart. "Surely," I thought, "this means that
the Word of God is of no avail to him?"

For some minutes we drove on in silence; I was deep in
thought. At last he looked at me and said, "What are you
thinking about?"

"Oh, all sorts of things!" I said, rather lightly.

"I don't believe it! I believe you are thinking about me."

"Well, yes, I am thinking about you."

"Tell me what you are thinking about me."

"Please don't be cross with me, brother, this is what I
have been thinking: You know the Scriptures, yet your
heart is full of resentment and anger, and you will not sub-
mit to God. Does this mean that all your reading of the
Bible has done you no good?"

Timofai wasn't angry with me, but his face darkened and
he said, "You don't know the Bible well enough to say this
kind of thing." Then he began to argue with me, trying to
justify himself. He said I was too ignorant of the Bible and
of the world, to understand him. I agreed. He went on to
say, "There are injustices which no honorable man can put
up with." Then he added, "I have never spoken about this to
any one, but because you are my friend I will tell you. My
uncle caused so much pain and sorrow to my father and
mother that in the end my mother died of it. My uncle slan-

dered my father; above all he spread such lies about me that he prevented me from marrying a young girl I had loved from childhood, and all this because he, an older man, wanted to marry her himself. Can anyone forget such an injury?" he asked. "I will never forgive him, ever!"

"You certainly have had a raw deal," I replied. "I agree, but this does not alter the fact that you aren't getting any help from all your study of the Holy Scriptures." Then he launched into a long argument about my scanty knowledge of the Bible and of all the passages in the Old Testament where good men stood up for themselves and even killed their enemies! The poor fellow was trying to justify himself in my eyes.

"Timofai," I said, "I know I am only a simple fellow, and not like you. Yet even I can see that there is a great difference between the Old and the New Testaments; there's a lot about revenge in the Old Testament, but in the New Testament it's all about love and forgiveness." He was silent. Then I went on, very quietly, to remind him of the way our Lord was treated in his Passion: how he was beaten and ill-treated and insulted and put to death by his enemies. But he forgave them all. Timofai was not offended by my frank speech. After further conversation he pressed my hand and said, "I can't help it! Stop talking about forgiveness, you are only making me very sad." I stopped at once, for I could see that he was very unhappy. But I was sure that one day he would change. Now this came about in a most remarkable way.

At that time Timofai had been in Siberia for sixteen years; he was about thirty-seven. He had a good wife, three children, and a pleasant life. He was very fond of flowers, especially roses – there were roses everywhere, in the garden, and in the house. Indeed, the whole house was full of their beauty and their fragrance. In summer he always went into the garden about sunrise. First he examined his roses, to see if they needed any attention, then he sat down among them on a bench, took out a book, and began to read. I believe he often said his prayers there as he sat in the early morning sunshine. One day he was sitting there as usual, reading his New Testament, and he came to the passage where Christ went to a rich man's house, and his host did not even give him water to wash his feet. Timofai put the book down and began to think, and as he brooded over the great poverty and love of the Lord he burst out, "Oh Lord! if you were to come to me I would give you all I have and am!" Suddenly a wind passed over the roses and he seemed to hear the words: "I will come."

Later in the morning Timofai came over to see me and told me what had happened. He said anxiously, "Do you believe that the Lord will really come to me as a guest?" I replied, "That, brother, is quite beyond my understanding! Is there anything about it in the Holy Scripture?" Timofai said, "Well, he is the same Christ, today and forever. I don't dare to refuse to believe it."

"Well, then," I said, "believe it!"

Timofai reflected for a few moments, then he turned to me and said, "I know what I'll do. I'll have a place set for him at our table every day." This did not seem to me quite the right line to take, but I felt I could not suggest anything else, so I shrugged my shoulders and said, "You must do what you think right."

Timofai told his wife that from the next day he wished an extra place to be prepared at every family meal; this sixth place was to be put at the head of the table for an honored guest, and a special armchair as well. She was astonished, and very curious. "Whom do you expect?" she asked. But Timofai kept his own counsel; he merely told her and the rest of the household that he had ordered this because he had made a vow, "for the most honored guest who may arrive." No one knew what he meant, and they were left wondering.

Day after day Timofai waited for the Lord: the next day, then the following Sunday, but nothing happened. Sometimes he waited in a fever of impatience, but he never doubted that the Lord would come, as he had said. One day he came to me and said, "Brother, day after day I pray, 'Lord, come,' and I wait, but so far I have never heard the answer for which I long: 'Yes, I will come soon.'"

Secretly I felt uncertain how to answer Timofai when he talked like this. Sometimes I was afraid that my friend had become "puffed up," and that this was a temptation which had come to him. But Providence meant it otherwise.

Six months passed, and Christmas was approaching. It was a hard winter. On Christmas Eve Timofai came to me and said, "My dear brother, tomorrow I am expecting the Lord!" I said simply, "And why are you so sure of it this time?" "This time," he said, "after I had prayed the usual prayer, my whole soul was moved, and I seemed to hear very clearly the words 'Yes, I am coming soon.' Tomorrow is his festival. Could there be a better day for him to come? I want you to be there, with all our relatives, for I feel awed and afraid."

"Timofai," I said, "you know that I don't profess to understand this matter, and I certainly don't expect to see the

Lord, sinful man as I am – but you are part of our family and I will come. But may I say something else? Since you expect such a Royal Guest would it not be wise to invite not only your own relatives and friends, but the sort of company that he would desire?"

Timofai smiled and said, "I see what you mean. Yes, I'll send out my servants into the whole village to invite all the exiles who are in need and poverty here, so far from their homeland. It is only fitting that when the Lord comes he should find the kind of guests he would want to see."

So on Christmas Day we all went to Timofai's house a little later than was usual, for a midday meal. We found all the large rooms filled with people, typical Siberians, that is, people who were exiles from their own countries. There were men and women, and many of the younger generation as well, people of very varied callings and from different regions, Russians, and Poles, and even some from far-away Estonia. Timofai had arranged that all the exiles who had not yet found their feet in a strange land should be invited. The long tables were covered with fresh white linen cloths, and all sorts of good things were placed there for the guests. The maids bustled about and brought in meat-pasties and kvass for the first course. Outside, the short winter day was drawing to a close, and all the guests were assembled. No one else was expected. Outside a snowstorm had begun, and the wind swept round the house; it was a terrible storm. Only the one Guest was missing: the One for whom they were waiting. The candles were lit, and the guests were about to take their places at the table. Outside it was not quite dark, and inside the house, apart from the candles, the rest of the rooms were in semi-darkness; the only light came from the little lamps burning before the icons. Timofai kept moving about from one room to another; he could not sit still, he was so agitated. "Could it be," he wondered, "that after all the Guest would not come?"

He whispered to me, "I can't make it out. Perhaps I have misunderstood the message? Well, we must go forward in God's Name. We must give thanks and start the meal."

Timofai stood up and went to the icon and began to pray the Lord's Prayer aloud. Then he added, "Christ is born to-day! Let us praise the Lord our God! Christ has come down from heaven, let us all rejoice that the Most High has visited us, and is even now in our midst."

He had hardly finished these words when there came a great gust of wind which shook the house, followed by a loud noise, as if something had fallen against the door; suddenly, the door burst open of itself. The guests were so frightened that they left the tables and huddled together in a corner; some fell down on the floor, others stood still and looked at the doorway. On the threshold stood a very old man dressed in rags; he was so weak that he could hardly stand. He was leaning on the nearest chair in the room; but behind him there was a wonderful light, and a delicate fragrance seemed to come in with him. Some people thought they saw a little lamp, burning with a steady flame unmoved by the wind.

As Timofai gazed at this strange figure, he cried out, "Lord! I see him, and I receive him in thy Name! Do not come to me thyself, for I am not worthy that thou shouldst come under my roof." He knelt down, and bowed his face to the ground. Then he cried out in a loud voice, "Let us rejoice, for Christ himself is among us!" And all the guests said, Amen.

Fresh candles were brought into the room, and Timofai stood up and looked intently at the old man. The radiance and the fragrance had faded; only the old man remained. Timofai went forward, took him by both hands and led him to the empty place reserved for the guest of honor. He knew who he was: his old uncle, who had done him so much harm. As they sat down together the other guests went back to the feast. Then the old man told Timofai that his whole life had gone to pieces; he had lost his family and all his possessions. For a long time he had been wandering about the forests and plains of Siberia, trying to find his nephew, for he wanted to ask Timofai to forgive him. He longed for this, though he was frightened of Timofai's anger. In the snowstorm he had lost his way completely, and he was so cold he was afraid he would freeze to death that night. "Suddenly," he said, "I met someone who said to me, 'Go to that house, over there, where you see the lights. Take my place, and you will be warmed and fed; you may eat out of my plate!' Then he took hold of both my hands and helped me. Somehow I reached this door."

"Uncle," said Timofai, "I know who led you here. It was the Lord who said that...so you are welcome to the best place at the feast. Eat and drink in his Name, and I invite you to stay as long as you like, to the very end of your life."

So the old man remained with Timofai and when he was dying he blessed his nephew. And Timofai had peace in his heart for he had learned to obey the words of the Lord: "Love your enemies, do good to those who ill-treat you..." "Come Lord Jesus! Come quickly and abide with me."

Christmas Day in the Morning

Pearl S. Buck

HE WOKE SUDDENLY and completely. It was four o'clock, the hour at which his father had always called him to get up and help with the milking. Strange how the habits of his youth clung to him still! Fifty years ago, and his father had been dead for thirty years, and yet he waked at four o'clock in the morning. He had trained himself to turn over and go to sleep, but this morning, because it was Christmas, he did not try to sleep.

Yet what was the magic of Christmas now? His childhood and youth were long past, and his own children had grown up and gone. Some of them lived only a few miles away but they had their own families, and though they would come in as usual toward the end of the day, they had explained with infinite gentleness that they wanted their children to build Christmas memories about *their* houses, not his. He was left alone with his wife.

Yesterday she had said, "It isn't worth while, perhaps – "

And he had said, "Oh, yes, Alice, even if there are only the two of us, let's have a Christmas of our own."

Then she had said, "Let's not trim the tree until tomorrow, Robert – just so it's ready when the children come. I'm tired."

He had agreed, and the tree was still out in the back entry.

He lay in his big bed in his room. The door to her room was shut because she was a light sleeper, and sometimes he had restless nights. Years ago they had decided to use separate rooms. It meant nothing, they said, except that neither of them slept as well as they once had. They had been married so long that nothing could separate them, actually.

Why did he feel so awake tonight? For it was still night, a clear and starry night. No moon, of course, but the stars were extraordinary! Now that he thought of it, the stars seemed always large and clear before the dawn of Christmas Day. There was one star now that was certainly larger and brighter than any of the others. He could even imagine it moving, as it had seemed to him to move one night long ago.

He slipped back in time, as he did so easily nowadays. He was fifteen years old and still on his father's farm. He loved his father. He had not known it until one day a few days before Christmas, when he had overheard what his father was saying to his mother.

"Mary, I hate to call Rob in the mornings. He's growing so fast and he needs his sleep. If you could see how he sleeps when I go in to wake him up! I wish I could manage alone."

"Well, you can't, Adam." His mother's voice was brisk. "Besides, he isn't a child any more. It's time he took his turn."

"Yes," his father said slowly. "But I sure do hate to wake him."

When he heard these words, something in him woke:

his father loved him! He had never thought of it before, taking for granted the tie of their blood. Neither his father nor his mother talked about loving their children – they had no time for such things. There was always so much to do on a farm.

Now that he knew his father loved him, there would be no more loitering in the mornings and having to be called again. He got up after that, stumbling blind with sleep, and pulled on his clothes, his eyes tight shut, but he got up.

And then on the night before Christmas, that year when he was fifteen, he lay for a few minutes thinking about the next day. They were poor, and most of the excitement was in the turkey they had raised themselves and in the mince pies his mother made. His sisters sewed presents and his mother and father always bought something he needed, not only a warm jacket, maybe, but something more, such as a book. And he saved and bought them each something, too.

He wished, that Christmas he was fifteen, he had a better present for his father. As usual he had gone to the ten-cent store and bought a tie. It had seemed nice enough until he lay thinking the night before Christmas, and then he wished that he had heard his father and mother talking in time for him to save for something better.

He lay on his side, his head supported by his elbow, and looked out of his attic window. The stars were bright, much brighter than he ever remembered seeing them, and one star in particular was so bright that he wondered if it were really the Star of Bethlehem.

"Dad," he had once asked when he was a little boy, "what is a stable?"

"It's just a barn," his father had replied, "like ours."

Then Jesus had been born in a barn, and to a barn the

shepherds and the Wise Men had come, bringing their Christmas gifts!

The thought struck him like a silver dagger. Why should he not give his father a special gift too, out there in the barn? He could get up early, earlier than four o'clock, and he could creep into the barn and get all the milking done. He'd do it alone, milk and clean up, and then when his father went in to start the milking, he'd see it all done. And he would know who had done it.

He laughed to himself as he gazed at the stars. It was what he would do, and he mustn't sleep too sound.

He must have waked twenty times, scratching a match each time to look at his old watch – midnight, and half past one, and then two o'clock.

At a quarter to three he got up and put on his clothes. He crept downstairs, careful of the creaky boards, and let himself out. The big star hung lower over the barn roof, a reddish gold. The cows looked at him, sleepy and surprised. It was early for them too.

"So, boss," he whispered. They accepted him placidly and he fetched some hay for each cow and then got the milking pail and the big milk cans.

He had never milked all alone before, but it seemed almost easy. He kept thinking about his father's surprise. His father would come in and call him, saying that he would get things started while Rob was getting dressed. He'd go to the barn, open the door, and then he'd go to get the two big empty milk cans. But they wouldn't be waiting or empty; they'd be standing in the milk house, filled.

"What the – " he could hear his father exclaiming.

He smiled and milked steadily, two strong streams rushing into the pail, frothing and fragrant. The cows were still surprised but acquiescent. For once they were behaving well, as though they knew it was Christmas.

The task went more easily than he had ever known it to before. Milking for once was not a chore. It was something else, a gift to his father who loved him. He finished, the two milk cans were full, and he covered them and closed the milk house door carefully, making sure of the latch. He put the stool in its place by the door and hung up the clean milk pail. Then he went out of the barn and barred the door behind him.

Back in his room he had only a minute to pull off his clothes in the darkness and jump into bed, for he heard his father up. He put the covers over his head to silence his quick breathing. The door opened.

"Rob!" his father called. "We have to get up, son, even if it is Christmas."

"Aw-right," he said sleepily.

"I'll go on out," his father said. "I'll get things started."

The door closed and he lay still, laughing to himself. In just a few minutes his father would know. His dancing heart was ready to jump from his body.

The minutes were endless – ten, fifteen, he did not know how many – and he heard his father's footsteps again. The door opened and he lay still.

"Rob!"

"Yes, Dad – "

"You son of a – " His father was laughing, a queer sobbing sort of a laugh. "Thought you'd fool me, did you?" His father was standing beside his bed, feeling for him, pulling away the cover.

"It's for Christmas, Dad!"

He found his father and clutched him in a great hug. He

felt his father's arms go around him. It was dark and they could not see each other's faces.

"Son, I thank you. Nobody ever did a nicer thing."

"Oh, Dad, I want you to know – I do want to be good!" The words broke from him of their own will. He did not know what to say. His heart was bursting with love.

"Well, I reckon I can go back to bed and sleep," his father said after a moment. "No, hark – the little ones are waked up. Come to think of it, son, I've never seen you children when you first saw the Christmas tree. I was always in the barn. Come on!"

He got up and pulled on his clothes again and they went down to the Christmas tree, and soon the sun was creeping up to where the star had been. Oh, what a Christmas, and how his heart had nearly burst again with shyness and pride as his father told his mother and made the younger children listen about how he, Rob, had got up all by himself.

"The best Christmas gift I ever had, and I'll remember it, son, every year on Christmas morning, so long as I live."

They had both remembered it, and now that his father was dead he remembered it alone: that blessed Christmas dawn when, alone with the cows in the barn, he had made his first gift of true love.

Outside the window now the great star slowly sank. He got up out of bed and put on his slippers and bathrobe and went softly upstairs to the attic and found the box of Christmas-tree decorations. He took them downstairs into the living room. Then he brought in the tree. It was a little one – they had not had a big tree since the children went away – but he set it in the holder and put it in the middle of the long table under the window. Then carefully he began to trim it.

It was done very soon, the time passing as quickly as it had that morning long ago in the barn. He went to his library and fetched the little box that contained his special gift to his wife, a star of diamonds, not large but dainty in design. He had written the card for it the day before. He tied the gift on the tree and then stood back. It was pretty, very pretty, and she would be surprised.

But he was not satisfied. He wanted to tell her – to tell her how much he loved her. It had been a long time since he had really told her, although he loved her in a very special way, much more than he ever had when they were young.

He had been fortunate that she had loved him – and how fortunate that he had been able to love! Ah, that was the true joy of life, the ability to love! For he was quite sure that some people were genuinely unable to love anyone. But love was alive in him, it still was.

It occurred to him suddenly that it was alive because long ago it had been born in him when he knew his father loved him. That was it: love alone could waken love.

And he could give the gift again and again. This morning, this blessed Christmas morning, he would give it to his beloved wife. He could write it down in a letter for her to read and keep forever. He went to his desk and began his love letter to his wife: *My dearest love…*

When it was finished he sealed it and tied it on the tree where she would see it the first thing when she came into the room. She would read it, surprised and then moved, and realize how very much he loved her.

He put out the light and went tiptoeing up the stairs. The star in the sky was gone, and the first rays of the sun were gleaming in the sky. Such a happy, happy Christmas!

The Other Wise Man

Henry van Dyke

You know the story of the Three Wise Men of the East, and how they traveled from far away to offer their gifts at the manger-cradle in Bethlehem. But have you ever heard the story of the Other Wise Man, who also saw the star in its rising, and set out to follow it, yet did not arrive with his brethren in the presence of the young child Jesus? Of the great desire of this fourth pilgrim, and how it was denied, yet accomplished in the denial; of his many wanderings and the probations of his soul; of the long way of his seeking, and the strange way of his finding, the One whom he sought – I would tell the tale as I have heard fragments of it in the Hall of Dreams, in the palace of the Heart of Man.

The Sign in the Sky

IN THE DAYS when Augustus Caesar was master of many kings and Herod reigned in Jerusalem, there lived in the city of Ecbatana, among the mountains of Persia, a certain man named Artaban, the Median. His house stood close to the outermost of the seven walls which encircled the royal treasury. From his roof he could look over the rising battlements of black and white and crimson and blue and red and silver and gold, to the hill where the summer palace of the Parthian emperors glittered like a jewel in a sevenfold crown.

Around the dwelling of Artaban spread a fair garden, a tangle of flowers and fruit trees, watered by a score of streams descending from the slopes of Mount Orontes, and made musical by innumerable birds. But all color was lost in the soft and odorless darkness of the late September night, and all sounds were hushed in the deep charm of its silence, save the plashing of the water, like a voice half sobbing and half laughing under the shadows. High above the trees a dim glow of light shone through the curtained arches of the upper chamber, where the master of the house was holding council with his friends.

He stood by the doorway to greet his guests – a tall, dark man of about forty years, with brilliant eyes set near together under his broad brow, and firm lines graven around his fine, thin lips; the brow of a dreamer and the mouth of a soldier, a man of sensitive feeling but inflexible will – one of those who, in whatever age they may live, are born for inward conflict and a life of quest.

His robe was of pure white wool, thrown over a tunic of silk; and a white pointed cap, with long lapels at the sides, rested on his flowing black hair. It was the dress of the ancient priesthood of the Magi, called the fire-worshipers.

"Welcome!" he said, in his low, pleasant voice as one after another entered the room – "Welcome, Abdus; peace be with you. Rhodaspes and Tigranes, and with you my father, Abgarus. You are all welcome, and this house grows bright with the joy of your presence."

There were nine of the men, differing widely in age, but alike in the richness of their dress of many-colored silks, and in the massive golden collars around their necks, marking them as Parthian nobles, and the winged circles of gold resting upon their breasts, the sign of the followers of Zoroaster.

They took their places around a small black altar at the end of the room, where a tiny flame was burning. Artaban, standing beside it, and waving a barsom of thin tamarisk branches above the fire, fed it with dry sticks of pine and fragrant oils. Then he began the ancient chant of the Yasna, and the voices of his companions joined in the beautiful hymn to Ahura-Mazda:

We worship the Spirit Divine, all wisdom and
   goodness possessing,
Surrounded by Holy Immortals, the givers of
   bounty and blessing,
We joy in the works of His hands, His truth
   and His power confessing.

We praise all the things that are pure, for these
   are His only Creation;
The thoughts that are true, and the words and deeds
   that have won approbation;
These are supported by Him and for these
   we make adoration.

Hear us, O Mazda! Thou livest in truth and
   in heavenly gladness;
Cleanse us from falsehood, and keep us from
   evil and bondage to badness;

Pour out the light and the joy of Thy life
  on our darkness and sadness.

Shine on our gardens and fields, Shine on our
  working and weaving;
Shine on the whole race of man, Believing and
  unbelieving;
  Shine on us now through the night,
  Shine on us now in Thy might,
The flame of our holy love and the song
  of our worship receiving.

The fire rose with the chant, throbbing as if it were made of musical flame, until it cast a bright illumination through the whole apartment, revealing its simplicity and splendor.

The floor was laid with tiles of dark blue veined with white; pilasters of twisted silver stood out against the blue walls; the clerestory of round-arched windows above them was hung with azure silk; the vaulted ceiling was a pavement of sapphires, like the body of heaven in its clearness, sown with silver stars. From the four corners of the roof hung four golden magic- wheels, called the tongues of the gods. At the eastern end, behind the altar, there were two dark-red pillars of porphyry; above them a lintel of the same stone, on which was carved the figure of a winged archer, with his arrow set to the string and his bow drawn.

The doorway between the pillars, which opened upon the terrace of the roof, was covered with a heavy curtain of the color of a ripe pomegranate, embroidered with innumerable golden rays shooting upward from the floor. In effect the room was like a quiet, starry night, all azure and silver, flushed in the east with rosy promise of the dawn. It was, as the house of a man should be, an expression of the character and spirit of the master.

He turned to his friends when the song was ended, and invited them to be seated on the divan at the western end of the room.

"You have come tonight," said he, looking around the circle, "at my call, as the faithful scholars of Zoroaster, to renew your worship and rekindle your faith in the God of Purity, even as this fire has been rekindled on the altar. We worship not the fire, but Him of whom it is the chosen symbol, because it is the purest of all created things. It speaks to us of one who is Light and Truth. Is it not so, my father?"

"It is well said, my son," answered the venerable Abgarus. "The enlightened are never idolaters. They lift the veil of the form and go into the shrine of the reality, and new light and truth are coming to them continually through the old symbols."

"Hear me, then, my father and my friends," said Artaban, very quietly, "while I tell you of the new light and truth that have come to me through the most ancient of all signs. We have searched the secrets of nature together, and studied the healing virtues of water and fire and the plants. We have read also the books of prophecy in which the future is dimly foretold in words that are hard to understand. But the highest of all learning is the knowledge of the stars. To trace their courses is to untangle the threads of mystery of life from the beginning to the end. If we could follow them perfectly, nothing would be hidden from us. But is not our knowledge of them still incomplete? Are there not many stars still beyond our horizon – lights that are known only to the dwellers in the far southland, among the spice trees of Punt and the gold mines of Ophir?"

There was a murmur of assent among the listeners.

"The stars," said Tigranes, "are the thoughts of the Eternal. They are numberless. But the thoughts of man can be counted, like the years of his life. The wisdom of the Magi is the greatest of all wisdoms on earth, because it knows its own ignorance. And that is the secret of power. We keep men always looking and waiting for a new sunrise. But we ourselves know that the darkness is equal to the light, and that the conflict between them will never be ended."

"That does not satisfy me," answered Artaban, "for, if the waiting must be endless, if there could be no fulfillment of it, then it would not be wisdom to look and wait. We should become like those new teachers of the Greeks, who say that there is no truth, and that the only wise men are those who spend their lives in discovering and exposing the lies that have been believed in the world. But the new sunrise will certainly dawn in the appointed time. Do not our own books tell us that this will come to pass, and that men will see the brightness of a great light?"

"That is true," said the voice of Abgarus; "every faithful disciple of Zoroaster knows the prophesy of the Avesta and carries the word in his heart: 'In that day Sosiosh the Victorious shall arise out of the number of the prophets in the east country. Around him shall shine a mighty brightness, and he shall make life everlasting, incorruptible, and immortal, and the dead shall rise again.'"

"This is a dark saying," said Tigranes, "and it may be that we shall never understand it. It is better to consider the things that are near at hand, and to increase the influence of the Magi in their own country, rather than to look for one who may be a stranger, and to whom we must resign our power."

The others seemed to approve these words. There was a silent feeling of agreement manifest among them; their looks responded with that indefinable expression which always follows when a speaker has uttered the thought that has been slumbering in the hearts of his listeners. But Artaban turned to Abgarus with a glow on his face, and said:

"My father, I have kept this prophecy in the secret place of my soul. Religion without a great hope would be like an altar without a living fire. And now the flame has burned more brightly, and by the light of it I have read other words which also have come from the fountain of Truth, and speak yet more clearly of the rising of the Victorious One in his brightness."

He drew from the breast of his tunic two small rolls of fine linen, with writing upon them, and unfolded them carefully upon his knee.

"In the years that are lost in the past, long before our fathers came into the land of Babylon, there were wise men in Chaldea, from whom the first of the Magi learned the secret of the heavens. And of these Balaam the son of Beor was one of the mightiest. Hear the words of his prophecy: 'There shall come a star out of Jacob, and a scepter shall arise out of Israel.'"

The lips of Tigranes drew downward with contempt, as he said:

"Judah was a captive by the waters of Babylon, and the sons of Jacob were in bondage to our kings. The tribes of Israel are scattered through the mountains like lost sheep, and from the remnant that dwells in Judea under the yoke of Rome neither star nor scepter shall arise."

"And yet," answered Artaban, "it was the Hebrew Daniel, the mighty searcher of dreams, the counselor of kings, the wise Belteshazzar, who was most honored and beloved of our great King Cyrus. A prophet of sure things and a reader of the thoughts of God, Daniel proved himself to our people. And these are the words that he wrote." Artaban read from the second roll: "'Know, therefore, and understand that from the going forth of the commandment to restore Jerusalem, unto the Anointed One, the Prince, the time shall be seven and threescore and two weeks.'"

"But, my son," said Abgarus, doubtfully, "these are mystical numbers. Who can interpret them, or who can find the key that shall unlock their meaning?"

Artaban answered: "It has been shown to me and to my three companions among the Magi – Caspar, Melchior, and Balthazar. We have searched the ancient tablets of Chaldea and computed the time. It falls in this year. We have studied the sky, and in the spring of the year we saw two of the greatest stars draw near together in the sign of the Fish, which is the house of the Hebrews. We also saw a new star there, which shone for one night and then vanished. Now again the two great planets are meeting. This night is their conjunction. My three brothers are watching at the ancient temple of the Seven Spheres, at Borsippa, in Babylonia, and I am watching here. If the star shines again, they will wait ten days for me at the temple, and then we will set out together for Jerusalem, to see and worship the promised one who shall be born King of Israel. I believe the sign will come. I have made ready for the journey. I have sold my house and my possessions, and bought these three jewels – a sapphire, a ruby, and a pearl – to carry them as tribute to the King. And I ask you to go with me on the pilgrimage, that we may have joy together in finding the Prince who is worthy to be served."

While he was speaking he thrust his hand into the inmost fold of his girdle and drew out three great gems – one blue as a fragment of the night sky, one redder than a ray of sunrise, and one as pure as the peak of a snow mountain at twilight – and laid them on the outspread linen scrolls before him.

But his friends looked on with strange and alien eyes. A veil of doubt and mistrust came over their faces, like a fog creeping up from the marshes to hide the hills. They glanced at each other with looks of wonder and pity, as those who have listened to incredible sayings, the story of a wild vision, or the proposal of an impossible enterprise.

At last Tigranes said: "Artaban, this is a vain dream. It comes from too much looking upon the stars and the cherishing of lofty thoughts. It would be wiser to spend the time in gathering money for the new fire-temple at Chala. No king will ever rise from the broken race of Israel, and no end will ever come to the eternal strife of light and darkness. He who looks for it is a chaser of shadows. Farewell."

And another said: "Artaban, I have no knowledge of these things, and my office as guardian of the royal treasure binds me here. The quest is not for me. But if thou must follow it, fare thee well."

And another said: "In my house there sleeps a new bride, and I cannot leave her nor take her with me on this strange journey. This quest is not for me. But may thy steps be prospered wherever thou goest. So farewell."

And another said: "I am ill and unfit for hardship, but there is a man among my servants whom I will send with thee when thou goest, to bring me word how thou farest."

But Abgarus, the oldest and the one who loved Artaban the best, lingered after the others had gone, and said gravely:

"My son, it may be that the light of truth is in this sign that has appeared in the skies, and then it will surely lead to the Prince and the mighty brightness. Or it may be that it is only a shadow of the light, as Tigranes has said, and then he who follows it will have only a long pilgrimage and an empty search. But it is better to follow even the shadow of the best than to remain content with the worst. And those who would see wonderful things must often be ready to travel alone. I am too old for this journey, but my heart shall be a companion of the pilgrimage day and night, and I shall know the end of thy quest. Go in peace."

So one by one they went out of the azure chamber with its silver stars, and Artaban was left in solitude.

He gathered up the jewels and replaced them in his girdle. For a long time he stood and watched the flame that flickered and sank upon the altar. Then he crossed the hall, lifted the heavy curtain, and passed out between the dull red pillars of porphyry to the terrace on the roof.

The shiver that thrills through the earth ere she rouses from her night sleep had already begun, and the cool wind that heralds the daybreak was drawing downward from the lofty snow-traced ravines of Mount Orontes. Birds, half awakened, crept and chirped among the rustling leaves and the smell of ripened grapes came in brief wafts from the arbors.

Far over the eastern plain a white mist stretched like a lake. But where the distant peak of Zagros serrated the western horizon the sky was clear. Jupiter and Saturn rolled together like drops of lambent flame about to blend in one.

As Artaban watched them, behold! an azure spark was born out of the darkness beneath, rounding itself with purple splendors to a crimson sphere, and spiring upward through rays of saffron and orange into a point of white radiance. Tiny and infinitely remote, yet perfect in every part, it pulsated in the enormous vault as if the three jewels in the Magian's breast had mingled and been transformed into a living heart of light.

He bowed his head. He covered his brow with his hands.

"It is the sign," he said. "The King is coming, and I will go to meet him."

By the Waters of Babylon

ALL NIGHT LONG VASDA, the swiftest of Artaban's horses, had been waiting, saddled and bridled, in her stall, pawing the ground impatiently and shaking her bit as if she shared the eagerness of her master's purpose, though she knew not its meaning.

Before the birds had fully roused to their strong, high, joyful chant of morning song, before the white mist had begun to lift lazily from the plain, the other wise man was in the saddle, riding swiftly along the highroad, which skirted the base of Mount Orontes, westward.

How close, how intimate is the comradeship between a man and his favorite horse on a long journey. It is a silent, comprehensive friendship, an intercourse beyond the need of words.

They drink at the same wayside spring, and sleep under the same guardian stars. They are conscious together of the subduing spell of nightfall and the quickening joy of daybreak. The master shares his evening meal with his hungry companion, and feels the soft, moist lips caressing the palm of his hand as they close over the morsel of bread. In the grey dawn he is roused from his bivouac by the gentle stir of a warm, sweet breath over his sleeping face, and looks up into the eyes of his faithful fellow traveler, ready and waiting for the toil of the day. Surely, unless he is a pagan and an unbeliever, by whatever name he calls upon his God, he will thank Him for this voiceless sympathy, this dumb affection, and his morning prayer will embrace a double blessing – God bless us both, and keep our feet from falling and our souls from death!

And then, through the keen morning air, the swift hoofs beat their spirited music along the road, keeping time to the pulsing of two hearts that are moved with the same eager desire – to conquer space, to devour the distance, to attain the goal of the journey.

Artaban must, indeed, ride wisely and well if he would keep the appointed hour with the other Magi; for the route was a hundred and fifty parasangs, and fifteen was the utmost that he could travel in a day. But he knew Vasda's strength, and pushed forward without anxiety, making the fixed distance every day, though he must travel late into the night, and in the morning long before sunrise.

He passed along the brown slopes of Mount Orontes, furrowed by the rocky courses of a hundred torrents.

He crossed the level plains of the Nisæans, where the famous herds of horses, feeding in the wide pastures, tossed their heads at Vasda's approach and galloped away with a thunder of many hoofs, and flocks of wild birds rose suddenly from the swampy meadows, wheeling in great circles with a shining flutter of innumerable wings and shrill cries of surprise.

He traversed the fertile fields of Concabar, where the dust from the threshing-floors filled the air with a golden mist, half hiding the huge Temple of Astarte with its four hundred pillars.

At Baghistan, among the rich gardens watered by fountains from the rock, he looked up at the mountain thrusting its immense rugged brow out over the road, and saw the figure of King Darius trampling upon his fallen foes, and the proud list of his wars and conquests graven high upon the face of the eternal cliff.

Over many a cold and desolate pass, crawling painfully across the wind-swept shoulders of the hills; down many a black mountain gorge, where the river roared and raced before him like a savage guide; across many a smiling vale, with terraces of yellow limestone full of vines and fruit trees; through the oak groves of Carine and the dark Gates of Zagros, walled in by precipices; into the ancient city of Chala, where the people of Samaria had been kept in captivity long ago; and out again by the mighty portal, riven through the encircling hills, where he saw the image of the High Priest of the Magi sculptured on the wall of rock, with hand uplifted as if to bless the centuries of pilgrims; past the entrance of the narrow defile, filled from end to end with orchards of peaches and figs, through which the river Gyndes foamed down to meet him; over the broad rice-fields, where the autumnal vapors spread their deathly mists; following along the course of the river, under tremulous shadows of poplar and tamarind, among the lower hills; and out upon the flat plain, where the road ran straight as an arrow through the stubble fields and parched meadows; past the city of Ctesiphon, where the Parthian emperors reigned, and the vast metropolis of Seleucia which Alexander built; across the swirling floods of Tigris and the many channels of Euphrates, flowing yellow through the corn-lands – Artaban pressed onward until he arrived, at nightfall of the tenth day, beneath the shattered walls of populous Babylon.

Vasda was almost spent, and he would gladly have turned into the city to find rest and refreshment for himself and for her. But he knew that it was three hours' journey yet to the Temple of the Seven Spheres, and he must reach the place by midnight if he would find his comrades waiting. So he did not halt, but rode steadily across the stubble fields.

A grove of date palms made an island of glooms in the pale yellow sea. As she passed into the shadow Vasda slackened her pace, and began to pick her way more carefully.

Near the farther end of the darkness an access of caution seemed to fall upon her. She scented some danger or difficulty; it was not in her heart to fly from it – only to be prepared for it, and to meet it wisely as a good horse should do. The grove was close and silent as the tomb; not a leaf rustled, not a bird sang.

She felt her steps before her delicately, carrying her head low, and sighing now and then with apprehension. At last she gave a quick breath of anxiety and dismay, and stood stock-still, quivering in every muscle, before a dark object in the shadow of the last palm tree.

Artaban dismounted. The dim starlight revealed the form of a man lying across the road. His humble dress and the outline of his haggard face showed that he was probably one of the poor Hebrew exiles who still dwelt in great numbers in the vicinity. His pallid skin, dry and yellow as parchment, bore the mark of the deadly fever which ravaged the marshlands in autumn. The chill of death was in his lean hand, and, as Artaban released it, the arm fell back inertly upon the motionless breast.

He turned away with a thought of pity, consigning the body to that strange burial which the Magians deemed most fitting – the funeral of the desert, from which the kites and vultures rise on dark wings, and the beasts of prey slink furtively away, leaving only a heap of white bones in the sand.

But, as he turned, a long, faint, ghostly sigh came from the man's lips. The brown, bony fingers closed convulsively on the hem of the Magian's robe and held him fast.

Artaban's heart leaped to his throat, not with fear, but with a dumb resentment at the importunity of this blind delay.

How could he stay here in the darkness to minister to a dying stranger? What claim had this unknown fragment of human life upon his compassion or his service? If he lingered but for an hour he could hardly reach Borsippa at the appointed time. His companions would think he had given up the journey. They would go without him. He would lose his quest.

But if he went on now, the man would surely die. If he stayed, life might be restored. His spirit throbbed and fluttered with the urgency of the crisis. Should he risk the great reward of his divine faith for the sake of a single deed of human love? Should he turn aside, if only for a moment, from the following of the star, to give a cup of cold water to a poor, perishing Hebrew?

"God of truth and purity," he prayed, "direct me in the holy path, the way of wisdom which only Thou knowest."

Then he turned back to the sick man. Loosening the grasp of his hand, he carried him to a little mound at the foot of the palm tree.

He unbound the thick folds of the turban and opened the garment above the sunken breast. He brought water from one of the small canals near by, and moistened the sufferer's brow and mouth. He mingled a draught of one of those simple but potent remedies which he carried always in his girdle – for the Magians were physicians as well as astrologers – and poured it slowly between the colorless lips. Hour after hour he labored as only a skillful healer of disease can do; and, at last, the man's strength returned; he sat up and looked about him.

"Who art thou?" he said, in the rude dialect of the country, "and why hast thou sought me here to bring back my life?"

"I am Artaban the Magian, of the city of Ecbatana, and I am going to Jerusalem in search of one who is born to be King of the Jews, a great Prince and Deliverer of all men. I dare not delay any longer upon my journey, for the caravan that has waited for me may depart without me. But see, here is all that I have left of bread and wine, and here is a potion of healing herbs. When thy strength is restored thou canst find the dwellings of the Hebrews among the houses of Babylon."

The Jew raised his trembling hand solemnly to heaven.

"Now may the God of Abraham and Isaac and Jacob bless and prosper the journey of the merciful, and bring him in peace to his desired haven. But stay; I have nothing to give thee in return – only this: that I can tell thee where the Messiah must be sought. For our prophets have said that he should be born not in Jerusalem, but in Bethlehem of Judah. May the Lord bring thee in safety to that place, because thou hast had pity on the sick."

It was already long past midnight. Artaban rode in haste, and Vasda, restored by the brief rest, ran eagerly through the silent plain and swam the channels of the river. She put forth the remnant of her strength, and fled over the ground like a gazelle.

But the first beam of the sun sent her shadow before her as she entered upon the final stadium of the journey, and the eyes of Artaban, anxiously scanning the great mound of Nimrod and the Temple of the Seven Spheres, could discern no trace of his friends.

The many-colored terraces of black and orange and red and yellow and green and blue and white, shattered by the convulsions of nature, and crumbling under the repeated blows of human violence, still glittered like a ruined rainbow in the morning light.

Artaban rode swiftly around the hill. He dismounted and climbed to the highest terrace, looking out toward the west.

The huge desolation of the marshes stretched away to the horizon and the border of the desert. Bitterns stood by the stagnant pools and jackals skulked through the low bushes; but there was no sign of the caravan of the wise men, far or near.

At the edge of the terrace he saw a little cairn of broken bricks, and under them a piece of parchment. He caught it up and read: "We have waited past the midnight and can delay no longer. We go to find the King. Follow us across the desert."

Artaban sat down upon the ground and covered his head in despair.

"How can I cross the desert," said he, "with no food and with a spent horse? I must return to Babylon, sell my sapphire, and buy a train of camels, and provision for the journey. I may never overtake my friends. Only God the merciful knows whether I shall not lose the sight of the King because I tarried to show mercy."

For the Sake of a Little Child

THERE WAS A SILENCE in the Hall of Dreams, where I was listening to the story of the Other Wise Man. And through this silence I saw, but very dimly, his figure passing over the dreary undulations of the desert, high upon the back of his camel, rocking steadily onwards like a ship over the waves.

The land of death spread its cruel net around him. The stony wastes bore no fruit but briers and thorns. The dark ledges of rock thrust themselves above the surface here and there, like the bones of perished monsters. Arid and inhospitable mountain ranges rose before him, furrowed with dry channels of ancient torrents, white and ghastly as scars on the face of nature. Shifting hills of treacherous sand were heaped like tombs along the horizon. By day, the fierce heat pressed its intolerable burden on the quivering air; and no living creature moved on the dumb, swooning earth but tiny jerboas scuttling through the parched bushes, or lizards vanishing in the clefts of the rock. By night the jackals prowled and barked in the distance, and the lion made the black ravines echo with his hollow roaring, while a bitter, blighting chill followed the fever of the day. Through heat and cold, the Magian moved steadily onward.

Then I saw the gardens and orchards of Damascus, watered by the streams of Aldana and Pharpar, with their sloping swards inlaid with bloom, and their thickets of myrrh and roses. I saw also the long snowy ridge of Hermon, and the dark groves of cedars, and the valley of the Jordan, and the blue waters of the Lake of Galilee, and the fertile plain of Esdraelon and the hills of Ephraim, and the highlands of Judah. Through all these I followed the figure of Artaban moving steadily onward, until he arrived at Bethlehem. And it was the third day after the three wise men had come to that place and had found Mary and Joseph, with the young child, Jesus, and had lain their gifts of gold and frankincense and myrrh at his feet.

Then the other wise man drew near, weary, but full of hope, bearing his ruby and his pearl to offer to the King. "For now at last," he said, "I shall surely find him, though it be alone, and later than my brethren. This is the place of which the Hebrew exile told me that the prophets had spoken, and here I shall behold the rising of the great light. But I must inquire about the visit of my brethren, and to what house the star directed them, and to whom they presented their tribute."

The streets of the village seemed to be deserted, and Artaban wondered whether the men had all gone up to the hill-pastures to bring down their sheep. From the open door of a low stone cottage he heard the sound of a woman's voice singing softly. He entered and found a young mother hushing her baby to rest. She told him of the strangers from the Far East who had appeared in the village three days ago, and how they said that a star had guided them to the place where Joseph of Nazareth was lodging with his wife and her newborn child, and how they had paid reverence to the child and given him many rich gifts.

"But the travelers disappeared again," she continued, "as suddenly as they had come. We were afraid at the strangeness of their visit. We could not understand it. The man of Nazareth took the babe and his mother and fled away that same night secretly, and it was whispered that they were going far away to Egypt. Ever since there has been a spell upon the village; something evil hangs over it. They say that the Roman soldiers are coming from Jerusalem to force a new tax from us, and the men have driven the flocks and herds far back among the hills, and hidden themselves to escape it."

Artaban listened to her gentle, timid speech and the child in her arms looked up in his face and smiled, stretching out its rosy hands to grasp at the winged circle of gold on his breast. His heart warmed to the touch. It seemed like a greeting of love and trust to one who had journeyed long in loneliness and perplexity, fighting with his own doubts and fears, and following a light that was veiled in clouds.

"Might not this child have been the promised Prince?" he asked within himself, as he touched its soft cheek. "Kings have been born ere now in lowlier houses than this, and the favorite of the stars may rise even from a cottage. But it has not seemed good to the God of wisdom to reward my search so soon and so easily. The one whom I seek has gone before me; and now I must follow the King to Egypt."

The young mother laid the babe in its cradle, and rose to minister to the wants of the strange guest that fate had brought into her house. She set food before him, the plain fare of peasants, but willingly offered, and therefore full of refreshment for the soul as well as for the body. Artaban accepted it gratefully; and, as he ate, the child fell into a happy slumber, and murmured sweetly in its dreams, and a great peace filled the quiet room.

But suddenly there came the noise of a wild confusion and uproar in the streets of the village, a shrieking and wailing of women's voices, a clangor of swords, and a desperate cry: "The soldiers! the soldiers of Herod! They are killing our children."

The young mother's face grew white with terror. She clasped her child to her bosom, and crouched motionless in the darkest corner of the room, covering him with the folds of her robe, lest he should wake and cry.

But Artaban went quickly and stood in the doorway of the house. His broad shoulders filled the portal from side to side, and the peak of his white cap all but touched the lintel.

The soldiers came hurrying down the street, with bloody hands and dripping swords. At the sight of the stranger in his imposing dress they hesitated with surprise. The captain of the band approached the threshold to thrust him aside. But Artaban did not stir. His face was as calm as though he were watching the stars, and in his eyes there burned that steady radiance before which even the half-tamed hunting leopard shrinks and the fierce bloodhound pauses in his leap. He held the soldier silently for an instant, and then said, in a low voice:

"I am all alone in this place, and I am waiting to give this jewel to the prudent captain who will leave me in peace."

He showed the ruby, glistening in the hollow of his hand like a great drop of blood.

The captain was amazed at the splendor of the gem. The pupils of his eyes expanded with desire, and the hard lines of greed wrinkled around his lips. He stretched out his hand and took the ruby.

"March on!" he cried to his men. "There is no child here. The house is still."

The clamor and the clang of arms passed down the street as the headlong fury of the chase sweeps by the secret covert where the trembling deer is hidden. Artaban reentered the cottage. He turned his face to the east and prayed:

"God of truth, forgive my sin! I have said the thing that is not, to save the life of a child. And two of my gifts are gone. I have spent for man that which was meant for God. Shall I ever be worthy to see the face of the King?"

But the voice of the woman, weeping for joy in the shadow behind him, said, very gently:

"Because thou hast saved the life of my little one, may the Lord bless thee and keep thee; the Lord make His face to shine upon thee and be gracious unto thee; the Lord lift up His countenance upon thee and give thee peace."

In the Hidden Way of Sorrow

THEN AGAIN there was a silence in the Hall of Dreams, deeper and more mysterious than the first interval, and I understood that the years of Artaban were flowing very swiftly under the stillness of that clinging fog, and I caught only a glimpse, here and there, of the river of his life shining through the shadows that concealed its course.

I saw him moving among the throngs of men in populous Egypt, seeking everywhere for traces of the household that had come down from Bethlehem, and finding them under the spreading sycamore trees of Heliopolis, and beneath the walls of the Roman fortress of New Babylon beside the Nile – traces so faint and dim that they vanished before him continually, as footprints on the hard river sand glisten for a moment with moisture and then disappear.

I saw him again at the foot of the pyramids, which lifted their sharp points into the intense saffron glow of the sunset sky, changeless monuments of the perishable glory and the imperishable hope of man. He looked up into the vast countenance of the crouching Sphinx and vainly tried to read the meaning of the calm eyes and smiling mouth. Was it, indeed, the mockery of all effort and all aspiration, as Tigranes had said – the cruel jest of a riddle that has no answer, a search that never can succeed? Or was there a touch of pity and encouragement in that inscrutable smile – a promise that even the defeated should attain a victory, and the disappointed should discover a prize, and the ignorant should be made wise, and the blind should see, and the wandering should come into the haven at last?

I saw him again in an obscure house of Alexandria, taking counsel with a Hebrew rabbi. The venerable man, bending over the rolls of parchment on which the prophecies of Israel were written, read aloud the pathetic words which foretold the sufferings of the promised Messiah – the despised and rejected of men, the man of sorrows and the acquaintance of grief.

"And remember, my son," said he, fixing his deep-set eyes upon the face of Artaban, "the King whom you are seeking is not to be found in a palace, nor among the rich and powerful. If the light of the world and the glory of Israel had been appointed to come with the greatness of earthly splendor, it must have appeared long ago. For no son of Abraham will ever again rival the power which Joseph had in the palaces of Egypt, or the magnificence of

Solomon throned between the lions in Jerusalem. But the light for which the world is waiting is a new light, the glory that shall rise out of patient and triumphant suffering. And the kingdom which is to be established forever is a new kingdom, the royalty of perfect and unconquerable love."

"I do not know how this shall come to pass, nor how the turbulent kings and peoples of earth shall be brought to acknowledge the Messiah and pay homage to Him. But this I know. Those who seek Him will do well to look among the poor and the lowly, the sorrowful and the oppressed."

So I saw the other wise man again and again, travelling from place to place, and searching among the people of the dispersion, with whom the little family from Bethlehem might, perhaps, have found a refuge. He passed through countries where famine lay heavy upon the land, and the poor were crying for bread. He made his dwelling in plague-stricken cities where the sick were languishing in the bitter companionship of helpless misery. He visited the oppressed and the afflicted in the gloom of subterranean prisons, and the crowded wretchedness of slave markets, and the weary toil of galley-ships. In all this populous and intricate world of anguish, though he found none to worship, he found many to help. He fed the hungry, and clothed the naked, and healed the sick, and comforted the captive; and his years went by more swiftly than the weaver's shuttle that flashes back and forth through the loom while the web grows and the invisible pattern is completed.

It seemed almost as if he had forgotten his quest. But once I saw him for a moment as he stood alone at sunrise, waiting at the gate of a Roman prison. He had taken from a secret resting place in his bosom the pearl, the last of his jewels. As he looked at it, a mellower luster, a soft and iridescent light, full of shifting gleams of azure and rose, trembled on its surface. It seemed to have absorbed some reflection of the colors of the lost sapphire and ruby. So the profound, secret purpose of a noble life draws into itself the memories of past joy and past sorrow. All that has helped it, all that has hindered it, is transfused by a subtle magic into its very essence. It becomes more luminous and precious the longer it is carried close to the warmth of the beating heart.

Then, at last, while I was thinking of this pearl, and of its meaning, I heard the end of the story of the Other Wise Man.

A Pearl of Great Price

THREE-AND-THIRTY years of the life of Artaban had passed away, and he was still a pilgrim, and a seeker after light. His hair, once darker than the cliffs of Zagros, was now white as the wintry snow that covered them. His eyes, that once flashed like flames of fire, were dull as embers smoldering among the ashes.

Worn and weary and ready to die, but still looking for the King, he had come for the last time to Jerusalem. He had often visited the holy city before, and had searched through all its lanes and crowded hovels and black prisons without finding any trace of the family of Nazarenes who had fled from Bethlehem long ago. But now it seemed as if he must make one more effort, and something whispered in his heart that, at last, he might succeed.

It was the season of the Passover. The city was thronged with strangers. The children of Israel, scattered in far lands all over the world, had returned to the Temple for the great feast, and here had been a confusion of tongues in the narrow streets for many days.

But on this day there was a singular agitation visible in the multitude. The sky was veiled with a portentous gloom, and currents of excitement seemed to flash through the crowd like the thrill that shakes the forest on the eve of a storm. A secret tide was sweeping them all one way. The clatter of sandals, and the soft thick sound of thousands of bare feet shuffling over the stones, flowed unceasingly along the street that leads to the Damascus Gate.

Artaban joined company with a group of people from his own country, Parthian Jews who had come up to keep the Passover, and inquired of them the cause of the tumult, and where they were going.

"We are going," they answered, "to the place called Golgotha, outside the city walls, where there is to be an execution. Have you not heard what has happened? Two famous robbers are to be crucified, and with them another, called Jesus of Nazareth, a man who has done many wonderful works among the people, so that they love him greatly. But the priests and elders have said that he must die, because he gave himself out to be the Son of God. And Pilate has sent him to the cross because he said that he was the 'King of the Jews.'"

How strangely these familiar words fell upon the tired heart of Artaban! They had led him for a lifetime over land and sea. And now they came to him darkly and mysteriously like a message of despair. The King had arisen, but He had been denied and cast out. He was about to perish. Perhaps He was already dying. Could it be the same who had been born in Bethlehem thirty-three years ago, at whose birth the star had appeared in heaven, and of whose coming the prophets had spoken?

Artaban's heart beat unsteadily with that troubled, doubtful apprehension which is the excitement of old age. But he said within himself: "The ways of God are stranger than the thoughts of men, and it may be that I shall find the King, at last, in the hands of His enemies, and shall come in time to offer my pearl for His ransom before He dies."

So the old man followed the multitude with slow and painful steps toward the Damascus gate of the city. Just beyond the entrance of the guard house a troop of Macedonian soldiers came down the street, dragging a young girl with torn dress and disheveled hair. As the Magian paused to look at her with compassion she broke suddenly from the hands of her tormenters and threw herself at his feet, clasping him around the knees. She had seen his white cap and the winged circle on his breast.

"Have pity on me," she cried, "and save me, for the sake of the God of Purity! I also am a daughter of the true religion which is taught by the Magi. My father was a merchant of Parthia, but he is dead, and I am seized for his debts to be sold as a slave. Save me from worse than death."

Artaban trembled.

It was the old conflict in his soul, which had come to him in the palm grove of Babylon and in the cottage at Bethlehem – the conflict between the expectation of faith and the impulse of love. Twice the gift which he had consecrated to the worship of religion had been drawn from his hand to the service of humanity. This was the third trial, the ultimate probation, the final and irrevocable choice.

Was it his great opportunity, or his last temptation? He could not tell. One thing only was clear in the darkness of his mind – it was inevitable. And does not the inevitable come from God?

One thing only was sure to his divided heart – to rescue this helpless girl would be a true deed of love. And is not love the light of the soul?

He took the pearl from his bosom. Never had it seemed so luminous, so radiant, so full of tender, living luster. He laid it in the hand of the slave.

"This is thy ransom, daughter! It is the last of my treasures which I kept for the King."

While he spoke, the darkness of the sky thickened, and shuddering tremors ran through the earth, heaving convulsively like the breast of one who struggles with mighty grief.

The walls of the houses rocked to and fro. Stones were loosened and crashed into the street. Dust clouds filled the air. The soldiers fled in terror, reeling like drunken men. But Artaban and the girl whom he had ransomed crouched helpless beneath the wall of the Prætorium.

What had he to fear? What had he to live for? He had given away the last remnant of his tribute for the King. He had parted with the last hope of finding Him. The quest was over, and it had failed. But, even in that thought, accepted and embraced, there was peace. It was not resignation. It was not submission. It was something more profound and searching. He knew that all was well, because he had done the best that he could, from day to day. He had been true to the light that had been given to him. He had looked for more. And if he had not found it, if a failure was all that came out of his life, doubtless that was the best that was possible. He had not seen the revelation of "life everlasting, incorruptible, and immortal." But he knew that even if he could live his earthly life over again, it could not be otherwise than it had been.

One more lingering pulsation of the earthquake quivered through the ground. A heavy tile, shaken from the roof, fell and struck the old man on the temple. He lay breathless and pale, with his gray head resting on the young girl's shoulder, and the blood trickling from the wound. As she bent over him, fearing that he was dead, there came a voice through the twilight, very small and still, like music sounding from a distance, in which the notes are clear but the words are lost. The girl turned to see if someone had spoken from the window above them, but she saw no one.

Then the old man's lips began to move, as if in answer, and she heard him say in the Parthian tongue:

"Not so, my Lord: For when saw I thee hungry, and fed thee? Or thirsty, and gave thee drink? When saw I thee a stranger, and took thee in? Or naked, and clothed thee? When saw I thee sick or in prison, and came unto thee? Three-and-thirty years have I looked for thee; but I have never seen thy face, nor ministered to thee, my King."

He ceased, and the sweet voice came again. And again the maid heard it, very faintly and far away. But now it seemed as though she understood the words: "Verily I say unto thee, inasmuch as thou hast done it unto one of the least of these my brethren, thou has done it unto me."

A calm radiance of wonder and joy lighted the pale face of Artaban like the first ray of dawn on a snowy mountain peak. One long, last breath of relief exhaled from his lips.

His journey was ended. His treasures were accepted. The Other Wise Man had found the King.

The Miraculous Staircase

Arthur Gordon

O N THAT COOL DECEMBER morning in 1878, sunlight lay like an amber rug across the dusty streets and adobe houses of Santa Fe. It glinted on the bright tile roof of the almost completed Chapel of Our Lady of Light and on the nearby windows of the convent school run by the Sisters of Loretto. Inside the convent, the Mother Superior looked up from her packing as a tap came on her door.

"It's *another* carpenter, Reverend Mother," said Sister Francis Louise, her round face apologetic. "I told him that you're leaving right away, that you haven't time to see him, but he says…"

"I know what he says," Mother Magdalene said, going on resolutely with her packing. "That he's heard about our problem with the new chapel. That he's the best carpenter in all of New Mexico. That he can build us a staircase to the choir loft despite the fact that the brilliant architect in Paris who drew the plans failed to leave any space for one. And despite the fact that five master carpenters have already tried and failed. You're quite right, Sister; I don't have time to listen to that story again."

"But he seems such a nice man," said Sister Francis Louise wistfully, "and he's out there with his burro, and…"

"I'm sure," said Mother Magdalene with a smile, "that he's a charming man, and that his burro is a charming donkey. But there's sickness down at the Santo Domingo pueblo, and it may be cholera. Sister Mary Helen and I are the only ones here who've had cholera. So we have to go. And you have to stay and run the school. And that's that!" Then she called, "Manuela!"

A young Indian girl of twelve or thirteen, black-haired and smiling, came in quietly on moccasined feet. She was a mute. She could hear and understand, but the Sisters had been unable to teach her to speak. The Mother Superior spoke to her gently: "Take my things down to the wagon, child. I'll be right there." And to Sister Francis Louise: "You'd better tell your carpenter friend to come back in two or three weeks. I'll see him then."

"Two or three weeks! Surely you'll be home for Christmas?"

"If it's the Lord's will, Sister. I hope so."

In the street, beyond the waiting wagon, Mother Magdalene could see the carpenter, a bearded man, strongly built and taller than most Mexicans, with dark eyes and a smiling, wind-burned face. Beside him, laden with tools and scraps of lumber, a small gray burro stood patiently. Manuela was stroking its nose, glancing shyly at its owner. "You'd better explain," said the Mother Superior, "that the child can hear him, but she can't speak."

Goodbyes were quick – the best kind when you leave a place you love. Southwest, then, along the dusty trail, the mountains purple with shadow, the Rio Grande a ribbon of green far off to the right. The pace was slow, but Mother Magdalene and Sister Mary Helen amused themselves by singing songs and telling Christmas stories as the sun marched up and down the sky. And their leathery driver listened and nodded.

Two days of this brought them to Santo Domingo Pueblo, where the sickness was not cholera after all, but measles, almost as deadly in an Indian village. And so they stayed, helping the harassed Father Sebastian, visiting the dark adobe hovels where feverish brown children tossed and fierce Indian dogs showed their teeth.

At night they were boneweary, but sometimes Mother Magdalene found time to talk to Father Sebastian about her plans for the dedication of the new chapel. It was to be in April; the Archbishop himself would be there. And it might have been dedicated sooner, were it not for this incredible business of a choir loft with no means of access – unless it were a ladder.

"I told the Bishop," said Mother Magdalene, "that it would be a mistake to have the plans drawn in Paris. If something went wrong, what could we do? But he wanted our chapel in Santa Fe patterned after the Sainte Chapelle in Paris, and who am I to argue with Bishop Lamy? So the talented Monsieur Mouly designs a beautiful choir loft high up under the rose window, and no way to get up to it."

"Perhaps," sighed Father Sebastian, "he had in mind a heavenly choir. The kind with wings."

"It's not funny," said Mother Magdalene a bit sharply. "I've prayed and prayed, but apparently there's no solution at all. There just isn't room on the chapel floor for the supports such a staircase needs."

The days passed, and with each passing day Christmas drew closer. Twice, horsemen on their way from Santa Fe to Albuquerque brought letters from Sister Francis Louise. All was well at the convent, but Mother Magdalene frowned over certain paragraphs. "The children are getting ready for Christmas," Sister Francis Louise wrote in her first letter. "Our little Manuela and the carpenter have become great friends. It's amazing how much he seems to know about us all..."

And what, thought Mother Magdalene, is the carpenter still doing there?

The second letter also mentioned the carpenter. "Early every morning he comes with another load of lumber, and every night he goes away. When we ask him by what authority he does these things, he smiles and says nothing. We have tried to pay him for his work, but he will accept no pay..."

Work? What work? Mother Magdalene wrinkled up her nose in exasperation. Had that softhearted Sister Francis Louise given the man permission to putter around in the new chapel? With firm and disapproving hand the Mother Superior wrote a note ordering an end to all such unauthorized activities. She gave it to an Indian pottery-maker on his way to Santa Fe.

But that night the first snow fell, so thick and heavy that the Indian turned back. Next day at noon the sun shone again on a world glittering with diamonds. But Mother Magdalene knew that another snowfall might make it impossible for her to be home for Christmas. By now the sickness at Santo Domingo was subsiding. And so that afternoon they began the long ride back.

The snow did come again, making their slow progress even slower. It was late on Christmas Eve, close to midnight, when the tired horses plodded up to the convent door. But lamps still burned. Manuela flew down the steps, Sister Francis Louise close behind her. And chilled and weary though she was, Mother Magdalene sensed instantly an excitement, an electricity in the air that she could not understand.

Nor did she understand it when they led her, still in her heavy wraps, down the corridor, into the new, as-yet-unused chapel where a few candles burned. "Look, Reverend Mother," breathed Sister Francis Louise. "Look!"

Like a curl of smoke the staircase rose before them, as insubstantial as a dream. Its base was on the chapel floor; its top rested against the choir loft. Nothing else supported it; it seemed to float on air. There were no banisters. Two complete spirals it made, the polished wood gleaming softly in the candlelight. "Thirty-three steps," whispered Sister Francis Louise. "One for each year in the life of Our Lord."

Mother Magdalene moved forward like a woman in a trance. She put her foot on the first step, then the second, then the third. There was not a tremor. She looked down, bewildered, at Manuela's ecstatic, upturned face. "But it's impossible! There wasn't time!"

"He finished yesterday," the Sister said. "He didn't come today. No one has seen him anywhere in Santa Fe. He's gone."

"But *who* was he? Don't you even know his *name?*"

The Sister shook her head, but now Manuela pushed forward, nodding emphatically. Her mouth opened; she took a deep, shuddering breath; she made a sound that was like a gasp in the stillness. The nuns stared at her, transfixed. She tried again. This time it was a syllable, followed by another. "Jo-sé." She clutched the Mother Superior's arm and repeated the first word she had ever spoken. "José!"

Sister Francis Louise crossed herself. Mother Magdalene felt her heart contract. José – the Spanish word for Joseph. Joseph the Carpenter. Joseph the Master Woodworker of...

"José!" Manuela's dark eyes were full of tears. "José!"

Silence, then, in the shadowy chapel. No one moved. Far away across the snow-silvered town Mother Magdalene heard a bell tolling midnight. She came down the stairs and took Manuela's hand. She felt uplifted by a great surge of wonder and gratitude and compassion and love. And she knew what it was. It was the spirit of Christmas. And it was upon them all.

You may see the inexplicable staircase yourself in Santa Fe today. It stands just as it stood when the chapel was dedicated except for the banister, which was added later. Tourists stare and marvel. Architects shake their heads and murmur, "Impossible." No one knows the identity of the designer-builder. All the Sisters know is that the problem existed, a stranger came, solved it and left.

The thirty-three steps make two complete turns without central support. There are no nails in the staircase; only wooden pegs. The curved stringers are put together with exquisite precision; the wood is spliced in seven places on the inside and nine on the outside. The wood is said to be a hard-fir variety, nonexistent in New Mexico. School records show that no payment for the staircase was ever made.

? bottom —

Vagrant staircase

No visible means of
support

Handel — Career
debt

Messiah — 24 days

142 people — debtors
prison (Ireland)

Hospital for women &
Children (London)

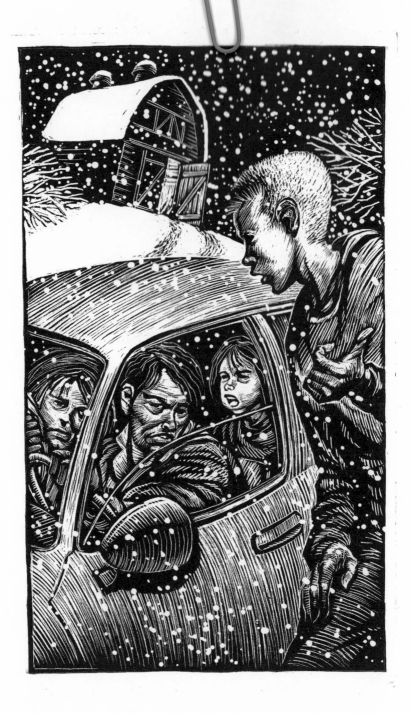

No Room in the Inn

Katherine Paterson

IN THE WINTER, our house looks like a Christmas card. It's an old Vermont farmhouse nestled into the woods, with a view of the snow-covered Green Mountains. The attached barn is now a garage, and my parents run a bed-and-breakfast in the house. My dad works full-time at a computer outfit, so, being both the only man and the only kid at home, I spend a lot of time splitting wood, making fires in the huge kitchen woodstove, cleaning rooms, changing sheets, washing dishes – you name it.

When I saw my parents off at Burlington Airport last week, I tried to look a little sad – as a Christmas present to my mother, who was feeling terrible about leaving me alone for the holidays. Can you imagine? An eighteen-year-old boy alone in a country inn with no guests to cater to, no wood to split, no beds to make – nothing to do for ten glorious days but eat, sleep, and ski. And a new Pontiac Grand Prix sitting in the other half of the garage whispering, "Use me! Use me! Use me!"

I had taken my folks to the airport in the 4 x 4. A good thing, too, because by the time I headed home, the snow was coming down hard. Great for the slopes, I thought, and switched on the radio, which was playing a sappy old-time number, "Let it Snow, Let it Snow, Let it Snow." I was feeling so good I listened to "White Christmas" and a jazzed-up version of "Away in a Manger" before I reached over to switch to my usual station. Ha! Ten days with no one complaining because I had switched the dial on the car radio.

I tried to figure out why I was feeling so great. Sure, I'd miss not having Christmas with the family. My sister's kids are terrific and they think their uncle Ben is God's gift to the world. But you have to understand. I never get time to myself these days. If I'm not working at school, I'm slaving away at the inn. It's really only a bed-and-breakfast, but my mother likes to call it The Inn. I'd have it all to myself, including the 4 x 4, which I have to share with my dad, and ta-da my mother's Pontiac, which for ten days was mine, all mine.

The euphoria had left me by the time I'd spent an hour and forty-five minutes driving what should have taken just over an hour. I was tired and hungry and feeling – could you believe it? – just a little bit sorry for myself in the blackness of a late winter afternoon, when I turned off the interstate and headed for the village. I decided to stop at Gracie's, the only restaurant around, for meat loaf and cheer. Gracie is famous for both.

The woodstove was crackling warm, and the smell of meat loaf and homemade bread filled the place. There were a couple of farmers, Ewell Biggs and Ames Whitehead, sitting at the counter drinking coffee when I got there. They nodded at me as I sat down. I nodded back, waiting for

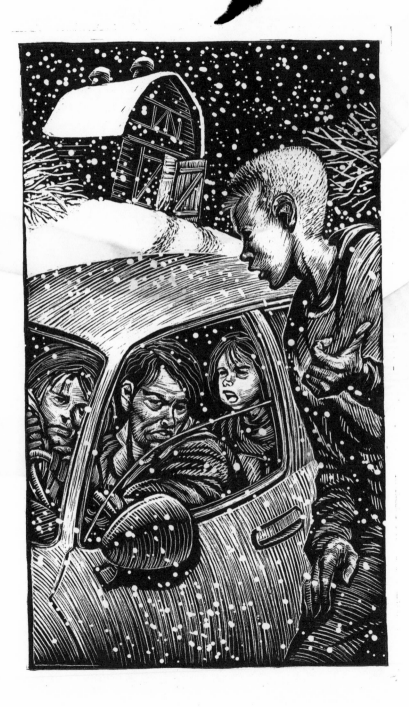

Pratt ton —

Vagrant Staircase

No visible means of
Support

Handel — Career
debt

Mession — 24 days

142 people — debtors
prison (Amband)

Hospital for women &
Children (London)

Gracie's usual "Hello, stranger!" But Gracie just stared at me sadly. "It's meat loaf tonight," she said, as though that would be the last thing anyone would want.

"That's fine," I said, and then, "is something the matter, Gracie?"

"Gracie's all worried about them Russians," Ewell explained to me between slurps of coffee.

"They're Armenians," Gracie said to him, and then to me, "I was just watching the news. Five hundred thousand with no place to sleep, and it's cold."

"It ain't like Vermont winter," Ames said. "Lord, it was seventeen below at my barn this morning."

"It's cold enough," Gracie insisted. "I saw this old woman on TV last night. They showed her hands. She was kinda holding them tight like this" – Gracie clutched her hands together in front of her ample bosom – "and she didn't have any gloves. She was just holding onto herself and shivering. It killed me. I couldn't sleep last night thinking about that poor old woman."

I thought Gracie was going to burst into tears, but she pulled herself together enough to get me a huge steaming plate of meat loaf, mashed potatoes, and beans, with three hot rolls on the side. She knows how I love her rolls.

Just then I felt a blast of air on my back. We all turned to look at the door. A man was standing there – a stranger. There was several days' growth of stubble on his face. He had on worn jeans and a flimsy baseball jacket and no hat or gloves. He was not anyone from around here.

"Take a seat," Gracie said. "Be right with you." Before I could ask for the ketchup, she was back to the Armenians. "And those children. Did you see those poor kids in the hospital with their legs all crushed? One little boy couldn't even remember who he was. The doctor didn't know if his parents were dead or alive."

I opened my mouth during the pause to ask for the ketchup, but by then she had turned to the stranger. "Now, what can I do for you?" she asked.

He was still standing in front of the door as though he couldn't remember what he'd come in for. "Coffee," he muttered at last. "To go."

"People who got through the earthquake are just freezing to death from the cold," Gracie went on as she filled a large Styrofoam cup from the coffee urn.

The man looked puzzled. "Armenians," I said. "She's all upset about the Armenians."

It was obvious he didn't know what we were talking about. "There was a big earthquake over there. They think about fifty to sixty thousand people died."

"And the rest are likely to." Gracie gave a huge sigh. "Right at Christmas. I can't get over those poor children. Cream and sugar?"

"Yeah," the man said. "Both. Double."

Gracie put two teaspoons of sugar and a huge dollop of cream into the cup and pushed on a lid. "That'll be sixty-three cents," she said as the man handed her a dollar bill. "This mason jar here is for the Armenians," she said, pointing to it. "I'm taking donations – if you'd like to put in your change…"

The man took the change she held out and stuffed it into the pocket of his jeans. "How far to Burlington from here?" he asked.

"Well," said Gracie – you could tell she was a little bit annoyed that the man didn't care anything about her Armenians – "you get back on the interstate, it's about forty miles."

"I just came from there," I said, sticking my two cents in like a fool. "Road's terrible."

"Ah, they'll plow soon," said Ewell.

"I need gas," the man said.

"Well, that might be more of a problem. Nothing open this time of night," Ames said.

The man shrugged. He looked at Gracie, but she ignored him, carefully refilling my water glass. "Ben," she said. "You feeling lonely in that big place, come have Christmas dinner here with me."

"Thanks, Gracie," I said, keeping my back to the stranger. "I just might."

I felt the cold air as he opened the door to go. He muttered something as he went out. It sounded like "Damned Armenians," but maybe I just imagined that.

"Friendly soul," Ewell remarked.

"Not too worried about your Russians, either," Ames teased.

"Armenians," Gracie said, looking sadder than ever, so when I was ready to go I stuffed all my change into the jar, even though I'd given her a twenty.

The first thing I did when I got back home was to hang out the "No Vacancy" sign. I wasn't likely to get any visitors on a night like this, but I wasn't taking any chances. I had the evening all planned: first a roaring fire in the woodstove, then a large bottle of Coke and a two-pound bag of potato chips, then three rented videos in a row, none of which I would have been able to watch had there been anyone else in the house.

I had no sooner popped the first tape into the machine and settled back to watch when the doorbell rang…and rang…and rang. There was nothing to do but go answer. I put on the chain and opened the door a crack. "Sorry, no vacancy," I said, and then I saw it was the stranger from Gracie's.

"How about if I just stay in the garage?" he asked. "Like you said, the interstate is terrible, and it's freezing out here in the car."

It wasn't my problem. "Sorry," I said. "No vacancies. There's Woodley's just off the interstate."

"I already tried there," he said. "I ain't got sixty-five dollars."

"Well, if I could let you stay, which I can't, it's sixty-five here, too."

"Look, I'm just asking to stay in your garage, so I won't freeze to death. You'd let a stray dog into the garage, wouldn't you, night like this?"

I hesitated. I didn't really like his looks. Besides, the Pontiac was in there. If anything happened to that car, my mother would kill me.

He smiled then – the kind of shifty-eyed smile that immediately makes you distrust someone. "Just think of me as one of them Armenians," he said.

He was right. Fake smile or not, he would freeze to death in his car on a night like this. "Okay," I said. "Wait. I'll have to get my car out to make room for yours." I closed the front door and carefully locked it before going out through the kitchen to the attached garage. I got in the 4 x 4, pushed the button for the electric door, and slowly backed out. A ten-year-old Chevrolet with rusted sides drove into the slot beside the Pontiac. I got the old blankets out of the cargo area, then locked the 4 x 4 and hurried into the garage.

I put the blankets on the back of the Chevy. "Here's some blankets in case," I yelled as I pushed the button to close the door. I couldn't look at his old car. I couldn't think of the man out here when I had a roaring fire going in the kitchen. But I sure wasn't going to let him inside. People get robbed and beaten up for that kind of stupidity – murdered, even.

He didn't say anything, not even thanks. But it didn't matter. I gave him what he asked for – more than he asked for.

I went in and turned up the VCR very loud...I don't know how long the knocking had been going on before I finally heard it. "Yeah?" I yelled through the closed kitchen door.

"Daddy said, could I use the bathroom?"

I was so startled to hear a kid's voice, I opened the door. Sure enough, there stood a dirty, skinny, red-faced kid. "Daddy said you'd let me use the bathroom."

I just opened the door wider and let him in. What was I supposed to do? Tell the kid to go out in the snow? Sheesh. I shut the door behind him and led him to the downstairs powder room. "Don't use the towels," I warned.

I waited outside the bathroom for what seemed like ten minutes. What in the world was the kid up to? Finally, he came out, walking tall and straight-backed like some little prince. He didn't say a word, not even thank you.

"You're welcome," I said loudly as I let him out the door, but he didn't look my way.

I just sat down. The guy hadn't said anything about any kid. I was sure he hadn't. I probably should call the welfare people or the police or somebody. I hadn't figured out what to do when there was another, softer knock on the kitchen door.

This time I just opened it. "You've been to the bathroom already," I started to say when I saw it was a different kid – a stringy-haired little girl with a runny nose rubbed raw. "Where did you come from?" I asked.

She whispered something.

"What?"

Again, I caught the word bathroom, so I shut the door and pointed her to the powder room. I didn't even bother to warn her about my mother's fancy guest towels. Somehow, I knew this was going to be a long night.

Before the kid had left the bathroom, there was another knock. I snatched open the door, all ready to give the guy a piece of my mind. But this time a woman stood there, holding a baby in a filthy rag of a blanket.

I couldn't believe it. This was like one of those circus acts where people just keep coming out of a car. "Would you warm it?" she asked. I looked down. She was handing me a baby bottle. It was about half full of frozen milk.

"You better do it," I said. I got her a saucepan, filled it with water, and turned on the burner. "The kid – the little girl's in the bathroom," I said, nodding in that direction. I waited, as patiently as I could, for the woman to test the milk on her wrist and shove the bottle into the baby's mouth, and for the little girl to finish wiping her grubby little hands on all four of Mom's embroidered Irish linen guest towels.

"Now," I said. "I'm very sorry, but you're going to have to go."

"It's cold out there," the little girl whined as I tried to gently urge her out the door.

"I know," I said grimly, going out with her around the Pontiac toward the Chevy. The man was sitting there behind the wheel, with all the windows rolled up. I went to the driver's side and tapped, but he didn't roll the window down. He looked straight ahead. I banged louder. "You're going to have to go." I said. "This isn't going to work. You didn't tell me you had kids with you."

The man turned slowly and opened the window a crack. He gave me a look – it was the most sarcastic expression I've ever seen on a man's face. "Just pretend we're some of them Armenians," he said and rolled the window up again.

I stood there for a minute, trying to figure out what to do next. It was so quiet I could hear the soft sounds of the baby drinking its milk. The little girl was watching me from the other side of the Chevy with big scared eyes. The woman hadn't moved. She was still standing in the doorway, the baby cradled in her arms, a dark silhouette against the light streaming from the bright kitchen. "...'Round yon Virgin Mother and Child..." A shiver went through me.

"I'm sorry," I said to her, and I really was. It wasn't her fault. "I'm sorry, but you're going to have to find someplace else. I don't own this place. I'm just taking care of it, and the owners wouldn't approve of me letting people stay in the garage."

No one moved, but the little girl began to whimper again.

"I think there's a shelter or something in Barre. I could call on the phone..." Still no one moved.

I went back to the kitchen door and pressed the opener button on the wall. The garage light flashed on and the door rattled up. The woman jumped, and the little girl started crying in earnest. "I'm sorry," I said again, although I was beginning to feel more angry than sorry. That jerk had really taken advantage.

Just pretend we're some of them Armenians. The nerve. I watched the woman help the crying child into the backseat of the car and climb in after her. The baby's blanket caught on something and she jerked it free. I could hear a tearing sound. At the front window the boy sat, his nose flattened against the pane.

I waited but nothing happened. The man was just going to sit there. Anger washed away what guilt I might have felt. I went around to the man's window again. "If you don't move out of here," I said, "I'm calling the police."

The man acted as if he hadn't heard. Suppose he just stayed there and they all froze to death right in our garage? Imagine the headlines – "No Room in the Inn: Homeless Family Freezes at Local B & B." "I'm not kidding," I shouted. "I'm calling the cops!"

Through the closed windows of the Chevy, I could hear the little girl crying. "Come on!" I yelled to block out the sound. "Get outta here!"

Finally, he started the motor and began to back out slowly. I ran to the 4 x 4. As soon as the Chevy was out of the way, I was going to drive it in and close the door. The snow had stopped. The plows would be out soon. They'd be okay. An unheated barn was no place for a baby.

And then I heard myself. "Away in a manger, no crib for his bed." No room in the inn, not for two thousand lousy years. Never.

The Chevy had stalled in the driveway. I jumped out and ran to the driver's window and pounded on it again. He stopped grinding the starter and turned to give me his sarcastic look. "We're going," he said.

"I changed my mind."

Now he opened the window. "What you say?"

"Put your car back in and come on in the house. It's freezing out here."

He smiled grimly. "Thinking about them Armenians, huh?"

"No," I said. "Actually, I was thinking about something else."

I led the way into the kitchen and found them chairs so they could sit around the stove and get warm. Then I went to the phone to call Gracie. I knew I needed help, and she was sure to come. I'd just tell her I had a houseful of Armenians.

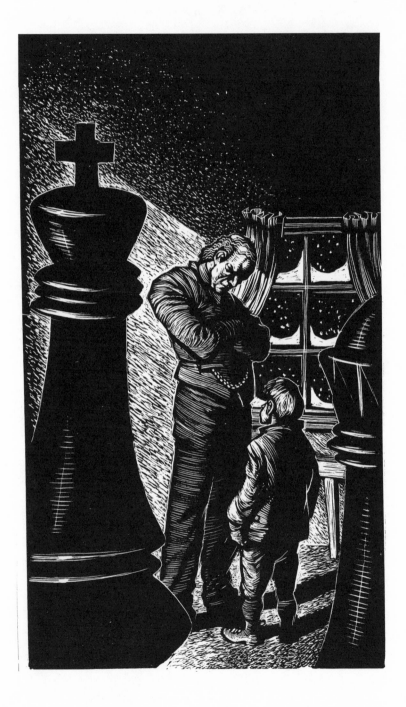

The Chess Player

Ger Koopman

IT WAS CHRISTMAS EVE. The whole day a cold wind had been blowing and now it had started to snow. Thousands – millions – of snowflakes came out of the sky and slowly covered the little village where Farmer Dyhema lived. They covered his fields, already plowed up for the next sowing; they covered his huge barns, full of hay or corn; they covered the yard, the big stable, and the house.

Old Farmer Dyhema had seen the snow coming down. He was sitting near the open fire in his easy chair. He liked the snow on his fields. It will make a better harvest next year, he thought. It was nice and warm in his room. On the table stood a chessboard. All the chessmen stood in their right places, four rows on the white and black squares of the board. Dyhema liked playing chess. He was waiting for the minister. Every Sunday evening the minister came to play chess with the old farmer, and also at Christmas time. He would come tonight. Oh, yes, Dyhema liked the game. He always won. There was nobody in the village who could play as well as he could. There was nobody in the village who was as rich as he was. He was the best farmer, the richest farmer, the best chess player; and he was honest and righteous, too. He lived alone with his servants. His wife had died years ago. But this Christmas he was not thinking of his wife. He was always alone, thinking about himself. How good the harvest had been this year! What an important man he was in the village! When he walked through the streets they took their hats off as he passed. When somebody needed help – *he* gave it. When somebody needed work – *he* gave it. If anybody needed money – *he* lent it.

Suddenly the door opened. A servant came in. "It is rather late, Dyhema. Shall I keep the Christmas tart hot in the oven?"

Dyhema looked at the clock. "The minister is late," he said. "Yes, keep the tart hot."

The servant, moving toward the doorway, said, "I am afraid the minister will not come. The snow is very deep."

Dyhema looked cross, but he only said, "I can wait."

When the servant had gone, Dyhema stood up and looked out of the window. "Dear me, what a lot of snow," he said. "I am sure the minister will not come. The snow is very deep." Dyhema looked at the chessboard with longing eyes.

BUT SOMEBODY was coming! The Christ Child!

The whole day the Christ Child had been very busy. Christmas is his time, for then the hearts of people open; and that is what the Christ Child needs: open hearts. People think of their youth, how nice Christmas was at home. They think about their lives, and how things have turned out wrong. They long to change, to start anew. Then the Christ Child comes.

The whole day the Christ Child had been very busy. One thing had still to be done: to go to the old farmer, Dyhema. When God had told him that, he had said, "But his heart is not at all open." But God had only said, "Go. It has been closed and hard for too long. It is time now."

As the Christ Child was walking through the snow, he thought this over. What could he do? But when God says, "It is time," then it is time. And so at once the Christ Child was in the room of the old farmer. Nobody had heard him coming; nobody had seen him, but suddenly he was there. "Good evening, Dyhema," he said, in his beautiful voice.

Dyhema looked, and looked again. "Who are you, little boy, and how did you come in?"

The Christ Child sat down on a chair, opposite Dyhema, near the fire.

"I am the Christ Child."

"The Christ Child? So. What do *you* need?"

"I only want to talk to you."

"There is nothing to talk about. I did everything a man can do. I gave five hundred guilders for the Christmas celebration in the church."

"I know," said the Christ Child, "and two hundred and fifty guilders for the Sunday School celebration."

"Yes," said the farmer again, "and five hundred guilders for the poor people in the village; and wherever there are sick people, I send my servants to bring them a parcel."

"I know it all," said the Christ Child, and he sighed. "You are like a king on a throne who gives little presents to all his people. Yet how small these gifts are if you think of the thousands of guilders which you earned this year. And all these gifts were given, not out of love for others, but only out of love to yourself, so that you can sit here, content and satisfied with yourself. Oh, if you only knew the Christmas story!"

"I know it. By heart. 'In the days of the Emperor Augustus...'"

"See, you are quite wrong!"

"Wrong?" Farmer Dyhema took the Bible which was lying near him. "See, here it is. 'In the days of the Emperor Augustus...'"

"Wrong! *I know* the story. *I* am the Christ Child! It was not long, long ago, in the days of Augustus. It happens every year anew. Somewhere every year a child is born, poor and without clothes, waiting to be helped, by you. Sometimes it is a sick child, or a poor man, or a poor woman, waiting to be helped, by you. That is the Christmas story."

"I know that I am a sinner before God," said Dyhema. "Every one is a sinner before God. But as far as I was able I did what I could. I cannot give all my money away, or anything like that. That is just nonsense."

"I do not ask only for money. I ask for much more than money. I ask for love! You said that you did everything you could? What about your daughter?"

The old farmer stood up angrily. "My daughter is dead. She is dead for me! If you were really the Christ Child you would know that ten years ago she married against my will. She married an artist, a musician, against my will. Children should obey their parents. No, do not speak about her."

"She is poor. She has a son."

"I know. It is her own fault. Not mine!"

The Christ Child looked at the clock. Half past seven.

And at eight o'clock – at eight o'clock Dyhema's daughter was to come here with her son. He had been to the place where she lived, and he had told her to go back to her father. He had said that everything would be all right when she came. And now there was only half an hour left, and the heart of the old farmer was harder than ever before. But he was not dismayed. God had sent him. He even smiled and said, "Let us play chess!"

"Can you play?"

"A little bit."

"Come on. That is better than all this talking."

They started. It seemed that the Christ Child was not a very good player. After ten minutes he had already lost two castles and a knight. Dyhema rubbed his hands. He would win the game. That was certain. When the Christ Child had lost nearly half his pieces, he suddenly spoke. "Imagine for a minute that your daughter came to you this Christmas Eve with your grandson. Would you receive them?"

"Stop that nonsense. Look at your game. You have nearly lost. And why should they come?"

"I have almost lost. Well, perhaps. But suppose I should win the game before eight o'clock, would you receive them?"

The old farmer laughed. "I would, because it is impossible."

The Christ Child smiled, too. It was one minute to eight. The Christ Child had only his king, queen and one bishop. Dyhema had almost all his men. Dyhema looked at the clock. "Eight o'clock," he said.

"Eight o'clock. And I think it's checkmate," said the Christ Child.

"Checkmate?" Dyhema looked at the board. His eyes widened. "Oh? Wait a minute. You have changed the positions of all my men. No, no! But what has happened?"

The Christ Child smiled again. "That is what happens in life," he said. Then he looked very earnest. "Often people think they are lost. They think that nothing in the world can help them. And then God looks and says, 'It is time.' And all at once everything looks different. Everything comes into a different light, and all at once you see that all is not lost, but won. Remember this, Dyhema! All is not lost in His eyes. The lowly shall be lifted up – the first shall be last." And then he was gone.

Dyhema stood up. He sat down in his chair near the fire. He closed his eyes. He would think this over.

SUDDENLY HE AWOKE. Somebody had knocked at the door. He rubbed his eyes. I have been sleeping, he thought. I had a wonderful dream about the Christ Child. He looked at the table. There was the chessboard. The two rows of white men and the two rows of black men stood neatly on opposite sides of the board. Yes, it had been a dream. "Come in," he said. A servant came in.

"Dyhema, here is a little boy. He says…"

Dyhema stood up in astonishment. "A little boy with his mother?"

"No, he is alone. But he says his mother had an accident. She has sprained her ankle. She is waiting in the snow about half a mile away. She sent the boy for help."

Dyhema laughed. He thought, of course it is not my daughter. And then he said, "Send the servants out with

the horse and cart. Make a room ready and bring her here.
Send for the doctor. Bring the boy here."

The servant went out. A moment later a boy of about
nine came in. Dyhema stood up. He was strangely moved.
The boy looked – yes, he looked just as he himself must
have looked long, long ago. "What is your name?"

"Sigurd," said the boy.

Dyhema sank back into his chair. He closed his eyes.
Sigurd, that was *his* name. His daughter had called her son
after him. But what about the Christ Child? It was a
dream, of course. But dreams are lies, nonsense. But still
there was the boy. His grandson. No. He would not receive his daughter. He stood up and went to the kitchen.
Only one old servant was there. "Where are the others?"
he asked.

"They are all with their families, of course, and two
have gone out to fetch the poor woman," she said.

"I do not want her here! They must take her somewhere
else!"

"Dyhema! On Christmas Eve you are going to refuse a
poor woman your house! Very well. You are responsible.
But I cannot go out and through the snow. Who will tell
them?"

"As soon as they are here, call me. But don't let the
woman come into the house."

Dyhema went back to the living room. The boy sat near
the fireplace. When Dyhema came in he stood up and, going to him, the boy said, "Are you my grandfather?"

"Of course not," Dyhema said angrily.

The boy looked sad. "Then I have come to the wrong
farm. You know, Mummy said, when she fell down, 'That

light over there is the farm. Run over there and ask for help.' But it does not matter. When Mummy comes here she can tell you where she wanted to go. She was born in this village, you know. My granddad is the richest farmer in the village. My mummy said, 'He is like a little king. Everyone asks for his advice. He is very clever, you know.'"

Dyhema suddenly said, "Why are you going to your grandfather?"

"Mummy said that the Christ Child had told her to go. We have never been there. We are very poor, you know. My daddy is dead. We had no money, but mummy always said, 'I will not take the first step.' And then all at once she told me that the Christ Child had told her to go."

"Did she see the Christ Child?"

"I don't know. Afterwards she said it was a dream. And on the journey she was very uncertain. She said to me, once, 'Do not be surprised if we only stay for a short time.'"

Dyhema said nothing. He looked into the fire. Suddenly the boy saw the chessboard. He went to the table. "My granddad can play chess! He always wins, my Mummy says! Can you play? I can. Mummy says that I play so well because I got it from my granddad. Shall we play? Do you know, I am hungry. We had no supper."

Dyhema looked up. "Can you really play? Such a small child?"

"I am not small. And I often win."

"Come on, let us try," Dyhema said.

After a short time Dyhema understood that the boy really could play. Almost without thinking he made the right moves. After half an hour Dyhema became restless. The boy was winning! Really, the small boy seemed to be a bet-

ter player than he was. And what annoyed him most was
that while he did his utmost to win, the boy just played,
without thinking it over. If Dyhema made a move, after a
long time of consideration, the boy followed immediately,
and it was always the right move. Perhaps it was because
Dyhema was so annoyed that he suddenly made a wrong
move. The boy smiled. "That is a bad move," he said. "You
had better take it back."

"No, what I have done, I have done!"

The boy looked at him. Why was this old man so angry?
He could not help it, could he? Was it because he could not
win the game? A lot of people grew angry if they could not
win. It was interesting. You learned most in a game that
you lost. But this was an old man. Perhaps...

Suddenly the old servant came in. "Dyhema, what about
the Christmas tart? Can I bring it in now?"

Dyhema looked very angry. "Go away with your tart!"

What a pity, the boy thought. He was so hungry. How
angry the old man was. Was that only because he was not
winning? Suddenly he said, "I should like to have some
tart. I had no supper, you know."

Dyhema only said, "Your turn to play."

Sigurd sighed. Then he had an idea. He would let the old
man win. He would make a bad move. It was not easy to
do that. He sighed. It is Christmas Eve, he thought, I will
do it. And he made his move.

Dyhema laughed. "A bad move. See, I can take your
queen. Oh, I knew I could win. I have never yet lost a
game!"

Sigurd blushed. This was not fair. He had always been
told not to be sad if he lost, and not to be proud if he won.

Suddenly he smiled. If I can cheer him up, let him win, he thought, and he said, "You can never be sure who wins before it is checkmate."

All the time Dyhema had looked at the boy. He had seen the tears come into his eyes after he had spoken. And he had seen the change, the smile. And then the words of the boy. It was as if he saw the Christ Child again. He remembered the words of the Christ Child, "Sometimes you think all is lost." He stood up. He walked up and down the room. The boy looked at him in surprise. Dyhema saw his life – his long life – in a new light. No mistakes? Open and right? There was a fault, a great fault. How could he have been so blind? My heart has been cold and unmoved, yet I've always thought I was such a good man, with all my good deeds. What a wretched old man I am. All this he felt deep in his heart and he saw his dream again, heard the words of the Christ Child, "God comes. He brings something new into life. *Love!*" That was it. Love!

Dyhema went to the boy. He put his hand on his shoulder. "You have won," he said, "you and the Christ Child."

The boy looked up at him in astonishment. "What do you mean?"

Old Farmer Dyhema smiled. "It does not matter, my son," he said. "It does not matter. But remember this: the Christ Child brings new life, yet all seemed so lost to man when Jesus was born. Born in a stable, poor and cold. All seemed to have been utterly lost in the end, my son. A cross was the end. We must remember, Sigurd, remember the moment when God looked and said, 'It is the time.' And it was! The cross was not the end. And even today the Christ Child still comes to warm the hearts of men."

There was a hard knocking, and the door opened. The old servant said, "Tell me, Dyhema, where must I send this woman? She is here now."

"Bring her in here, of course."

"But you said…"

"It is my daughter! Didn't you know that? Bring her in here at once! Quick! And bring the Christmas tart. Quick, it is Christmas!"

The Christmas Lie

Dorothy Thomas

IT WAS THE LAST DAY of school before the Christmas holidays, and I, because I was only recently recovered from a weeks-long bout with tonsillitis and wearied on the walk home in the Alberta cold, rode with the Bunny children in their cutter, and so got myself into a world of trouble.

I found it very pleasant riding with Madge and Ben behind the foal-heavy cayuse they were let drive to school. It was good to glide effortlessly along, the buffalo robe they had brought from the States tucked around us, and look on the wall of timber to either side of the line our sleigh trail followed, and listen to rhythmed bell and hoof. I was ready to fall asleep when the thought of Christmas came to me and I asked suddenly, "What are you having for Christmas dinner?"

The Bunny homestead was in the long Battle Lake valley, and they had wide, sloping gardens in summer, and a cave for storing food, a much larger meat house than ours, and they butchered more often from an ampler herd.

Madge, a literal-minded but kindly child, told me of the dinner plans in detail, and my mouth watered, listening. When she finished with "squash pie and whipped cream, and walnuts from our folks in Missouri," I, who could barely remember such meals from that past that was Kansas, burst out, "Oh, I wish I could be there!"

A brief silence followed my cry, and in it I counted the hoofbeats and reminded myself that at nine I was too big a girl to be bidding for an invitation, and blessed my luck in there being no brother or sister by to go home and tell on me.

"Come on, Babe," Ben said to the mare and gently touched her with the whip tip. "Sky looks like more cold." I wondered whether they were thinking what being led into politely asking me to dinner would entail – that it would mean asking my eight brothers and sisters and my parents as well.

"I wish that you could come," Madge said kindly.

Ben began to draw on the reins toward stopping the mare and letting me out at my corner for the quarter-mile walk home alone, through the timber.

The dinner pails were handed me to carry. I clamped a mittened hand about the bail of each, waved them goodby and stood to watch them over the nearest knoll and turned toward home. There was a windswept treeless strip before I came to the rise that ran down to the timber edge. I left the heavier of the pails on a stump beside the trail, where it would not be missed by the others when they came along, and whispering a prayerful charm to ward off wolves, went on. To jog, as did the others, jarred my throat. I had found a hurt-saving gait of my own that did not let me lag behind and kept my feet from getting too cold – a gentle prance. My moccasined feet made only the slightest sound on the icy runner path. To myself I recalled the Bunny Christmas-dinner menu, improving on it somewhat by adding my favorites of the preserves and pickles I knew were on the Bunny pantry shelves. I was not a child to eat much, for eating, like talking, was doubtfully worth the discomfort it cost, but I liked to think about food.

When the light from the clearing shone through the latticed slits between pine and spruce, I began to chant aloud. There, where a cry could summon Rats, our dog, nothing could harm me.

As always, my heart lifted when I saw the low log house and the smoke rising from the pipe at the end of the snowladen roof. I passed under the moose horn and along the snow-walled canyon to the door and went in. My mother looked up from her knitting, smiled and said, "Hang your mittens and oversocks on the line and put on dry moccasins. Don't wake the baby." I waited for her to ask why I had come in alone and whether my throat hurt, but she went on counting stitches with so purposed a calm that I knew she was working on someone's Christmas present.

When I had changed my moccasins I went to look at my sleeping little brother. He lay under a folded blanket on a lower bunk. His hands were curled in dainty fists beside his golden head. His black lashes lay long on his cheeks. I carefully lifted the blanket and crept in beside him, not quite touching him, to spare him my outdoor coldness, and fell asleep.

When I awoke, the others were home, laughing and talking, and mother was getting supper. The baby was with them.

"Wake up, lazybones!" someone called to me when I sat up. My elder sister had set the lamp on the table and its light glowed on her braid-crowned, amber hair and in her hazel eyes. She smiled at me and asked, "Was it fun, riding with the Bunnys?"

I knew that Ben would much have preferred my sister in my place. He blushed sometimes when the children at school teased him about her, but she was too shy and too sturdy and kind ever to have left the younger ones to walk alone. Often she carried the youngest one pickaback for better than half the way.

"Did you sleep in the cutter too?" a brother teased. "You sleep half the time."

"No, we talked," I said.

"So? What did you talk about?"

He was ribbing me. Always it hurt my throat to talk, and only having a very good story to tell made it worthwhile. "We talked about Christmas," I said and then, to my amazement and theirs, "They want me to come for Christmas dinner."

"You?" a brother asked. "Just you?"

I considered his question and a suitable answer while they all looked at me. I found it impossible to own, at once, that I had all but asked myself, and that Madge's invitation was a purely rhetorical one.

I swallowed and said, "They want us all to come."

I waited for someone to say, "Here now! Of course, they don't! Just what did they say?" and break me down. Was I not a child given to sudden fantasies after long silences?

My mother turned from the breadboard where she was cutting out biscuits with an empty baking-powder can to say happily, "I only wish they had told us, asked us sooner. There will be so much to do, to get you all ready. I'll need to wash and iron, do a lot of baking, and wash your hair." She cut the remaining biscuits with a flourish, set the can down and pressed her floury hands together – almost, she clapped them. She smiled, and looked very pretty and young enough to be one of us rather than the mother of the nine of us. "Last year the Hagens asked us, and now the Bunnys! It will be more like Christmas!" Her dark eyes shone with Kansas joy.

All the year long we had remembered, retold those two wonderful days and nights at the Hagens', and relived the brightness of their Scandinavian Christmas. Having enjoyed that holiday largess, why should an invitation by the Bunnys be cause for doubts and questionings now? They all – and first and most happily my mother – gladly joined me in wishful thinking. Along with my dread of the web I should likely have to weave if I did not quickly find the courage to own I was fabricating, I felt a tender pity for them and especially for my mother – for so many months at a time she did not leave the clearing.

Mother looked to see that Maud, our cat, was not sleeping on drying mittens in the oven, and slid the big pan of biscuits in. She straightened up and looked at me seriously, and I thought, half in dread, half in hope, now it occurs to her that I made this up. She will ask, "Is it really true?" and I will tell her it isn't and I must brace myself to weather the family derision, and it will be over at last.

Instead, she said, "You, child, must have a new dress. You were sick when I made the other girls' dresses and I put your dress lengths away. Which do you want, the red or the brown?"

Mother was smiling at me, trusting, happy, wanting to do something for this slightest, thinnest, least useful of her children. I looked toward the door. If only my father would come in quickly! He would understand, surely, that I'd got myself into a fix, and help me. But the door stayed closed, the latch unmoving. "Well, which?" mother asked, with her not unkind impatience.

"The red," I whispered.

"The red it will be," mother said. "I'll cut it out after supper...Boys, tomorrow you must go out and shoot partridges for some big partridge pies. I'll make light rolls. I am so glad I saved enough of the raspberries for some tarts. Tonight, bring in snow to melt, so that I can wash in the morning. Now go to the barn and tell papa! We'll have supper as soon as the biscuits are done!"

"We'll have our own Christmas here Christmas Eve, won't we?" someone asked mother.

"Yes, of course," mother said, and exchanged glances with my older sister; she was her confidante and, we little ones knew, shared the holiday secrets with her.

When father came in, he said, "So, we're asked out to Christmas dinner!"

"Yes," mother said. "Likely there will be a letter, when you go for the mail tomorrow."

"I doubt it," father said. "Mrs. Bunny is not of epistolary bent...Boys, which shall it be tonight, history or algebra?" Father was giving a high-school course to his older sons; each night after supper the table was cleared and under the hanging lamp father had made, they worked to-

gether or we all listened while he read aloud to us, then
questioned the boys.

"I'll need the table to cut out a dress for this girl," mother
said. "You'd better read aloud, if you will."

In my place at table, between my two oldest brothers, I
bowed my head for the blessing and felt that deep unwor-
thiness that was to grow, with each prayer raised, from
that meal onward toward Christmas.

I waited to see which of the books father would choose
from the shelf above the window, and was somewhat disappointed when he took down Ivanhoe. The people of Scott's
stories were so undaunted and husky – men of deeds and
few but honest words, but all so long in the telling!

I fell asleep and was dreamily grateful when my eldest
brother lifted me in his arms, carried me to my bunk that I
shared with my two sisters, undressed me and got me into
my gown and tucked the covers about me. In bed I
strained to listen and heard "'Only a change of raiment,
only a change of raiment,' the old man said." The words
struck me as terribly sad. Tears came to my eyes, and
weeping for beautiful Rebecca's father, in his fear and per-
fidy, I fell asleep.

I woke to hear Rats barking his particular bark that
went with the rifle and shotgun being taken down from
their pegs above the door; my brothers were going out to
shoot partridges. My younger sister was setting the breakfast table, and already my older sister was taking her turn
at the steaming tub of wash water, rubbing clothes on the
board to help mother get the washing done and onto the
lines that were strung overhead.

Little was expected of me at that time in my growing. I

was not strong enough to carry in wood or water. I could not even feed the hens: the rooster chased me. He had chased my younger sister, too, when he was first brought home to shepherd our little flock, but she fought him with a birch switch and vanquished him, and was paid a thin Canadian dime for her courage. After that he prudently looked the other way and let her pass. Once I thought to fool him by wearing her coat, but he found me out, and with head lowered and neck ruffled, he ran at me. I stood, paralyzed with fear, my hands over my face, until brother arms lifted me high and set me on a shoulder, where I buried my face in a sheepskin cap, and from that vantage peeked to see the rooster lifted by a shoepack kick and sent, squawking, over the jack-pine stump.

I was good for nothing but to set the table or mind the babies. A hewer of wood and drawer of water I never became. The youngest of my four older brothers more than a little resented this partiality shown me, and made me suffer for it by teasing me. It was first on his account and my dread of his scorn, or so I told myself, that I nightly repented the day's cowardice and resolved in my prayers to muster the courage, by dawn, to tell my parents that I had lied, that we had not been asked to the Bunnys for Christmas dinner. But always the smile that twitched the corner of my brother's mouth silenced me before I could begin, and I let the days go by, sorrowful but unconfessing.

When she is pinning up the hem of my dress, I shall tell mamma, I deceived myself. I shall be standing on the table, looking down on her dark head, and I shall say, "Mamma, I can't bear it any longer. I must tell you..." But she said, "Be still, child," and I was still.

I shall tell her when she is working the buttonholes, I

said, and stood near where she sat in the rocking chair, the only piece of furniture besides the sewing machine brought with us from the States, and watched the needle dip, dart, loop and taut the thread and pull away in swift rhythm. Mamma, oh, mamma, I said in my mind, willing her to look at me and see my misery and ask, "What is it, child?" but instead of looking at me, she began to sing Thomas Moore's sad song:

> I never nursed a dear gazelle
> To glad me with its soft black eye,
> But when it came to know me well,
> And love me, it was sure to die.

I dropped down, placed my head in her lap and cried. She smoothed my hair and laughed fondly, and asked, "Want me to sing it again?" I knew then that I could not tell her.

I began to follow my father about, hoping, without believing now, that I could tell him. Father seldom let an opportunity pass to teach me and try to make up to me the weeks or months of schooling I missed. "Spell 'ill,'" he would say and when I had complied, "Now, 'bill.'" Then he would leave off spelling to ask me to tell him the different kinds of bills there were, and perhaps to describe the muscles in the neck, back and shoulders of a woodpecker that made possible the power and rapidity of his rat-a-tat-tat on a tree trunk.

I felt some embarrassment that he should waste these digressions on the likes of me. Because the others all knew so much more, and were, some of them, ready to remind me of this fact, I had got a very humble opinion of my own mental prowess, and saw my father's bothering to tell me such things as a measure of his loving kindness and his need to talk with someone, and I was comforted a little. Why I did not tell him, I do not know. It could be that I tried, only to find him too deep in his own thoughts to hear what I was saying. So often mother told him things of importance to her, only to have him look up from his carpentry or book to ask, "What did you say, my dear?" or, a week later, "Why did you tell me nothing of this?"

The partridges were plucked and the soft breast feathers put in the feather poke to be saved for pillows. The birds were cooked and the meat stripped from the bones, for pies. I helped. And whatever I did, I did sorrowing, fearing.

My sister ironed while mother sewed. It was not enough for mother to make the dress. No, she must embroider it in wools, in a design of her own making. It seemed to me that never had she shown me such special attention and creative kindness.

Our Christmas Eve was dwarfed by the prospect of the morrow's outing. We all knew where the gifts were hidden. Had we not seen our mother making them? We had watched her knitting, seen her whittling the white birchwood with the knife father carefully whetted and sharpened for her. But we had not seen the finished gifts. We knew that she had turned the heel and narrowed the toe of many a stocking, and sandpapered the little carved toys while we were away at school or while we slept, and wrapped each in saved tissue wrappings and tied it with ribbons or lengths of bright yarn.

There was, of course, the package from the States. Our little Aunt Bird, mother's sister, worked in a millinery store, and twice a year she sent a package made up of bits of tulle, lace, rolls of straw braid, feathers and plumes, and satin and velvet ribbons. The winter package we opened on

Christmas Eve. Few of these treasures were suitable for personal adornment, but mother used them where she could, and the rest were for us little girls, for our dolls. I remember my mother lifting a nosegay of violets from the package, shaking the flowers into looseness, then pinning them in her hair and singing gaily:

> Violets, violets, bring me blue violets –
> Some for their fragrance and some for my hair!

"Elegant" and "refined" were words frequently on our mother's lips. Though she never openly reproached him for it, we all knew that she deplored our father's taking us from our parsonage home in Kansas to homestead in the Alberta brush country. All unintentionally, she falsified, glorified the life that had been ours in the little Kansas towns where father had taught and preached, and brought us little ones to think of Kansas as another word for heaven – a heaven where we should all be transplanted, in some not too distant life, to enjoy perpetual plenty and culture.

After the supper dishes were put away, the box of presents was brought out and, beginning with the baby, we opened our gifts. Mine was a doll with china head and hands, and shanks that tapered to high-heeled slippers. Mother apologized for the doll's nakedness and not having found time to dress her, and said, "Bring me the scrap bag and I'll make her a dress right now!" Immediately, her scissors snipped out a pattern from saved brown paper, and the minute yoke, sleeves and skirt length were cut from a large scrap left over from my new dress.

Watching mother dress my doll, I forgot, for moments, my guilt. I played at rolling out dough with the tiny rolling pin mother had carved for me and was briefly happy. I looked up to find father's eyes fixed on me, and hope sprang up when he said to mother, "Do you think this child is well enough to go out in the cold tomorrow?"

Mother motioned me to her, touched my brow, turned my face up to the light and said, "Open your mouth. Let me look at your throat." They exchanged a long parental look. "I think she is better," she said.

"Good," father said. "It would be a shame, after they asked for her especially."

I had only to throw myself on my mother's breast and mercy, and sob, "But they didn't ask me!" I let the moment pass. Mother had worked so hard and so happily. And I had almost come to believe in our having been asked, myself.

"You had as well read while I finish this dress," mother said to father. "The iron will be hot, and I can press it by the time you have finished." Agreeably, pleasantly, she fitted her work to the reading of the Word, her hands, her needles still only for the prayer.

My older sister brought the Bible and father opened it to the second chapter of Luke to read the Christmas story, and again, for moments, I forgot, while I soundlessly whispered the words I knew by heart, along with my father. But when we knelt to pray, guilt lowered on me and I pleaded, "Help me, and forgive, forgive!"

We little girls had had our baths in the afternoon while father and the big boys were outdoors. Then our hair had been done up in rags, to have curls the next morning. Now a tub of snow was brought in and set on the stove for the boys' baths and shampooing. After we were in our beds, we little ones sang Christmas carols, dropping out one by one, as sleep claimed us. Mine was the last voice I heard. I woke once in the night to feel mother's hand on my forehead.

What is this awful weight on my heart? I woke wondering, and remembered and sat up. I had let the day come, and now there was nothing to stop our going to the Bunnys and bringing them bewilderment and our parents embarrassment. It was only for an instant that I sat up, then I snuggled down under the covers: the room was terribly cold.

My mother came on tiptoe, holding my dressed doll in her hand, to whisper, "Merry Christmas, daughter."

I held the doll's cold, smooth head against my cheek.

"Come to the stove to dress," mother said. "Papa and the boys are out milking. Be very quiet. The longer the little boys sleep, the more I can get done." She leaned to draw the covers closer about my sister's shoulders. "Let her sleep too. She's worked so hard."

When I was setting the breakfast table mother began to sing, very softly, a mournful Christmas song that began:

The travelers, weak and sad and worn,
Approached the crowded town,
So friendless, homeless and forlorn,
The sun was going down.

And ended, in its first verse:

No room, no room for Jesus,
Nowhere to lay his head…

I had heard this song numberless times, but never before had its full pathos smitten me. I wiped my sleeve across my eyes. I must have sighed. Mother turned from the stove to ask, "Does your throat hurt?" I set down the stack of oatmeal bowls I was carrying and started toward her, my arms held out. I did not tell her, for at that moment the baby fell out of bed.

Then suddenly I was given a dawn-to-dusk reprieve. Father came in carrying two pails of milk on which, in the journey from barn to house, a skim of ice had formed at the edges, and said, while he stood by the stove to melt the ice his breathing had made in his beard, "I'd say it is a good forty-five below, and dropping. We can't take these little children, and especially this one, out in this!" He looked down at me, and mother looked at me, too, as though in my thin throat she saw a barometer.

"No, I suppose not," she said slowly. "Do you think the Bunnys will expect us, now it's this cold?"

"I doubt it," father said. "But in case they should, we'll send a couple of the boys down on their skis, with our regrets."

"And the carrying bag," mother said, "filled with things I've baked, and the gifts for Madge and Ben." She could not keep the tremor from her voice. She turned her head away. "The children! I mind so, for the children!"

"There will be other Christmases," he said gently, and went to her and leaned to kiss the part in her dark hair.

I went to kneel on the window seat, and with a spoon scraped a peephole in the thick and ferny frost pattern and looked out into the saving cold of Christmas.

I was past trying to confess my fault though my sin was ever before me. I watched the boys leave, skimming over the crust beside the sleigh trail in the deceptively shining morning, and tried not to think of the moment when the Bunnys' dog, mother of our dog, Rats, would run barking to meet them, and one of the older Bunny boys – Illo, Ivo or Jasper – would come out to greet them, and, when they had leaned their skis against the house wall, they would go in to the warmth of Mrs. Bunny's kitchen and welcome. Standing by the range, they would melt the frost from their eyebrows and nostrils, and warm their hands while the Bunnys asked about us all and heard from them our parents' apologies for not bringing us, and Mrs. Bunny said whatever came into her head to say, on hearing we had planned to come.

Mother said that we should have the nicest Christmas possible at home. She brought from the trunk her long, white, hemstitched linen tablecloth that had been the congregation's parting gift to her, and let my little sister and me help her spread it on the table. She took down from the top shelf of the corner cupboard a hand-painted china bowl and carefully washed and dried it and set it in the center of the table. It would hold the mashed potatoes in a knife-smoothed mountain from whose crater a lava of pale winter butter would overflow. There would be two vegetables, saved against this day, cranberry sauce and light rolls. To make up for her having sent one of the two partridge pies down to the Bunnys, mother had baked a hen, and there would be chicken gravy.

After she had freed our curls from their long, hard co-coons and brushed them about her finger, and had buttoned us into the dresses we were to have worn to the Bunnys, and the long-sleeved pinafores we wore over them, mother re-tired to the dormitory end of the house and did her hair and changed her dress and came out in her red cashmere princess and blushed at our cries of admiration and father's poetic approval. The brief train of the dress swished after her, its tiers of satin piping ashine, brightly crimson against the pine of the puncheon floor. It had been her best dress down in the States, the one she wore when she sang the alto part in a church quartet, and we had not seen her in it since the Christmas before.

We had only sat down to dinner when a shadow moved past the frost-darkened window, and Rats set up his angriest growling. Father went to the door, thinking, perhaps, that some homesteader had made his way to us through the cold.

There stood an Indian, the first ever to come to our house. Father quieted Rats and asked the Indian in. The boys helped him with his blanket and shoepacks, and had him warm himself. Mother whispered for us to slide our plates along to make room for him at the table and motioned for the boys to hang his blanket on the line. We waited. Mother set the platter and the other serving dishes on the back of the stove, where they would keep warm.

When at last the Indian was seated between my younger sister and me, we bowed our heads for the blessing. The instant the amen was said and the platter that held the golden baked hen was set before father again, my little sister, wanting to show her friendliness, quickly lifted the platter with its uncarved bird and held it before our guest. Whether it was her intent to have him admire it or to ask him to carve it there was no time to ask. Instead of taking or refusing the platter, he grasped the bird in both hands and bent his head over it. He hesitated and lowered it to his plate, and lifted his knife and fork and considered their use. He touched his thumb to the knife blade and silently laid it down again. He took up the bird and with his teeth tore a strip of white meat from the breastbone, and, the chicken still in his hands, chewed ravenously while we all watched, rapt. No one, not even the baby, so much as gasped.

Mother got up from her chair and took the remaining partridge pie from the oven and cut it at the worktable.

She set it before father and said, "Will you serve us now?"

Then our wordless guest, his first hunger assuaged, looked around on us and saw our empty plates and that he had taken and eaten the best of our dinner. A deeper red suffused his near-frozen cheeks, and he looked down at the bird and the inroads he had made on it, and held it out toward father, his eyes asking pardon.

I felt his humiliation as though it were my own. I knew what it was to want, and to act on impulse, and then to see what had been done and want to make amends. He had come, snow-blinded, into our house, stupid with cold and hunger and strangeness, and had been offered food. I, who had sometimes run to hide when a stranger came, and found it difficult to speak up at any time, said with gestures, "We have a partridge pie. The chicken is for you, and the dressing too. We want you to eat it." Then I looked at my father, fearful of having said the wrong thing, and was relieved when he smiled and said to the Indian, "Yes, eat."

Our plates were heaped with food and passed to us, and we, too, began to eat, glancing often at our hungry guest.

Mother cut the pies before she brought them to the table. When the Indian had finished with his piece, which he ate from the palm of his hand, he wiped his hands on his trouser legs and took from his shirtfront a short-stemmed pipe, and, with signs, asked father for tobacco. Told that father did not smoke, he pointed to the boys in turn, and made to understand there was no tobacco in the house, he delved for and found his own tobacco pouch and filled his pipe and smoked.

This was too much for my brothers. They got up to put wood into the stove, and the one bending over the wood box was taken with a fit of pretended coughing and had to be pounded on the back, and that was excuse for us all to laugh. Father kept a straight face, but his eyes twinkled. And I thought that the Indian's eyes were laughing too.

Satisfied with food and tobacco, the Indian got around to telling us why he had come. He had lost his ponies – a black, a bay, a tan, a pinto. This he let us know by laying his hand on first my head, then my younger sister's, then my older sister's, and then on all three in quick succession. Father had not seen his ponies, and tried to make it clear that, should they come our way, the boys would return them to him at the reservation on Pigeon Lake.

When he had gone, with one of the boys holding Rats until he was safely from the clearing, we little girls helped mother clear the table.

The lamp was lighted. Mother took up her knitting and recited for us some Christmas poems learned in her early childhood from her mother's mother. Always I had loved that evening hour when the outdoors was periwinkle blue beyond the patterned frost and a quiet fell on us and we were aware of the crackling of the fire, the tink of sparks in the stovepipe, the sound of whittling knife and the click of knitting needles. How precious and safe a time it had always been – that hour in a winter Eden. And now the sword was at the gate.

As though she read my thought, though not its dread, mother said, "The boys will be coming any time now, and will tell us about the Bunnys' Christmas dinner. And we will have something to tell them, won't we, children?"

"Yes, how we lost our chicken," my brother said, and looked at me and clicked his tongue. "If only the little girls hadn't passed it to him. If only she hadn't said we wanted – "

Father stopped him. "Come here, little girls," he said to us, and held out his hands and drew us onto his knees and stroked our hair. "We have so few guests I couldn't have blamed you if you had not known at all what to do, how to behave. And here, your mother couldn't have been more gracious and kind." He raised my hand and pressed it to his cheek. "You, especially, treasure," he said to me. "This must all have meant much to you, this day, and you took the disappointment of not going to the Bunnys like a little woman. How honest and warm a heart you have, to feel that Indian's uncertainty and hunger as you did, and to speak up and tell him to eat our chicken, and make him feel at ease. That's the sort of goodwill toward men to set the angels singing." He stopped, his voice shaken, and looked at mother. She was smiling, nodding agreement.

My father's words made the circle of his arm, always the safest place in my world, untenable. And my mother's loving pride in me and all that she had done for us all toward that day, that was in no way rightly mine, split my world apart. Better was the outer darkness of their disregard, their wrath. I flung myself from my father's embrace and stood alone, halfway between my parents, and with all the others looking on, wondering, I cried aloud, "They didn't ask us! They didn't even ask me! I made it up!"

Astonished and awful silence followed. No one laughed. No one derided or reproached me. I shut my eyes, trying to gather strength for whatever was to be. Then my mother was kneeling on the frosty puncheon floor and taking me to her heart to forgive me and to let me weep.

It was in that blessed moment of relief, release, that Rats set up his barking and ran down the trail to meet the boys, home from the Bunnys. There was more for me to suffer, but now I could endure it. Almost, I could welcome it.

"Hold her, papa," mother said. "This crying is very bad for her throat." She went to the stove to slide the teakettle forward and to put food into the oven to reheat.

Through my tears, I saw the others' solemn faces. I strove to hush my crying before my brothers came in. Mother waited until they had slid their skis onto the rafters and had hung up their coats and were warming themselves at the stove before she said quietly, "What did Mrs. Bunny say?"

"That you make the best light rolls ever," my brother said, smiling.

"What else did she say?"

"That she was sorry it turned too cold to bring the children out, and that we're all to come the first fit Sunday."

"And she sent candy, cakes and walnuts from the States, for the little ones," our other brother said. "They're in the carrying bag." At the goodness and kindly quick thinking of Mrs. Bunny I wept anew. Mother said to father, "Hadn't you better put her down and stay with her until she goes to sleep? This has been terrible for her."

Then the brother who liked to tease me came to me and thrust the little sleeping colt mother had carved for him into my hand and said gruffly, "You can hold him awhile!"

Father carried me and laid me down on the bunk and covered me with the folded crazy quilt. He leaned to kiss me, and the loop of his watch chain touched my arm and I heard the good ticking of his watch. Then he lay down beside me and moved my head to his shoulder.

"Will God forgive me?" I whispered between shaken sobs.

"Absolutely," he said.

I quieted, thinking on the goodness of God, Mrs. Bunny and my people. I was so humbly glad of peace on my earth once again, and of being one of the least of those sinners with whom, at Christmastime, God saw fit to be reconciled! The little wooden colt in my hand and my brow pressed to my father's beard, I went to sleep.

The Riders of St. Nicholas

Jack Schaefer

THE DAY DAWNED still and clear, with the winter-night chill of the high country lingering in the air. Stringy clouds clung to the tops of the mountains to the west, but that was nothing unusual in late December. The sun below the horizon to the east sent edgings of color along the high-hanging clouds, and the first pink flush of a fine morning touched the roof of the cookhouse in which the men of the Slash Y were finishing a particularly hearty breakfast.

Range manager Cal Brennan set down his coffee cup and pulled a paper bag from a jacket pocket and shook it gently. A soft rattling sound came from it. "I ain't takin' the trouble," he said, "of decidin' who's goin' an' who's stayin'. I'm makin' it an even chance for everybody, includin' Cookie here an' myself too. There's thirteen of us, an' there's thirteen beans in here. Ten white an' three brown. White ones go. Brown ones stay."

He held the bag up in his left hand above eye level and reached into it with his right hand. The hand emerged holding a white bean between thumb and forefinger. "Well, well," he said. "Bein' nice about this's paid off nice too." He passed the bag to foreman Hat Henderson.

Hat held it up, reached into it. A white bean. "Reckon I live right," he said, and passed the bag to Monte Walsh.

Monte held it up. "Gambling's a sin," he said. "That's what my mother used to say. Must be true 'cause I never have any luck at it." He reached in. A brown bean. "See what I mean?" he said. "And I got new boots too."

"No bellyaching," said Powder Kent, taking the bag. A white bean. "Don't fret, Monte. Miss Annie won't even miss you. Not with me there."

The bag passed on around the long table. White beans. Sunfish Perkins held it up. A brown bean. "Aw, hell," he said. "I ain't much on dancing and such anyways."

The bag passed on. Chet Rollins held it up. Two beans left in it – a white and a brown. Chet's glance flicked across the table at Monte – slumped on the bench staring down in disgust at the bean in his hand – and flicked back to the bag. He reached in. It could have been a white bean emerging between his thumb and forefinger, but before anyone was quite certain it slipped from his fingers back into the bag. "Damn," murmured Chet cheerfully, and reached in again. A brown bean. He tossed the bag to Skimpy Eagens, the cook. "It's all yours," he said.

THE SUN WAS AN HOUR UP, warming the air, driving the night chill back into the mountains. Monte Walsh and Chet Rollins and Sunfish Perkins sat on a top corral rail, watching the ten white-bean winners saddle up. The ten had a forty-five mile ride ahead of them, but what was a mere forty-five miles to the prospect of Christmas Eve festivities at the headquarters of the Triple Seven, for which folks were gathering from an even wider radius?

"You know," said Monte, morose, "I been thinking. That bag game wasn't exactly fair. First pickers had best chances, what with more white beans still in there. I'll bet Cal had that figured."

"Sure," said Chet. "But you can't squawk much. You were one of the first."

Monte gnawed on a knuckle. "That just goes to show," he said. "Luck and me ain't even acquainted. Someday I'm going to – " He stopped. Skimpy Eagens had left his horse and was calling to him.

"Come along, Monte," said Skimpy. "Something to show you." He led the way toward the cookhouse.

Inside, on the plank shelf near the big wood stove, limp, well-washed flour sacks were tucked down over two humped objects. Skimpy removed one with a flourish, disclosing the plump carcass of a wild turkey in a battered roasting pan. "Cal brought that in two days ago," he said. "It's stuffed. All you got to do is get a good fire going and put it in. About two hours. A little basting'd help."

"Basting?" said Monte, somewhat brightened.

"Just scoop up hot juice and dribble it over," said Skimpy. He lifted the second covering, disclosing a squat, dark ball of pudding in another pan. "Course those plums ain't fresh, only canned. But there's a snitch of brandy in it. Just warm it up some."

"What do you know," said Monte, brightening more.

"Not till tomorrow," said Skimpy. "That's what they're

for. And maybe I'll show you something else. Cal figured to let you just find it when you started rooting for food, but maybe he's hoping you'd just miss it." Skimpy pulled open a bulging potato bag under the shelf and took out an unopened bottle of whisky.

"That," said Monte, beaming, "is the best yet. I'll just take charge of that right now."

"You can read, can't you?" said Skimpy, holding the bottle up. A small piece of paper was flattened around it with a tag end of string. On the paper was written in Cal Brennan's crabbed scrawl, "Not to be opened till Christmas."

"All right," said Monte. "But put that thing back quick."

"Too late," said Sunfish Perkins from the doorway. "I got a good look."

THE SUN WAS AN HOUR and a half up, warming the air, reaching for the rim of frost left by the night chill around the inside of the corral water trough. Monte Walsh and Chet Rollins and Sunfish Perkins sat on the same top rail, watching the dust of the ten white-bean winners fade off northward.

"Hope that horse of Powder's stumbles and breaks a leg," said Monte. "The leg being Powder's."

Silence along the rail.

"Know what I'm going to do?" said Monte. "Soon as it warms up more, I'm going over to the house and bring that leather chair of Cal's out on the porch and sit in the sun. I'm going to catch up some on the sitting I ain't done in a long time. I'm going to sit there thinking of how Hat's been working us these last weeks. I'm going to sit there thinking up ways of talking you two into bringing me food so I don't even have to move none. Then I'm going to sit there some more, trying to make up my mind should I slip into town tonight or just take over that bed of Cal's and catch up on all that sleep I missed last month riding line extra for Dobe 'cause of that bad ankle of his."

Silence along the rail.

"Yep," said Monte. "That's it. And tomorrow if I feel up to it, maybe I'll show you two how easy I can beat you at horseshoes. That seems kind of strenuous right about now, but maybe I'll do it just to work up the right kind of appetite for that turkey and pudding and the other fixings you two'll fix."

"Sounds terrible exciting," said Sunfish. "Then what'll you do?"

"Why, shucks," said Monte. "Then I'll just sit some more and see how much mileage I can get out of my third of that bottle."

Silence along the rail.

"Well, now," said Chet, staring down solemnly at his hands on his knees. "Hat mentioned something about rehanging those crooked barn doors. Also something about working over the harness gear."

Monte shifted sideways some to stare at Chet.

"And also again and likewise," said Chet, "something about putting a new gate on that other corral."

Monte stared at Chet, horrified. "You mean," he said, "you're thinking of us killing ourselves working while the rest of 'em are off having fun?"

"Why, no," said Chet. "Did I say I was? But Hat mentioned those things, so I figured I ought at least do the same."

"Right," said Monte. "You've mentioned 'em. Now what's it really you're thinking of doing?"

"Sitting on that porch in the sun," said Chet. "Maybe playing a little euchre with you two so's to settle who cooks when. But mostly just sitting."

"Me too," said Sunfish Perkins.

THE SUN WAS WELL PAST noon, the sunlight warm and reassuring. Monte Walsh sat on the ranch-house porch, limp and lazy, in the mouse-chewed remnants of a once-imposing leather-covered armchair. A few feet away Chet Rollins leaned back, equally limp and lazy, in a rocker padded with the remains of old saddle blankets. Both chairs were placed at precise angles for maximum sunlight benefit. A few more feet away Sunfish Perkins sat cross-legged on the porch floor, leaning forward to play solitaire with an old, worn deck of cards.

"My, oh, my," murmured Monte. "It tires me just to hear him. Where's he get the energy to slap those cards so loud? How's he doing it with all that fat around his middle?"

"No fat," said Sunfish without looking up. "Muscle."

"Oh, my, yes," murmured Monte. "The kind of muscle they pack into lard pails."

Silence on the porch – a companionable silence broken only by the soft plop of old cards on old cards.

Over in the first corral a horse whinnied. On the porch three heads lifted some and looked into the distances of the big land. A darkish speck moved against the seemingly endless reaches of plain to the southeast.

"He got a late start," said Monte. "That is, if he's aiming at the doings up north."

"What's he doing heading over here then?" said Chet.

Silence on the porch. Sunfish gathered up the cards and leaned back against the porch post. The speck became larger and was a man on a horse.

"Simple," said Monte. "The horse's lame."

"G'wan," said Sunfish. "You can't tell this far."

"Want to bet?" said Monte. "It's favoring the off fore-foot."

Silence on the porch. The man and the horse came closer, and they were Sonny Jacobs of the Diamond Six and a smallish neat sorrel definitely favoring its off forefoot. They stopped by the porch, and Sonny surveyed its occupants. A wide smile creased his broad young face. "I never thought to see the day," he said. "Damned if you don't look like three old ladies sitting around at a sewing circle."

"That's better'n you look," said Monte. "Which is plain foolish, expecting to get anywheres on one of those bat-brained horses you raise down your way. What'd it do, step in a badger hole?"

"Hell, no," said Sonny. "Shied at a rabbit and into some damned cactus. I worked on that pastern maybe half a hour, but must be some spines still in it. You got anything particular to say about which one of yours I take?"

"Shucks, no," said Monte. "Any one you want in the corral there, long as it's the gray."

Three heads turned slightly to watch Sonny ride to the corral, dismount, open the gate, lead the sorrel in. His saddle rose into view from inside, heaved up to rest on a top rail. Dust rose over the corral, and a rope flashed through it. The saddle disappeared down inside, and Sonny came out leading a biggish, mean-looking gray. He swung up and rocked in the saddle as the horse plunged forward, bucking. Four lively minutes later he sat serenely in saddle by the porch as the horse stood quivering under him. "You sure can pick 'em, Monte boy," he said. "He'll be right interesting."

"And go the distance," said Monte. "You sure you ain't afraid of him?"

"Plumb scared to death," said Sonny. He reared the gray spinning on hind legs and started away fast and swung back in a short circle. "Almost forgot to tell you. I came up your east range. Following the drift fence. There's a stretch of it down." He swung again and was gone.

Silence on the porch. Three men sat still, very still, looking at one another and away. "Damn," said Sunfish.

"No, sir," said Monte. "I ain't going to move. Let it stay down awhile. When the others get back'll be time enough."

Chet sighed. "Yes-s-s-s," he said. "Yes, I guess maybe it will."

THE SUN WAS WELL into the afternoon, the sunlight full on the porch. Monte Walsh reclined in the remnants of an armchair, eyes closed. Chet Rollins reclined in the old rocker, head dropped sideways, breath coming in sighs not quite strong enough to be called snores. Sunfish Perkins lay full length on a doubled-over old quilt, definitely snoring in long, slow rhythm.

Monte opened his eyes, blinking into the sunlight. "Funny," he murmured. "Sun's right up there right on the job, but I feel kind of chilly around the edges." He closed his eyes again.

Slowly, then with increasing swiftness, the sunlight faded. Over by the other buildings a loose piece of roofing tin rattled. A gust of wind, whirling, picking up dust, swept past the porch. Monte opened his eyes and raised his head some. He sat up straighter. His eyes focused into distance to the west. "Chet," he said, voice low and urgent. "Take a look."

Chet snapped out of sleep and straightened, looking. Off to the west the mountains were gone, erased in a great drab grayness that filled the horizon and obscured the sun. Another gust swept past, and in the following stillness, suddenly heavy and ominous, Sunfish Perkins grunted and pushed up from the porch floor and stood looking too.

"Coming this way," said Sunfish, shivering. "And colder by the minute. Must be snow in it."

"That ain't good," said Monte. "It ain't good at all."

"Sure not," said Chet. "If this turns into something and any cows get through that fence, they'll drift with it clean over into Texas."

"Aw, hell," said Sunfish. "And I was dreaming so nice."

"Finish it later," said Chet. "What've we got in the corral?"

"Two apiece," said Monte. "That is, we did have before Sonny stole one. Come along."

Ten minutes later the three of them, in heavy jackets, gloved, hats pulled well down, led three horses, saddled, out of the near corral. Over the saddle horn of Monte's rat-tailed roan hung a coil of light baling wire. The wind came in long sweeps now, and the sky steadily darkened.

"Sunfish," said Chet. "This gets bad like it looks it could, we'll be needing plenty of relays the next day or two. You swing out and bring in some more of the saddle stock. Six or eight, anyway. Then you can get a fire going in the house where likely we'll hole up and get something hot cooking. Monte and me, we'll get that fence."

"Got you," said Sunfish. He swung up and left at a lope around the corner of the corral.

"Shucks," said Monte. "Looks like his bean wasn't as brown as mine. Yours too. Bring in a few horses. Cook a meal. And we got five, six miles just to get there. Then there's ten miles of fence."

"Sonny rode it," said Chet. "Mentioned one stretch down. One. Could be in the first mile." He swung up and started off.

"With my luck," said Monte, mounting, "it'll be the last mile."

UNDER THE DARKENING SKY, wind moved over the big land, whipping the short winter-cured grasses. The first flurries of snow skittered with it, big-flaked, hardening as the temperature dropped. Like a long, blurred pencil mark across the bigness, the drift fence came out of distance and went into distance, not so much a discernable fence as a line of tumbleweed banked against the poles and wires. Where some violent freak of wind, likely an oversize dust devil, had smashed sometime recently against massed tumbleweed and used it as a battering ram to rip the wires loose from the posts, a rat-tailed roan and a chunky bay stood, heads drooping, rumps hunched into the wind. Not far away two men worked rapidly, alternating at posts, wire cutters in hand, tugging to lift the sagging barbed wire, and snipping short lengths of bailing wire with which to lash each strand back into place on the posts.

The wind rose, and the snow increased, small-flaked now and hard and stinging, and two tough little cow ponies waited, and two men, fingers numbing, worked steadily on down the line. And across the darkening miles, back by the ranch buildings, another man, big barrel body swinging in saddle, raced on a sweat-streaked mottled roan to pocket a batch of skittery horses in an angle of fence, push them through a gate into the big holding corral, follow them in and close the gate, open another at the other end and work them on into the smaller, regular horse corral.

SWIRLING SNOW, wind-driven, filled the darkness of early night, making a grayness in which vision died at fifteen feet. A rat-tailed roan and a chunky bay, sleet-crusted, pushed through the grayness at a steady jog. The men in the saddles were hunched low, jacket collars up, hats pulled down with short lengths of baling wire over the crowns and ends twisted together under their chins, holding the brims down over their ears.

The roan raised its head and looked to the right, snorting snow out of its nostrils and whinnying.

"Look there," said Monte Walsh, drawing rein. "What now?"

"What say?" shouted Chet Rollins, stopping beside him.

Off to the right, lost in the swirling grayness, a horse whinnied. They swerved right and advanced slowly, peering ahead. They stopped. Directly in front of them stood a small, scrawny horse, showing pinto through the patches of snow gathering on it.

"Ain't that one of Gonzales's?" said Monte.

"And saddled," said Chet. "What's holding him?"

The horse sidled around to face more toward them and

raised its head. One rein hung limp. The other drew taut, fastened to some object on the ground rapidly becoming indistinguishable under a mantle of snow.

In one swift motion Monte was down and striding forward. In one swift matching motion Chet had swung down in the saddle and scooped up the reins of Monte's horse. He watched as Monte bent low, following the taut rein of the other horse down, fumbling to untie it from around a man's wrist. He watched as Monte brushed snow aside and heaved, rolling the object over so that the whiteness of a face under an old cap looked up into the swirling snow.

"José?" said Chet.

"Who else?" said Monte, dropping to his knees and bending lower.

"Alive?" said Chet.

"Yeah," said Monte. "And drunk. Smells like a damned saloon."

"Sober enough to hang onto the horse," said Chet. "Maybe the cold caught him too. That ain't much of a coat he's got."

"Yeah," said Monte. "Be stiffer'n a poker in another hour like this." Moving swiftly, Monte stepped to the roan and, with fumbling gloved fingers, began to unloosen the cinch. "What d'you figure he's been doing out here?"

"Been into town," said Chet. "Stayed too long. Too many primos and too much vino. Likely he was getting some things for the kids. Tomorrow's Christmas, or have you forgot?"

"I been trying to forget," said Monte, pulling the saddle blanket from under his saddle. He spread the blanket on the snow-covered ground and rolled the limp body of José

Gonzales onto it. "Funny, ain't it," he said, "the fool things people'll do for kids." He wrapped the blanket around tight. "That'll help some around the middle anyways," he said, and picked up the wrapped body and laid it, belly down, over the saddle on the pinto. A half-full burlap bag hanging from the saddle horn was in the way. He unlooped it and handed it to Chet.

THE CENTRAL ROOM of the old adobe ranch house was warm and cheerful in the light of two kerosene lamps and a fire in the huge stone fireplace. Three straw mattresses and a pile of blankets from the bunkhouse were ranged on the floor along the wall. A fair-sized iron kettle and a wide flat pan and a big coffeepot sat on the raised hearth. One whole front corner of the room was filled with fragrant piñon firewood.

Monte Walsh sat in the mouse-chewed remnants of armchair on one side of the fireplace, working on his seventh biscuit, his third cup of coffee, his second bowl of the Sunfish specialty – stewed beef swimming in a sauce of mashed beans. Sunfish Perkins himself sat in the old rocker on the other side of the fireplace, watching with considerable interest the activity near the closed front door. There, well away from the fire, the meager body of José Gonzales, stripped naked, lay on the floor. His worn clothing, patched long underwear and ragged jeans and shirt and thin coat, was draped over a ladder-back chair before the fire. His half-full bag sagged against the front wall by the door. Beside him knelt Chet Rollins, rubbing his bare arms and legs with melting snow from a nearby pail.

"Gosh," said Sunfish. "There ain't much of him, is there?"

"Not exactly in your overweight class," said Monte. "But there's enough of him to have more'n any of us's got – a wife and two kids."

"And a sister," said Sunfish. "Dobe'd never let you forget that."

José moaned and kicked feebly with one foot. "Go ahead, kick," said Chet. "I know it hurts like hell thawing out."

"And he eats prodigious," said Monte. "Looks like we got another boarder till this thing lets up."

"I ain't hauling in no other mattress," said Sunfish. "He can have yours. We'll just take you up on that talk about Cal's bed. You'll freeze your gizzard in that little room with no fire, but you'll freeze fancy."

José's head raised a bit and thumped back on the floor, and he began to thrash about in aimless motion. "Well, well," said Chet. "So you're wiggling all of them now." He picked up a piece of toweling and began rubbing with it.

"Shucks, Chet," said Monte, ambling over. "You got to eat too. I'll wrassle with him some."

Sunfish heaved to his feet and began to serve up stew and biscuits and coffee. "What's he got in that bag?" he said.

"A little food," said Chet, settling into the armchair to start on his first bowl of the Sunfish special. "A few things for the kids."

"It ain't much," said Monte suddenly, sharply, looking up from his rubbing. The other two stared at him. "Aw, shucks," he said, returning to work. "Tomorrow's Christmas, ain't it?"

Silence in the big old room.

"It's sure doing things outside," said Sunfish. "Must have been four inches already when you came in. Maybe it'll be like that one two years ago."

"Colder," said Chet. "That ought to mean less snow."

José opened his eyes and stared unaware at the ceiling. He turned away on his side, muttering bitterly in Spanish.

"No cussing," said Monte. "That ain't polite. Reckon you're about ready to try navigating some." He slipped an arm under the thin shoulders and rose, bringing José up with him. José wobbled on bare feet and reached out instinctively to brace himself against the front wall.

"Exercise," said Monte. "That's what you need. Walking'll do it." He began propelling him across the floor, back and forth.

"Easy," said Chet around a mouthful of stew. "Slow down. He ain't made of cast iron like you."

Moving his feet mechanically, José looked up vacantly at Monte.

"Aw, come on," said Monte cheerfully. "You're doing fine. Stepping out like a trooper." He propelled José over by the ladder-back chair and released the arm holding him, ready to grab again.

José stood steady enough, staring down at the clothes on the chair as if unaware of what they were.

"Quit it now," said Monte sternly. "Don't you go being stupid on me. It's plumb indecent the way you're parading around here. Put those things on."

Mechanically, moving out of old habit, José began dressing.

"Well, lookathere," said Sunfish. "Monte, you get too old to straddle a hoss, you can hire out as nursemaid."

José had on the patched underwear, the ragged pants and shirt. He picked up one of the boots and sat down on the chair as if to put it on and simply sat there, holding the boot, staring into the fire.

"Still being stupid, eh?" said Monte. "I ought to bat you one. Want to roast yourself?" He took hold of the chair and pulled it and José in it back to a safe distance, and José simply sat there, holding the boot, staring into the fire.

"All I got to say," said Sunfish, "is he's going to be mighty exciting company if he stays that way."

"He'll snap out of it," said Chet. "Shock, I guess."

On the ladder-back chair José stirred, and the boot fell to the floor. His head rose higher. "*Gracias – muchas gracias*," he said, and he was José Gonzales again, the quiet little man whose ancestors had come into the big land with the early conquistadors and who clung now in this Yankee-invasion time to his one remaining piece of small, sparse valley on the western edge of the Slash Y range and there scratched out a living for his family with a few chickens and a garden and a few goats and a rare willingness to haul firewood the long way into town on his one old burro. "I theenk there was snow," he said. "I theenk I fall from the horse." He smiled a small, apologetic smile. "I be dead, no?"

"Not no," said Monte. "Yes. Oh, my, yes, yes...Sunfish, I reckon he's ready to eat. That is, if Chet left him anything."

Silence in the big old room, warm and cheerful, as three men watched the fourth finish the last of the stew, the last biscuit, and his third cup of coffee. José leaned down to set his cup on the floor and pick up one of the boots. "*Gracias*," he said. "I theenk I go now."

"Whoa there, José," said Monte. "You ain't going no-wheres. It's colder'n an icehouse outside. Snowing to beat hell."

José, bent over, boot in hand, looked at Monte.

"Damn it!" said Monte sharply. "I ain't going to cart you in a second time."

José let the boot drop and sat very still, looking into the fire.

"You're beat up, and that horse of yours ain't got much," said Monte. "Tell you what. When this thing lets up, I'll ride over with you."

José sat very still, looking into the fire. "*Los niños,*" said José. "I theenk I go." He picked up the boot.

"Two women," said Chet softly. "And a couple of kids. José, have they got food and firewood?"

"*Un poco,*" said José. He picked up the other boot.

"The hell with him," said Monte, rising and striding to the window to look out into the swirling grayness.

"Can't let him go like that," said Sunfish. "Hey, Chet, ain't Cal's bearskin somewhere around?"

"Must be," said Chet, pushing up from the armchair and heading for the closed door of the left side room. "And he sure could use some socks."

"Give the fool one of our horses," said Monte savagely, without turning from the window. "But I ain't having a thing to do with it."

Five minutes later José stood in the center of the room, a shapeless small bulk in a long, old bearskin coat that came down to his ankles, an old pair of Cal Brennan's gloves, cap on head with the piece of toweling down over it and his ears and tied under his chin.

"Ain't he something?" said Sunfish. "Looks like a mangy he-bear with mumps."

"I nevair forget," said José. He started toward his burlap bag by the door, and Monte Walsh, leaving the window in long strides, was in the way.

"You damned little gamecock," said Monte bitterly. "You really set on it?"

"*Sí*," said José simply. "*Los niños.*" He shrugged. "Ees Chreestmas." He started around Monte, but was stopped by a lean, hard-muscled arm clamped over his shoulders. Monte drew a deep breath and looked across the room at Chet.

"All right, Monte," said Chet. He sighed. "Looks like it's us again."

"And me," said Sunfish Perkins. "Maybe you two can take care of José. But somebody's got to take care of you."

OUT THROUGH THE GATE, from the partial protection of the high-railed first corral into the swirling snow and wrenching wind, four men, bundled thick against the cold, led four saddled horses.

"Shucks," said Monte Walsh, hefting the half-full burlap bag. "This thing's mighty puny. Rest of you wait a minute." He strode off, carrying the bag with him to the bunkhouse. Inside he lighted the lantern on the old kitchen table.

"What do you think you're doing?" said Chet Rollins from the doorway.

"I got two pair of socks I ain't ever wore," said Monte, heading for his bunk and squatting to reach under. "And a deck of cards that's almost new."

"Whatever for?" said Chet.

"For this bag," said Monte. "Ees Chreestmas."

"Darned if it ain't," said Chet, watching Monte pull a box of checker men from under Dally Johnson's bunk and a mouth organ from under Powder Kent's pillow. "I got a pair of spurs I ain't used yet," Chet said, heading for his own bunk. "And some tobacco I been hiding from you."

Two minutes later the bag was two thirds full. "What they really need is food," said Chet, picking up the lantern and leading the way out and over to the cookhouse. Inside he took an empty burlap bag off a chopping block in a corner and, with Monte helping, began to stuff it with cans from the cupboard nearly filling one end of the room. He stopped. He was looking at two humped objects under limp, well-washed flour sacks on the shelf by the stove.

"Now wait a minute," said Monte. "Don't go getting foolish complete."

"Ees Chreestmas," said Chet, taking the larger of the two objects out of its pan and wrapping its flour sack around under it.

"Aw, hell," said Monte. "You're going to be so smart, do it right." He picked up the other object.

FAR OUT IN THE storm-clogged darkness of night four men on four tough cow ponies, sleet-crusted beyond recognition, slugged through snow up the side slope of a long ridge. Monte Walsh in the lead on a leggy dun peered from under the rim of his pulled-down hat, picking the way. Behind him Chet Rollins on a thick-necked black rode close beside José Gonzales, shrunken down inside the old bearskin coat on a short, sturdy roan. And behind them came Sunfish Perkins, a big, solid shape on a rangy bay.

As they came out on the bare-swept crest, the wind beat at them, and they dropped down the other side. The wind was less brutal here, rushing past overhead. Monte stopped, and the others pulled up with him to breathe the horses.

"He's doing it on nerve alone," said Chet. "But he's doing it."

They pushed on, and José dropped his reins and took hold of the saddle horn with both hands and clung to it, head down. Chet leaned over and grabbed the trailing reins, leading the roan close in beside him, and Sunfish Perkins closed in on the other side. Steadily they pushed on, following Monte's lead.

The swirling snow slackened some, and vision lengthened, and out of banked snow ahead rose the top rails of a rickety corral with an open-end shed at one end and a burro a dim shape in it, and beyond that a low, three-room adobe house.

They stopped by the corral, and Chet pulled José out of the saddle and set him on his feet. Chet took one arm and Sunfish the other, and they moved toward the house. Monte unlooped two burlap bags from saddle horns and followed.

"Hello, in there!" shouted Chet. He began stomping and shaking to get rid of crusted snow. "Hello, in there!" he shouted again, and the door opened. In the doorway stood a woman with a blanket wrapped around her and up over her head, eyes peering out bright and frightened at them. Behind her they could see in the light from a small fire another woman, standing by the fireplace, wrapped in a shawl, an old single-shot rifle in her hands. The first woman backed away as they pushed forward. "Madre mía!" she said. "José!"

"He's all right, ma'am," said Chet quickly. "Just wore out mucho trying to get home. Some rest is all he needs. That your bedroom over there?" With the woman leading, he and Sunfish took José through the inner door to the right.

The other woman had set the rifle somewhere. She had looked at each of them in turn and now looked past Monte out the open front door. "Dobe?" she said.

"Shucks, no, ma'am," said Monte, reaching back with one foot to close the door behind him. "But if he'd known about this storm, he'd of sure been here. Now where'll I put these things?"

She pointed to the left inner doorway. Bags cradled in his arms, Monte strode over to the doorway, into it and stopped. Dimly he could make out a mattress on the floor, close to a wood stove in which the remains of a fire still glowed. On the mattress, from under the edge of a ragged quilt, two small heads, stocking-capped, peered up at him. "*San* Nicholas," said one in an awed whisper, and both of them ducked down under the quilt.

Monte looked down at the old quilt and the tiny quiverings that marked two small shapes beneath it. Carefully he stepped over a corner of the mattress and set the two bags against the wall. Carefully he stepped back, still looking down. He began to back out through the doorway and whirled, startled. The other woman had been close behind him.

In the faint light from the fireplace he saw her face, tired and sagging in the relief of long waiting over, smiling at him. " *San* Nicholas," she said softly.

"Aw, shucks, ma'am," said Monte, embarrassed. "Kids say the silliest things." He fidgeted. "I got to go unsaddle that horse José rode," he said quickly. "José can swap him back for his pinto first good chance he gets." Monte fled to the door and out.

The snow had stopped now, and high overhead the wind sighed long and seemingly mournful. Monte strode to the corral and led the roan into the open-end shed and the low nickering welcome of the old burro. He removed the saddle and looked around in the near darkness. "Where's the hay?" he said. "Ain't he got any?"

Something tickled his nose, and he looked up. A few wisps showed sticking through the cracks between the poles of the roof. He strode outside and reached up and pulled from the conical pile covering the roof poles a plentiful supply and a cascade of snow. He scooped up a double armful and took it in. He stood watching the horse and the burro start on the hay, feeling weariness creep along his muscles in the absence of motion. "My, oh, my," he murmured. "Kids sure are crazy sometimes."

From over by the house came a new sound, and he hurried toward it. In the lee of the end wall, where the snow was thin, Sunfish Perkins had scraped a bare spot and pulled there a batch of dead piñon trunks from a pile nearby and was working on them with an old rusty ax. "They ain't got much in there," he said. "Grab yourself a load."

Monte bent over, picking up stove lengths, and moved toward the house and met Chet coming out for more of the same.

Ten double trips later they stood in the central room surveying a shoulder-high stack ranked along the wall between the fireplace and the corner. "That ought to hold 'em for a spell," said Sunfish.

Scuffling sounds came from the room to the right. José Gonzales, thin and meager and indomitable in patched long underwear and a pair of Cal Brennan's socks, struggled into the doorway with two women trying to hold him back. He pulled free and braced one hand against the doorjamb and stood straight. His head rose, erect and somehow dignified. "Señores," he said. "Thees ees your house."

"That's mighty kindly of you, José," said Chet quickly. "Sometime maybe. But we got a ranch to think of. We got a break in this storm too."

"Get back in that bed," said Monte. "Ain't you been fool enough for one night?" He turned. "Come on, let's scat."

Out by the corral three men swung up on three tough cow ponies and headed for the horizon. And back at the house a woman with a blanket wrapped around her stood in the doorway and watched them go. "*Vayan con Dios,*" she said softly.

FAR OUT BEYOND the ridge wind whistled in long, fierce sweeps, blowing the brittle snow into drifts belly-deep on the three horses slogging patiently through them, needing no guidance, driving straight for the home corral. The bay led, the black followed, and the leggy dun moved in sturdy stride behind. No more snow fell, but the cold was steadily deepening.

Monte Walsh caught himself toppling slowly forward in the saddle. He shook himself vigorously. "Watch it," he muttered. "That's bad." He tried to wriggle his toes inside his boots. There seemed to be no feeling in them.

He looked ahead and saw Chet Rollins swaying some,

catching balance in jerky movement. He slapped spurs to the dun and came alongside Chet. "Wake up!" he shouted. "Get down and walk!" He looked ahead. The big body of Sunfish Perkins, hunched down, was rocking slowly forward, jerking back, rocking forward again.

"You too," muttered Monte. He slapped spurs again and was alongside Sunfish. "Snap out of it!" he shouted.

Sunfish's head turned slowly. "What's eating you?" said Sunfish drowsily.

"Damn it!" said Monte, reining in the dun, forcing his reluctant body to swoop down so he could take the reins of the bay close by the bit and yank the horse to a stop. "Tired and cold," he said. "Hell of a combination. Get down and walk!"

"Yeah," said Sunfish. "Reckon you're right." He climbed down and started to shuffle forward, leading the bay.

Monte turned back. The black had stopped. Chet sagged in the saddle, blinking at him. "What you stopping for?" he said drowsily.

"Good gosh!" said Monte. He dismounted and in one furious heave yanked Chet out of the saddle. "Give out on me now," he said grimly, "and I'll bust you one you'll remember." He yanked Chet up to his feet. "Ain't you got ears? I said get walking!"

Monte took the reins of the black and put them in Chet's hand. He turned Chet forward and gave him a push that sent him stumbling ten feet through the snow, the black jerking on the reins and stepping out to follow.

"Keep moving," said Monte. He took the reins of the dun and moved up by Chet and reached out to push him again. He moved up and pushed once more.

"Quit that," said Chet, standing straighter and moving under his own power. "Keep it up, and I'll try kicking your teeth in."

"That's the talk," said Monte. "But just keep moving."

Silent in the great white cold of distance fading away across the long miles into distance, three men leading three horses in single file pushed forward, intent on the effort of driving one foot ahead of the other through the resistant snow.

Monte Walsh felt the blood moving in his legs, lean energy building again in hard muscles of his body. He looked ahead and saw that the same was happening to the others. He saw the big barrel body of Sunfish Perkins smashing steadily through the drifts, breaking trail. "My, oh, my," he murmured. "I'd never tell him, but that sure ain't lard he's packing on that carcass of his."

COLD HAD CREPT into the main room of the old ranch house. The fire in the fireplace had dwindled to a few faint embers. Sunfish Perkins, still bundled, knelt in front of it, whittling shavings over the embers from a piece of piñon with clumsy stiffened fingers on the knife. Monte Walsh was lighting one of the lamps. Chet Rollins, finishing shedding his jacket and hat and the bandanna that had been tied over head and ears under it, was starting to unfold blankets and lay them on the mattresses.

Chet stopped, then straightened. Slowly he picked up his jacket and started to put it on.

"Hey," said Monte. "You locoed?"

"We ain't fed the horses," said Chet.

"Think I'd forget that?" said Monte. "Why'd you think I ain't stripped down? Just thawing out a little first. You get busy with those beds."

He pulled up his jacket collar, slipped on his gloves, and went out the door. Down by the first corral he looked through the rails at the dark shapes crowding close, expectant, and began counting. "Six and Sonny took one and left his," he muttered, "and Sunfish brought in seven, and José swapped even." He nodded and went to the barn and pushed open one of the protesting doors. "That thing ain't going to be fixed soon," he said, and went on in, reaching with experienced hands in the dark to pull down a bale of hay. He carried it out by the rails, slipped off the twin cords, and heaved it over, a half at a time.

He leaned on the rails, looking through at the horses jostling one another to get at the hay. Suddenly he pushed out and returned to the barn and took two battered pails from nails on a beam and lifted the lid of a big, tin-lined wooden bin and dipped the pails in. One weighing heavy in each hand, he went out to the corral and in through the gate and to a trough along one side and emptied the pails into it, scattering the contents along the full length. "Come and get it," he said. "You're too stupid to know, but it's a Christmas present."

He watched the horses catch the meaning of the rattle of the pails; they drifted over, crowding one another. He saw the pinto, coming late and wary, ease in between two others. He saw the smallish, neat sorrel approach cautiously and slide in too. "When I wake up," he said, "if I ever do, maybe there'll be some more." He left the corral, dragging his legs, and moved up to the house.

Inside Sunfish Perkins sat on the hearth out of range of a now-healthy fire, slumped back against the fireplace, head dropped sideways, snoring in steady rhythm. Chet Rollins sat in the remnants of an armchair, head nodding, but still awake, waiting.

"I thought maybe you'd bring that bottle," said Chet.

"Shucks," said Monte. "I'm too tired even to drink. Likely it's froze solid anyways, and the bottle broke, and we'd have to get a pail and thaw it. Come on, let's tuck him away. Take the head. There ain't much in that part of him."

Together they lifted Sunfish and carried him to one of the mattresses and laid him down and spread a blanket over him. "If he dies in his sleep," said Monte, "at least he'll have his boots on."

There was silence in the big old room, except for slight rustlings as two men pulled off each other's boots and one blew out the lamp and both lay down on mattresses and reached to draw blankets up over them. Then there was silence in the big old room except for the outside sound of wind hunting along the eaves and finding no entrance.

Monte lay flat, looking up at the old beamed ceiling. "Know what we'll be doing when we get up?" he said. "We'll be eating beef and beans and riding out to thaw windmills; and if that crust that's starting already on the snow out there gets bad, we'll be hauling feed to a lot of hungry cows."

"Yeah," said Chet drowsily. "That's about it."

Monte raised himself on one elbow to look over at Chet stretched out flat. "You think I don't know," he said, "you fixed it someway for that brown bean just 'cause I already had one. Well, it kind of got you a bellyful."

"It ain't been so bad," said Chet drowsily. "Somehow, wherever you are, things are always happening."

"Shucks," said Monte. "That just goes to show. That's what I keep telling you. Luck and me, we – " He stopped. Chet was asleep.

Monte lay back and stared up at the shadows flickering between the beams. "Santo Nicholas," he murmured. "That's me."

CHRISTMAS DAY DAWNED cold and clear over the frozen white wonder of the big land. The first light of the morning sun touched the capped peaks of the mountains to the west and moved down them, pink-flushed, and moved over the badlands at their base and a small valley where a three-room house sent smoke drifting up from chimney and stovepipe and moved on over the long ridge that screened this and other valleys and on across the wide, white miles where the blurred tracks of three men and three horses showed in the snow and moved on to glow softly on the drifted flat roof of an old ranch house where three men slept the deep, dreamless sleep of tired muscles and the simple, uncomplicated assurance that they had done and would do whatever needed to be done.

Grandfather's Stories

Ernst Wiechert

It is Christmas Eve on a large Prussian estate shortly after the great upheaval now known as World War I, and several tenants have gathered with their masters – three brothers – for the evening. Christoph, their elderly coachman, has been coaxed into telling a story for old times' sake.

CHRISTOPH SAT on the edge of the hearth next to the forester's wife, smiled and filled his short pipe with fresh tobacco. His threadbare coat of blue cloth was properly brushed and the light of the candles shone on the buttons with the coat of arms and on his white hair. Behind him his shadow fell large and silent on the bright wall.

He smiled at the brothers one after the other and then he looked into the lights and shadows of the tree.

"My grandfather told us this story," he began. "When his father's father drove the horses, they had a master who was strict and sharp with his tongue. He had been long in military service, right back to the time of the Emperor Napoleon. He was not a hard master, but he had seen much that was hard and cruel during his campaigns, and he was used to order and not to obey.

"One Christmas Eve the grandfather came driving with him from a little town and he drove fast, for it was already time to light the tree. They had been delayed and the snow was falling fast. At that time there were still wolves in the forest, and they had lit the lanterns on the sleigh and the master held a rifle on his knees.

"When they drove out of the forest and were in sight of the dimly lit windows of the manor house, the grandfather all of a sudden stopped the four horses, for in the light of the lanterns a child stood by the road. It was a small child, a boy, and snow lay on his shoulders. The grandfather said that he was amazed, because there was no snow on the boy's hair, only on his shoulders. And it was snowing fast. But the boy's hair was like gold without a single snowflake on it.

"The child stretched out his right hand – palm upward – as if he wanted to have something put in it. He looked like a laborer's child, only more delicate. He had a happy, smiling face, though he was all alone on the edge of the deep forest, and now when the bells of the sleigh were not ringing any more, they could hear the wolves howl in the distance.

"The horses stood still and were not frightened.

"'Drive on, Christoph,' called the master impatiently. 'It is late.'

"But the grandfather did not drive on. He had folded his hands in the fur gloves over the reins and gazed at the child. Later he said that it had been impossible to take his eyes off the child.

"'Drive on, Christoph,' shouted the master and stood up in the sleigh.

"But the grandfather did not drive on. He took the rug from his knees and lifted it a little, and the child put his foot on the runner of the sleigh and sat down at the side of the grandfather. The boy was smiling all the time.

"The master was so angry that he forgot himself. He was not angry over the child, but because the grandfather had not been obedient, and the child had been the cause of the disobedience.

"So the master stood right up in the sleigh in his splendid uniform and his fur coat, grasped the child's shoulders and tried to throw him into the snow.

"But the child did not move. There he sat smiling and gazing at the horses and their large shadows thrown by the light of the lanterns. The grandfather holding the reins looked on. He said that he could not raise even the little finger of his hand. He was rather taken aback but he was not afraid.

"Then the master jumped out of the sleigh with a terrible curse, a curse which perhaps he had learned in the times of war and death. He stood at the side of the runner, and raised both his arms, meaning to pull the child out of the sleigh.

"But the child did not move. He even raised both hands as if he wanted to show that he was not holding onto anything. And he smiled.

"The snow was still falling in the light of the lanterns, and it was so quiet that the grandfather could hear his heart beat.

"'Get in, sir,' he said in a low voice, 'for Christ's sake get in.'

"And the miracle was that the master obeyed. He got in and they drove on.

"The grandfather could move his hands again. The child sat quietly at his side. No snowflake was to be seen on his golden hair. But when they drove into the courtyard, they were very much afraid. For in the moment when the sleigh drove below the coat of arms on the archway all the windows suddenly were lit up: the windows of the great house and the windows of all the cottages and the stables. It was so bright that the whole yard was bathed in light – a brightness, the grandfather said, that was not of this earth. All the cottagers came out of their houses, and the animals' heads appeared at the stable doors, as if they had been untied: the horses' heads, the cows', the sheep's. Without making a sound men and animals gazed at the sleigh, which drove up in a sweeping curve and stopped before the flight of steps in front of the manor house. And they all saw the Child – all of them. There was not one who did not see Him.

"The Child was the first to get out of the sleigh. But He did not step down, said the grandfather, He floated – without weight – like a snowflake. He turned round once to the sleigh and smiled, and then He went across the courtyard to a cottage where a little boy lay dying. They all knew that he would not live through the night.

"And when the Child from the sleigh stepped over the threshold of the cottage, the lights round the yard suddenly went out, and the people were as if dazzled and groped their way to the stables to tie up the animals.

"But the grandfather got down from the sleigh and helped his master up the steps, for he could not walk alone. Inside in the large hall where the tree was and where the antlers and the pictures hung on the wall, and where the stuffed birds stood, the master looked about him, as if he were in a dense, unknown forest, and in quite a strange voice he said: 'I thank you, Christoph.'

"But the cottager's child was well again by the morning.

"Yes," concluded Christoph in his low, gentle voice, "that was the night when the grandfather drove the Christ-child."

He got up, took a cinder from the fire for his pipe and sat down again by the hearth.

The candles burned down without a flicker, and in the hush they could hear how the frost was splitting the trees in the forest...

After a long pause, one of Christoph's listeners speaks up and requests another story. He agrees.

"My grandfather also told this story," Christoph began. "When the grandfather of his father drove the horses, they had a vicar at the church on the estate who was a shy, humble man and very poor. And he had seven children. In the castle there lived, after a good master whom they had called 'the Saint,' a harsh master as happens now and again in wild times. It was still the time of serfdom.

"On Christmas Eve, because he felt lonely, the master had detained the vicar in the manor house and had kept him back, as if he were a sort of toy, which he could take out of a box or put back, when he so minded.

"When the master had drunk a great deal of the hot punch, he wanted to play at dice with the vicar for a couple of gold coins, although he knew that the vicar was as poor as a church mouse.

"The vicar refused. As long as he had been on the estate he had never refused anything, and he knew that it was dan-

gerous to have a will of one's own. He did not refuse because he was poor. He refused – so he said in his humble
way – because the soldiers had cast lots for the garments of
Him who was born this night and had lain in a manger.

"The master looked long at him while he shook the dice
in the leather box.

"'Cast the dice, vicar!' he said.

"But the vicar shook his head.

"'Once more I say: cast the dice, vicar!' said the master,
and his lips were pale and thin.

"But the vicar shook his head and only folded his hands
on the white tablecloth.

"'If you do not cast the dice – and thus refuse to do what
your master commands you,' said the master, 'I shall have
you whipped like any disobedient servant, and you will be
given as many strokes with the whip as I shall throw pips on
the dice out of this box. Once more: cast the dice, vicar!'

"But the vicar shook his head.

"Thereupon the master got slowly up, shook the box and
let the dice roll on the white cloth. He kept his eyes fixed on
the vicar's face, and only after a long pause did he count the
pips on the dice. 'Seven, vicar,' he said. 'As many as you
have children, for each child the whip will strike you once.'

"He roused all his household and all the serfs on the estate, men and women, and ordered them to come into the
large hall. 'This man,' he said, 'has refused to play at dice
with me, and thus has treated me, his lord, with contempt.
Bind him so that I can have him whipped, seven strokes,
one for each of his children, and so that you may learn
what it means to treat me with contempt.'

"But none of the people stirred. The grandfather in the

foremost row heard how the men groaned and the women wept. But they did not move.

"The master looked sharply at each one of them and then he smiled. 'Your turn will come, too,' he said. And then he called the overseer. The overseer was a hard man, even harder than the master himself, and he stepped forward.

"He bound the vicar to one of the two columns which supported the ceiling of the hall, tore his clothes from his shoulders and struck him seven times across his back. The blood ran from the vicar's white skin, and the men and women went down on their knees and prayed. They had covered their eyes with their hands. The vicar did not utter a sound.

"When they had unbound him, he walked to the table and looked down on the dice which still lay there as they had rolled out of the box – two – three – two – and then he looked at the master: 'Pray,' he said in a low voice, 'that the Child may look at you tonight, or it will never look at you again.'

"Then he went out of the hall with the others.

"The next morning the master drove to church, as had been the custom since time immemorial.

"He did not walk, though it was not farther than one could throw a stone from a sling. The grandfather went behind him into the church, and left his grandchild with the horses.

"The church was crowded, and the master sat in his carved pew and had folded his hands in their white gauntlets over his prayer book. It was as quiet as the grave.

"The vicar was pale, but otherwise there was nothing to show that anything had happened to him.

"After the prelude, when the little organ began to play the melody of the opening hymn, the vicar raised his eyes from his folded hands and looked at his congregation. For the congregation did not sing. No mouth opened, and everybody's eyes were fixed on him. They heard how the master stamped his foot once. They heard it, because the wheel of his silver spur clicked.

"But then the master sat quiet and sang. He sang the three verses of the hymn in his high-pitched, melodious voice, and he sang alone with the vicar. No other lips moved. The grandfather said that few events in his life had been as awful as this.

"But the vicar did not look at him who alone sang the Christmas song with him.

"He saw his seven children who sat with their mother opposite the pulpit, and the mother was a thin, bent woman.

"Then the vicar read the Christmas Gospel according to St. Luke; everything was as it always had been. When he had finished reading, something happened at which the hearts of the faithful trembled once more, for the vicar did not go on to interpret the Gospel, but in a low voice began a solemn memorial address on the life and body of the late Hjalmar von Liljecrona, and the deceased man was sitting opposite him in the old, carved oaken pew and staring as on one whose senses God had darkened.

"'He died,' said the vicar, 'because he had thrown dice for the swaddling clothes of the Child in the manger, and because the Child had turned his eyes away from him. He died, because he had not only thrown dice for the clothes of this holy Child, but for the clothes of seven poor children of this world and with them for the clothes of seventy times seven children.'

"'And he had died in such a terrible way that he was walking about like a living person without knowing that he was dead, while everyone in the congregation beheld his living corpse and turned away from him shuddering, because he was stinking like the dead man in the story of Lazarus.'

"And the vicar had got so far, when the master jumped to his feet with a frightful curse, pulling his sword out of its scabbard. 'Take back that word, you devil of a vicar!' he shouted in a hoarse voice, 'take back that word!'

"But the vicar did not heed him any more than he would have heeded a breeze wafting through the church, and he folded his hands to pray for the dead and asked the congregation to do the same.

"Then the most terrible thing happened; the master sprang to the foot of the pulpit and, grasping his sword in the middle of the blade, hurled it at the vicar's heart.

"Now beautifully carved in wood in the wall of the pulpit was the mother of Christ holding the Child in her arms and lovingly protecting Him. And the sword – though hurled from so near – missed the vicar and buried its point in the heart of the Child Jesus, quivering there for a time, like the shaft of an arrow; then it slowly sank, drawn down by the heavy baskethilt, fell on the pine boards of the floor and broke into a thousand pieces. And my grandfather as well as many others saw a thin trickle of blood run down from the wound in the wood and drip onto the floor and onto the steel of the blade which turned crimson.

"Then for the first time that morning the vicar looked at the master who stood below him. He did not look at him angrily – there was not even reproach in his glance. He only looked at him in deep sorrow, as one may look at a picture of someone who is dead, and he remained so, when the master had fallen on his knees and covered his face with his hands in the long, white gauntlets.

"And so the vicar led him out of the church, slowly, step by step through the kneeling congregation. When the master refused to get into the sleigh, they led him through the snow to the manor house, the vicar on one side, bareheaded, and my grandfather on the other side, the whip in his free hand and an expression of consternation on his face.

"From that hour the master was a 'changed' man, as many of his line before him had been 'changed,' because it lay in their blood.

"Yes," concluded Christoph in his low, gentle voice, "that was the night when they cast dice for the Christ-child in the old house."

Then he took another cinder from the fire for his pipe and sat quietly on the edge of the hearth looking into the candles which were burning down.

Soon after the people started for home, and as they slowly walked through the snow, it was as if the old stories went with them, the stories of the old, gloomy houses, where so much happened, but where men could still be changed, if a voice could touch their hearts.

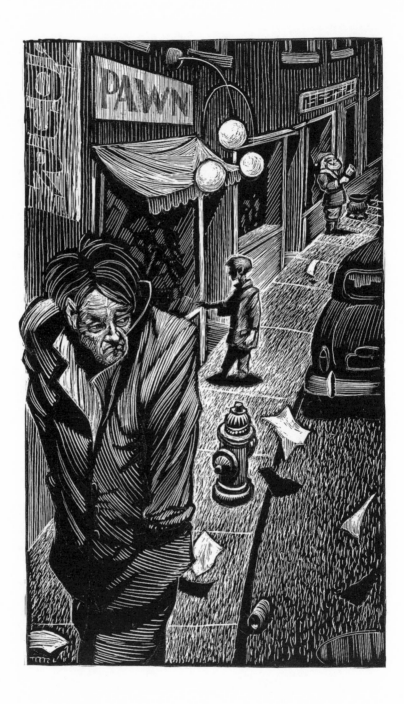

The Vexation of Barney Hatch

B. J. Chute

THE BIG BELL CLANGED in the church tower, and all the pigeons gossiping on the roof flew up in a violent state of nerves, as if the Day of Judgment had come upon them.

This created a fine rumpus of snow-gray wings in the snow-gray sky over Barney Hatch, but it confirmed him in a private theory that pigeons were not quite right in the head. The church had been around for more than a century, and the bell gave its great shout every hour, which meant that twenty-four times a day for over a hundred years the pigeons or their ancestors had been blowing their tops. Barney was not mathematically an able man, but even he could see that the thing had got out of hand.

A panhandler himself, Barney had a certain professional sympathy for pigeons, birds with an eye to the main chance and an alert capacity for spotting likely crumb-droppers.

He stared down at them now, bobbing and clucking around his shoes, and rubbed his nose thoughtfully with the back of his hand. His nose was cold, and he rubbed it some more, turning it from a melancholy blue to quite a cheerful red, but his mind was on neither the pigeons nor his nose. Barney Hatch had a project, and the project required cash.

Not a large fortune, but a sum of that size affectionately known as tidy. This project was going to cost three dollars and forty-nine cents, and since he had only forty-seven cents in his pocket he still needed three bills and two pennies. The trouble was that time was running short, tomorrow being Christmas Day and Christmas Day being the cause of the whole thing.

Christmas was all over the city – wreaths in doorways, tinsel and red ribbon and holly berries bursting out at odd corners, a piney, citrony, maddening jumble of sights and smells, tugging and nudging like a persistent cat at an ashcan. It had roused in Barney a sudden determination to do some celebrating himself for once and to join in the general exuberance of warmth and good cheer.

The very notion of a celebration had automatically pointed his toes toward the nearest liquor store, and he was engaged in a conscientious survey of the stock of whisky in the glittering window, with an eye toward economy, when the gold seal on a front-row bottle winked at him. It was a fat bottle, nicely shaped to accommodate the hand, and in addition to the gold seal it had a fancy label and a scarlet ribbon in a Christmas bow around its neck. It was plainly a bottle designed for good cheer, and judging by the price, its contents had been knowingly distilled.

On the other hand its price was outrageous.

Barney's struggle with his good sense was brisk but brief. After all, a Christmas treat was a Christmas treat, and what good was a celebration unless it was done right? He thought about the glow there would be in a bottle of good whisky like this one, and how the glow would last and spread and get deeper and wider. Nothing in the world could give you a glow like that, one you could count on, and a whole bottle to himself would very probably produce the finest glow in the history of man.

All he had to do was raise the money.

Contemplating the financial aspects now, among the cooing, huffing pigeons, Barney did comforting sums in his head. After all, it was Christmas, a time when any competent panhandler can count on a certain amount of soft-headedness among his clientele. Estimating, he decided that six suckers at fifty cents each would just do him nicely. He raised his eyes from the improvident birds and took a good look around.

A man went by, briefcase in hand, a rolled-up newspaper under one arm. A literate gent, well-heeled. Barney got his feet moving fast and performed a sort of flanking movement. Barney smiled an ingratiating, a calculating, smile. He said, "Sir," like a cooing dove, imagining for a moment that the man would press a five-dollar bill into his hand, touched by the general lunacy of Christmas.

The man stepped neatly around Barney, said, "Left my wallet home," and departed. Barney said, "Yah!" to the tails of the gentleman's overcoat. Left his wallet home! He'd be as apt to set sail without his trousers as without his money.

Expressing dissatisfaction in a low mutter, Barney left the pigeons and the church bell and tried another street. A lady in a squirrel neckpiece gave him a dime and a lecture, leaving him with two ninety-two to go and a bad taste in his mouth, which came not from remorse or shame but from biting the dime.

Business seemed suddenly to have turned sour, but the gold-seal bottle hovered in the air above him, slightly to one side of his right eyebrow. He walked up one street and down another. The professional shamble became quite sincere, his feet hurt, he had never had such a bad day. One would think, with Christmas practically ready to pounce, that people would be digging deep into their purses and handing over dollar bills with warm enthusiasm. Lock and key on 'em, Barney grumbled to himself. Lock and key on every purse and wallet in town. The whole city dizzy with Christmas and good will, and what did he get? Ten cents from a squirrel neckpiece, with a lecture thrown in.

He walked through a transported grove of pine trees on a street corner, little fat trees and tall lean trees, all waiting for the tinsel and the star and the fancy trimmings that were nice enough when you had four walls to wrap around them. "Knickknacks," said Barney scornfully. "Jinglejangles." And he thought of the knickknack and jinglejangle of a gold seal on a whisky bottle. He thought of waking up on Christmas morning and taking his first drink, savoring it in a gentlemanlike manner, not gulping, the whole bottle to go through and the whole day to go through it. He thought of how he would admire the label and the seal and the Christmas ribbon before he pulled the cork and had himself his first Christmas drink, spreading warm and bright.

He walked on, and the gold-seal bottle kept just one step ahead of him, out of reach, an air-borne promise. He stopped outside a department store, its windows shimmering and quivering with light and glitter, people rushing inside where it would be nice and warm, with their purses gaping, and then coming out and quickly closing the purses again so the loose change wouldn't catch cold.

Barney swore. It began to look as if he was going to spend Christmas with fifty-seven cents and no gold seal, no cork, no different from three hundred and sixty-four other days.

He stepped into the doorway of the store, out of the way of the wind. He thrust his hands deep into his pockets and glared at his reflection in the store window.

A fat man with a busy face came lumbering out of the store. He stared up the street, down the street, and then he stared at Barney. His eyes narrowed like he was doing sums on his fingers, and he shook his head and sighed. "You want a job for a couple of hours?" said the man.

Barney looked back over his shoulder, figuring the man was talking to someone behind him, but there was no one there. He wasn't used to being offered jobs, and a wary look came into his eyes, because you never know about offers. Like a dime, the thing to do was take a bite of it and see if it bit solid.

"How much?" said Barney.

"Dollar fifty an hour."

Two hours at a dollar fifty was three bucks, and he only needed two dollars and ninety-two cents. Profit, eight cents. He was rich. "Okay," said Barney.

"Thank goodness," said the fat man with real sincerity, and added, "You're skinny, but we can stuff you."

"Eh?" said Barney, recoiling.

"Come on, come on." The man took his elbow and piloted him into the store and down the crowded aisles.

"What you hiring me for?" Barney asked plaintively. "What you want to stuff me for?"

"Santa Claus, of course." The man's voice implied that any fool should know that. "Ours has gone home sick. We called the agency, but they can't get the substitute here until one-thirty. Line of kids a mile long, yapping and yelping. Mothers getting so mad they'll yank them out of line and go somewhere else. They go somewhere else, we go broke. How we going to pay our taxes?" He glared at Barney.

Barney was not tax-conscious. He was, however, conscious that he had no wish to play Santa Claus for a mob of children. His instinct warned him to escape while escape was still possible, and he was about to take its advice when – in a rather peremptory manner – the vision of the gold-seal bottle appeared in the air above him. Barney relaxed.

His escort pushed him through a doorway into what appeared to be a dressing room. A scarlet suit, furred and benevolent, hung from a hook. "I'll help you get dressed," said the man, calmer now that he had caged his Christmas spirit. "On account of the pillow."

Barney took off his coat and thought hard about the money he was making. Even with two pillows under his belt, there was something faintly melancholy about his shape. He tested the pillows against slippage. "What do I have to do when I get out there?" he said nervously.

"You sit in a chair by the Christmas tree," said the man, frowning at Barney's front, "and you talk to the kids and you give them each a lollipop."

"What do I say?"

"Promise them anything they ask for. Especially if it's in the store."

"I don't know what's in the store."

"Promise them anything."

This pie-in-the-sky approach seemed slightly sinister. "When do I get my money?" said Barney, leaning toward the mirror and tying on his beard. It was a splendid beard, long and white and fluffy, but self-esteem was not going to hinder self-interest.

"Oh, that." The man scribbled something on a piece of paper. "Give this to the cashier when you leave. You come back here and give the new man your suit (and I hope to God he's got more shape than you have) and then you can get your money and be on your way."

Barney grinned and took another look in the mirror. There was something not quite right about the beard; it looked more like some strange white thicket behind which he was lurking. And his nose had faded, being indoors. Still, he looked more like Santa Claus than he looked like anything else, and when the business was over and done with he would be three dollars richer.

Patting his front with a certain anxiety, Barney let himself be shepherded back through the store to where a glittering Christmas tree touched the ceiling and a small jungle of assorted children milled about, shouting their boredom and their lack of faith.

Barney had an impulse to run, but his guide, perhaps sensing it, shoved him briskly into the thronelike chair and anchored him by putting a small child on his knee. The infant was fat, fair and female, and Santa Claus regarded her with marked distaste. He then thought of the three dollars and pulled himself together enough to inquire what the little lady wanted for Christmas.

The little lady sounded off like a clockwork mouse, her list of vital necessities having apparently been ready for days and her memory excellent. When he took her off his knee and forgot to give her a lollipop, she demanded that too, and Barney had to admire the tough grip she had on the situation.

In about ten minutes he was pretty well into the swing of things, the Santa Claus racket being somewhat easier than expected. If a toddler wanted a grizzly bear in his Christmas stocking, all Santa had to do was pat his head, promise a den of bears and hand him back to his mama. This grandiloquent largess with no responsibility speeded the passage of the two hours, and Barney had just promised a little girl with pigtails that she would have curly hair for Christmas when the small boy turned up.

He was a very small boy, even smaller than the other children, and he looked out of place in the line among the well-brushed, neatly dressed household creatures who were patrolled by parents. His hair, if it had been combed at all, had been combed by his fingers. His pants were too short and his coat sleeves too long, his face was dirty, and he stood with his hands thrust in his pockets and his chin sticking out.

Barney recognized him. He was a street sparrow, and wherever else he might belong, he didn't belong in the warm, rich aisles of a big department store.

The boy stood and stared at him, and Barney stared back. There was something about this kid's stare that was different from the others', and it took a moment for Barney to place it. Then he realized that the boy was looking at him as if he were real. The other children had looked at him as if he were a handy device for registering propositions.

He felt a vague embarrassment, very foreign to him. He rubbed his nose with the back of his hand, causing his whiskers to lurch sideways. "Well, my little man," he said, because that was more or less what he had been saying for almost two hours, "and what do you want for Christmas?"

"What I didn't get last year," said the boy. He looked at Santa Claus long and hard. "What you promised me last year and I didn't get."

Barney pulled his beard back into position and tried to think of some way of counteracting this very unfavorable propaganda. Several children in the line were giving him rather cool up-and-down looks, and Barney wished no complaints made to the management before he pocketed his money.

He said with false cheer, "Well, well, we'll do better this year, won't we? Just what was it you wanted?"

"You know," said the small boy quietly. "The harmonica."

It was a long word, but he didn't miss a syllable. It took Barney a moment to identify a harmonica as the small musical instrument which was played like corn on a cob. "Must've slipped down to the bottom of my pack," he said cleverly. "Imagine that happening!" He gave a conciliatory, unsuccessful chuckle. The boy regarded him calmly but with unnerving watchfulness.

"Well, you'll get it this year for sure," said Barney defensively.

"You said that last year."

"I told you. It slipped down to the bottom of my pack. Here." He handed over a green lollipop. "Take this and go away and be a good boy. If you aren't a good boy, you won't get anything for Christmas at all." Even as he said this, it struck him as a revolting philosophy, but it was backed by tradition. He said hopefully, "Two lollipops?"

The boy shook his head and backed off. "No, I don't want them. I want the harmonica."

The line behind him was growing restive, and there was a faint murmuring of parents. "Go away," said Barney.

"Okay. I'll see you later."

Not if I see you first, thought Barney, and turned with considerable relief to his next customer. The clock told him he had ten minutes to go, and then the world in a gold-seal bottle would be his.

When the clock hand moved into place, Santa Claus's eagerness to quit his duties was such that he nearly dumped the last child on the floor. In the dressing room his replacement was waiting calmly, a cozy gentleman with a twinkle in his eyes and a curve like a robin's under his waistcoat. The beard and his red suit merely confirmed that here was Santa Claus. Barney frankly admired him and hoped the small harmonica-seeking boy would turn up in the line again, pitted against a Santa who would know how to deal with him.

Whistling, he sought out the cashier's desk, and in a few minutes he had exchanged his white slip of paper for three pretty green ones, underwritten by the Treasury of the United States.

He now had three dollars and fifty-seven cents. He would walk slowly to the liquor store; he would stroll, savoring every moment. The very magnificence of the gesture would lay out a red carpet for Christmas. It would be glorious.

Floating on a cloud of anticipation, Barney Hatch walked out of the department store and into the street.

"There you are," said the small boy, rising at his elbow.

Barney leaped and came down quivering, like a spring stretched too far. For a moment he thought he must still be wearing his whiskers, but a hand to his chin reassured him. Case of mistaken identity, he told himself quickly; probably looked like the kid's grandpop. Privately he didn't think he looked like anybody's grandpop, but the alternative was even more fantastic.

The boy took hold of Barney's coat and gave it a good sharp tug, endangering a vital button. "Come on."

"Scram," said Barney, resorting to simple English. "You've got me mixed up with someone else."

"No, I ain't."

Barney stopped in his tracks and stared down at the top of the head that needed a haircut. "Who do you think I am?"

"Santa Claus," said the boy.

He knew he shouldn't have asked. He couldn't even figure out how the kid had been able to spot him without his beard and his furred suit. He said, "Look, kid, I saw your friend Santa Claus just a minute ago. He's in the store. You go back in the store and you'll find him there under the tree."

"That ain't Santa Claus," said the boy.

"It is so," said Barney indignantly.

"It ain't."

All right, it ain't, thought Barney. "You shouldn't say 'ain't,'" he said to the boy.

"Santa Claus is up at the North Pole. He don't get into town nowadays."

"Yes, you do."

"Listen," said Barney, "you're making me very nervous. Go away or I'll call a cop." He looked up the street in a threatening manner, and his eye lit on the happy sight of a fine specimen of a Santa Claus, halfway up the block, standing by a phony chimney and ringing a bell. Barney put a hand on the boy's shoulder and give him a fervent push. "There's your Santa Claus, up there. See, I told you you'd got the wrong guy."

"That ain't Santa Claus."

"Geez," said Barney with some passion, "can't you get a new record? What makes you think the guy up there ain't Santa Claus?"

"Because you are," answered the boy.

Barney shook his head hard, feeling life getting complicated, and then he had a bright idea. He surrendered suddenly. "Okay," he said, "so I'm Santa Claus. How'd you guess?"

The boy shrugged. "I don't know – I just did."

Reindeer fur got shed on my trousers, I suppose, thought Barney with some bitterness. Aloud, he said, "Well, it was real smart of you. I'm sort of anonymous, you know. That means nobody knows I'm in town." He put a hand on the boy's shoulder, and the boy squirmed away. "Now, look, son. That guy in the store, the one that's wearing my costume – well, he's one of my special assistants."

"Yeah?"

"Yeah." Barney felt exasperation crawling up inside his collar. What was the matter with modern youth anyway? No faith. He said, "Yeah," twice more, just to make things clear. "Well, he handles the musical-instrument side of the business, see? So you go back in the store and tell him I sent you, and everything will be okay. See?"

"No."

"Whaddya mean no!"

The boy said stolidly, "You promised me my harmonica

last Christmas, and I didn't get it. I've waited a whole year."
He looked up suddenly. "I've gotta get it this year, I've
wasted a whole year when I could've been playing. You
promised me."

Barney's voice rose. "I wasn't even around last year!"

The boy just looked at him, in the patient way children
look at grownups who make silly remarks. Barney began
to feel haunted. A man might as well try to get a wad of
chewing gum out of his hair as this little squirt. For a moment, he toyed with the idea of turning tail and running,
but there is nothing that attracts a policeman like a running
object.

The situation required something more subtle. Barney
heaved a sigh. "How about your ma and pa buying a harmonica for you?" he said hopefully.

The boy's eyes slid sideways. For just a second Barney
was sorry he'd asked, there being so many homes in the
world where stockings never hang at Christmas time.
Then he cheered himself with the thought that the kid had
probably long since driven all his relatives into the loony
bin with his persistence, and so he was able to hurl his
bombshell without a qualm. "I didn't bring no harmonicas
with me this trip," he said crushingly. "You're out of luck
this year."

"You c'n buy it."

The mere suggestion of parting from any cash caused a
cry of anguish to rise to Barney's lips. He said in one outraged defiant breath, "See here, you! You're too old to believe in Santa Claus, and furthermore there ain't no Santa
Claus," and then he waited stoically for the expected broken heart.

It failed to materialize. The boy nodded calmly. He said,

"Like you told me, you have to be anonymous." He called it "anon-y-mouse," like something a cat would be watching for.

Barney sighed heavily and stroked the end of his nose. He was not an expert on harmonicas, but he was pretty sure you could buy one at a dimestore toy counter. Take away one dime from his cash on hand, it would leave him three forty-seven, only two cents short of his ticket to Christmas Day. If he couldn't make a two-cent touch in the next couple of hours, he deserved to be read out of the panhandlers' club anyway.

He sighed again. "All right," he said glumly. "Where's the nearest dimestore?"

The boy started to say something and then changed his mind. He took Barney's hand, not in the least trustingly but plainly to prevent his escape. They walked down two blocks, one over, turned sharply into a grubby side street, and stopped in front of a store.

"Hey," said Barney. This was no dimestore. This was a kind of store Barney knew inside and out: a pawnshop, and not a classy one. Its fly-specked dusty windows were piled high with objects as miscellaneous as a junkman's dream: old tired medals on faded bits of ribbon; an alarm clock with no hands; a china lamp with a Cupid base and dirty blue ruffles; a handful of painted brooches; a snuffbox with no lid; a silver mug inscribed 1887–1907; a stuffed and lopsided owl.

"There," said the small boy. "There, by the owl."

Barney looked. A beat-up tarnished harmonica lay in a satin-lined box. The lining had been red once, but the sun through the window had faded it to pink like a raspberry stain, and there was a big dent in the harmonica's side. It looked like a long time since anyone had played it or wanted to.

A connoisseur of old age and unwanted objects, Barney figured a quick guess that the harmonica had been lying there anyway five years. It was a weather-beaten shipwreck washed up on a pawnshop beach. Junk, really junk.

Barney looked down at the head just under his elbow. "Is that what you've been yammering about?"

The head nodded. Its nose pressed against the windowpane. "I told you about it last Christmas. That was when you promised – "

Barney bit the tail off an expletive, calling down a justified imprecation on some previous hired Santa Claus who must have been throwing out promises like confetti. He stared at the harmonica and worried the tip of his nose. It was hard to know with pawnbrokers; this one might charge as much as a quarter.

"Been there a long time," he said. "Wouldn't you rather have a nice clean harmonica from the dimestore?"

The small boy said scornfully, "They're just toys. This is a real one."

Real like his Santa Claus was real. Two pieces of junk. "This is awful old. Been there years."

"Don't hurt it," said the boy. "Not if it's a good one." He moved back from the window a little, unconsciously cupping his hands as though the instrument already lay in their grubby palms.

The most the pawnbroker could possibly charge for that piece of junk was fifty cents. Fifty cents was an awful thought; fifty cents was outrageous for a skinny piece of music-making tin. But on the other hand the essence of a pawnshop was bargaining, and no one knew this better than Barney Hatch, who, in his day, could have bargained a sparrow out of its beat in the gutter. Starting at fifty cents, he would begin to work downward. The dent in the harmonica, the dust, the years it had been there with no one wanting it, the tarnish, even the pathetic satin lining of the box. Mentally Barney talked the price down to thirty-five cents.

Thirty-five cents was still too much. At the thirty-five-cent level he would begin to apply sentiment. It's Christmas, ain't it? Here's a little boy believes in Santa Claus. Here's a moldy old harmonica, no good to anyone, taking up space. No class to a piece of junk like that. Make it twenty cents, we'll take it off your hands.

Twenty cents. That was the sky.

"Awright," said Barney dismally, and pushed the boy through the door. The shop was full of shadows. The fattest shadow detached itself and came forward. "Want somep'n? Oh, it's *you.*"

"Me?" said Barney.

"Nah. The kid." The man had a flat face like a moon. "Comes here all the time. Nose sticking right through the plate glass." He looked at the small boy, from whom, suddenly, a quiver of electric current seemed to be flowing. "Listen!" said the pawnbroker, outraged by so much intensity. "I'm not gonna haul that thing out of the window for you again. I told you last time – "

The boy said, "He's going to buy it for me." He said it quite quietly. The songs of all the golden trumpets must have come from somewhere else.

The pawnbroker looked at Barney sharply. "That right? You gonna buy it?"

"Got to look it over first," said Barney. He reached into his pocket, past the cool crackle of his beloved dollar bills, and found a quarter, which he rubbed tenderly between his fingers. When it came back to him, it would be shrunk to a nickel. A sad end for a lovely object.

The pawnbroker waddled toward the window, talking to himself. "Gives me the creeps, that kid does, staring inna window all the time. Comes in, says, 'Can I see it again?' I got nothing to do but run around hauling the thing outa the window. Been there so long, fits so nice."

"Spoils the window," said Barney, sensing conflict.

"Props up the owl," said the pawnbroker, sighed heavily and justified his gloom at once by removing the harmonica and causing the owl to fall onto the china Cupid-lamp. "You see?" he said with a kind of melancholy pride. He blew dust off the box and the harmonica, waddled back and planked the box down. The small boy put his chin on the counter and stared so hard it looked as if his ears might fly off.

Barney reminded himself that twenty cents was an outside price.

The boy's dirty paw reached up, and one finger touched the deep dent in the side of the instrument. "Don't touch!" said the pawnbroker crossly.

The boy put his hands in his pockets, because, uncaged, he could not be responsible for them. Barney kept thinking about the twenty cents; the old harmonica was so busted up it probably couldn't even carry a tune. "Piece of junk, ain't it?" said Barney, very loud and affable. "Pay you to let the kid cart it away, huh?"

The pawnbroker gave a short, unpromising laugh.

Barney shrugged; he had not expected the gambit to work. "Whadda you want for it?" he said casually.

He had expected the pawnbroker to hesitate, sizing up his customer's affluence according to immemorial pawnbroking custom. The pawnbroker did not hesitate. He said crisply, "Three bucks."

Barney gave a wild, incredulous howl. "Three bucks! You're outa your mind."

"Take it or leave it," said the man. "That's the price."

"You're outa your mind," said Barney.

There was a small bubble of sound down at counter level. The kid had reached up and taken the harmonica into his hands and was now rubbing it tenderly against his coat sleeve. The pawnbroker said, "Put it down!" with weary irritability.

"Bet it don't even blow," said Barney indignantly. "Piece of junk. I'll give you two bits for the piece of junk."

"It blows," said the pawnbroker, unmoved.

"Bet it don't." Barney was wondering what had got into him to make him offer two bits when his outside limit was twenty cents. This crazy three-bucks talk must have addled his brain.

"Blow it yourself," said the pawnbroker coldly.

Barney stretched out his hand. The small boy pulled away and put the harmonica to his own lips. There was a small breathy sound, wheezy like an old organ, as the little instrument breathed out the dust of the window, breathed in something new. Then it piped, a sweet little pipe like a bird in a meadow, following a thread of tune, a tiny melody that went up and down, miniature but recognizable.

"Don't breathe so light," said the pawnbroker fretfully. "Makes it sound like a sick cat. You've got to fill your lungs."

"Ain't used to me yet," said the small boy in the smallest of whispers.

"Where'd you learn to play a tune?" said Barney.

"Fella taught me once." He volunteered no more. His eyes were enormous; his hands were cradles. He talked gently to the harmonica.

The pawnbroker and Barney looked at each other. "Thirty cents," said Barney. "That's my last word."

"Listen." The pawnbroker leaned across his counter, master of all his objects. "You hear how good she plays? Six years inna window and still as sweet as a bird."

"No volume," said Barney.

"Get the dust outa its innards and some breath into the boy, you'd get plenty of volume. Three bucks, nothing less."

"Who," said Barney rhetorically, "do you think you're kidding?"

The pawnbroker waved a hand. "A dollar a year I take off. Last Christmas, she was four bucks. This Christmas, three. Next Christmas, two. See you next Christmas, Santa Claus."

The kid's head jerked up. Barney leaped like a flea. "Don't call me that!" he yelped.

The boy looked at the pawnbroker with interest. "How'd you know who he was?"

"Who?"

"Him. Santa Claus."

"Listen!" said Barney hysterically.

"He's anon-y-mouse," said the boy pleasantly. He lifted the harmonica to his lips again, and this time the tune didn't sound so thin anymore but almost like a real piece of music. Over his cupped hands, his eyes were as bright as a squirrel's.

"Three bucks," said the pawnbroker.

"Talk sense," said Barney.

The pawnbroker shrugged, then turned to the kid. "Gent ain't gonna invest," he said indifferently. "Give her here. I'll put her back in the window."

The kid backed away, the harmonica held tight. He looked up at Barney. "You promised."

Barney glared at him. Maybe the whole thing was a racket; maybe the kid and the pawnbroker were in cahoots. Only a sucker would be expected to pay three dollars for a piece of junk, even if the piece of junk did have a tune inside it.

Barney Hatch was smart and Barney Hatch was getting out, his money tight in his pocket, his Christmas Day all spelled out for him, the glow of his own private bottle of good whisky just around the next corner.

"Thirty-five cents," said Barney coldly. "Not a nickel more."

"Three bucks."

"Thirty-five cents."

The pawnbroker said to the boy, "Put the harmonica down, kid. The gent ain't interested." He spread his hands on the counter, watching the boy, and after a minute he said, "I told you, put it down."

The boy, moving so slowly he hardly moved at all, put it down. He reached up and placed the shiny little piece of junk, value three dollars, on the counter, and then he opened his hand and let it go like it was a baby rabbit or something. Then he touched the dent in it with one finger, like smoothing a baby rabbit's ears. The pawnbroker took it up and put it back in its box and snapped the lid down hard.

The kid looked at Barney.

It all of a sudden became very clear to Barney that he didn't have to stand there in a dirty old pawnshop with a skinny little kid staring at him. He pushed his hands down deep into his pockets and felt the lovely, crackling reassurance of his money, and that did it. He spun on his heel and left the shop, and he walked down the street in such a hurry that you would have thought there was a pack of angels snapping at his heels.

He didn't stop and he didn't look back, and he turned a corner so fast that he bumped into a fat lady with a lot of packages who gave him a huffy look like her mouth was full of pins. He didn't pay any attention. The corner he was turning was the corner by the liquor store, and the one thing that was clear in his mind was that he was going to convert his dollars into Christmas and convert them quickly.

There, in the window, was the bottle he had picked out, gold seal, fancy label, red Christmas bow, and, inside it, Barney's passport to Christmas. He could imagine its glow, spreading and comforting, making the twenty-fifth of December something to remember. Just looking at it made him feel better.

He reached into his pocket, taking out the bills, smoothing them, putting the change on top. Three dollars and forty-nine cents, the price of a good bottle of whisky, only forty-nine cents more than a cheap, beat-up harmonica in a satin-lined box.

Barney made a cross sound. He hadn't intended thinking about the kid. He looked at the whisky bottle again, it not being shaped like a harmonica at all. The kid must be used to waiting by now; he could wait another year. It would learn him not to believe in Santa Claus. Kids had no business going around believing in Santa Claus anyway. Probably just a gag. Who believed in Santa Claus?

Suppose this kid did? Well, then, it was high time he stopped believing. High time he grew up!

Barney looked down at the dollar bills and the loose change, and then he looked past them, at the whisky bottle. Kids like that one never grew up; they didn't have to. They were born old. What Barney knew about people not caring, what the whisky bottle knew, that was what the kid knew too.

Today, just in case he'd forgotten his lesson, the kid had learned it again.

The whisky bottle glittered in the window. The gold seal shone like a star. Barney swore. Barney said, "The hell with it," and a passerby gave him a shocked look which Barney didn't see.

He turned on his heel and he started walking fast, walking back the way he had come. The last couple of blocks he ran, because the kid might be gone.

The kid wasn't gone. He was standing there outside the pawnshop window, hugged up close to the glass, waiting for next Christmas. The hand that Barney put on his shoulder was rough. It was rough the way Barney marched him into the store. It was rough the way he slammed down three dollars on the pawnbroker's counter and the way he said, "Get that junky thing outa the window again." It was a roughness like shattered glass, like a broken whisky bottle.

The pawnbroker scooped up the money first. Then he went to the window and took the satin-lined box out and put it in front of Barney. Barney pushed it over with one angry hand, not looking at the kid.

The kid didn't ask. He knew it was his. He put out both hands, and it almost seemed, though it wasn't possible, that the harmonica jumped up into them. He turned his back to the counter, and he pressed his shoulders against it. He held the harmonica up to his mouth, but his hands were shaking, and the silly little tinny thing wabbled and shook too.

He put his hands down level with his chest, the harmonica tight and safe in his fingers.

The pawnbroker brushed some imaginary crumbs off the counter. The room was getting dark with twilight, and outside the wind was worrying the big window, trying to get at the stuffed owl and the china lamp and the silver mug.

Barney stood in the middle of the pawnshop and listened to the wind. If it had come into the shop and laid its cold finger on his shoulder, it couldn't have told him more plainly what a fool he'd been. Money gone, whisky gone, Christmas gone. The Christmas that would have been a real one, the Christmas that would have kept the cold out.

He hunched up his shoulders. The pawnbroker and the kid were both looking at him, and suddenly their staring made him angry. What did they have to be gaping at him for? Kid had his harmonica, pawnbroker had his money, everybody was sitting pretty except Barney Hatch.

He opened his mouth to shout his anger at them, but the kid spoke first. "I'm awful sorry," the kid said anxiously. "I didn't say thank you." After a moment, he tried again. "I c'd play a tune for you," he said hopefully. "Only I don't know but the one."

The pawnbroker leaned abruptly across the counter. "'Tisn't suited," he said firmly. "Don't you know any Christmas tunes, like – " he thought for a moment " – like 'Hark the Herald Angels Sing'? That's a good tune."

The boy shook his head. "I don't know it. I never heard it."

"Imagine that," said the pawnbroker wonderingly. "Imagine that." He straightened up from the counter and drew a deep breath, and from inside him there came a sort of rumble. The rumble was just a little bit off key, but the herald angels were clearly on their way.

For a moment the kid listened with his head tilted on one side, and then he cupped the harmonica and put it to his lips. At first he had a little trouble making the tune come right, and then it began to grow until the harmonica was singing glory to the new-born King as if it had been silent for six years just for this moment.

The pawnbroker beat one hand on the counter, keeping time, and the chorus of Christmas angels came up so fine and strong that the dust danced on the pawnshop shelves.

Barney stared. Very slowly, all through him, there began to spread a glow, warm and golden and quite unmistakable. It was the glow he had planned to buy for three dollars and forty-nine cents, the glow he had thought came only in a bottle.

He stood there, listening, and he let it warm him. Outside the wind shook hard at the window, wanting to come in out of the cold.

The Empty Cup

Opal Menius

NEVER DID ANY MAN love a woman as I loved my dark-eyed Rachel. When I wooed her, the light winds of spring were gently stirring the olive leaves in the garden of her father where her little sisters played. When I won her, the quiet evening star shone clear from the deep velvet of a summer sky. We were, that night, two shadows in a garden of shadows, but the gloom was only beauty to us in that time when no shadows lay across our lives. Rachel's laugh was as clear as the song of birds, and I prayed that it would ever ring as joyous and as sweet.

It was in October, in the time of the Feast of Booths, that I talked with her father. In that week spent by the Jews in remembering and in giving thanks for the joys of home and fireside, I spoke to him of the home I had made ready for Rachel. It was built of finest cedar, and my vine and fig tree flourished, though they were yet young and small. The old man's eyes were sad when he thought of the long, long journey from his house down to mine. But he was not blind to the unveiled joy in his daughter's eyes when she looked upon me, and her happiness was dear to his heart.

Soon we were no longer man and maiden, but bridegroom and bride. Then, the week of feasting over, we began the journey to our home.

We traveled slowly down the winding and dusty road, stopping often to let the donkeys rest, or for no other reason than that we wished to explore some tempting hillside and valley. We would romp and race across the grassy meadows. She could run like the wind, but I, too, was fleet of foot. Sometimes, when I had finally caught her in my arms and stilled her laughter with a kiss, I would whisper the words of the good King David, "My cup runneth over."

Who would have thought that even greater joy was yet to be mine? We came, one day, to the end of our journey, and Rachel became the mistress of my home. She was like that proverbial woman made famous by our great King Solomon – she looked well to her household. My house of cedar was always clean. My table was loaded with the best of food. My own grapes quenched our thirst. My wife made sure that this was so; and she provided kisses and laughter and love as freely as she provided food.

Our neighbor, the good mother Hannah, used to say to me, "It is a noble woman you have taken to wife, my son. Her price is far above rubies." Hannah loved my Rachel and spent many happy hours with her. Hannah had borne sons and daughters, but they had in the fullness of time gone forth into homes of their own. Now Hannah had lonely hours to fill, and Rachel was the sunshine of her days.

I thought I knew all there was to know of joy. Then came October and the Feast of Booths again. This time, we had a new blessing for which to give thanks. Our newborn child lay in the fine fir-wood cradle I had so carefully made for him in the long months of waiting for his coming. There had been a day when, for the first time, Rachel's laughter was stilled, for she went down into the very valley of the shadow of death; and the child was precious to us not only because he was the firstborn but also because we knew that Rachel would never have another.

As the days went by, the joy of motherhood brought swift healing to my lovely wife, and soon the house rang with her happy laughter day and night. The child was gentle and sweet like his mother, but strong as a young fir tree. There never was a finer baby! My work at the carpenter shop suffered in those days, for I would suddenly find myself leaving a yoke for oxen half done while I fashioned a toy for the baby. When he waved his tiny fists in the air and crowed for joy over some simple gift of mine, and when his mother's smiling eyes met mine across his little cradle, I knew no happier man had ever lived.

Another October, with its Feast of Booths, came round, and we slept beneath the stars in the shelter I had prepared for my wife and my son, and we gave thanks from grateful, reverent hearts. I think it was during that week that I spoke to my wife of my plan to go over into Lebanon and buy cedar for some new building soon to begin. She was disturbed at the thought of the months we would be separated, but she saw it was needful that I should go. She agreed that, with old Hannah to be with them at night, she and the boy should manage at home.

I left them in Hannah's care. Only business of greatest importance would have taken me away from them. Though there were many strange and wonderful things to see on the journey, I lived only for the day of return. My thoughts were ever with my loved ones. Often I dreamed of the hour when I should reach home. For my son I had carved a toy lamb from the finest wood in Lebanon. Sometimes, in my dreams, he ran to meet me as I turned in at the gate. I would hold the lamb high above his head and he would reach for it and laugh. Sometimes, in my dreams, I would come home at evening and the child would be asleep in his fir-wood crib. I would gently place the lamb in his arms and he would smile in his sleep. But how he would crow with joy when he awakened!

Actually, I came home at noontide. I thought the boy might be playing in the garden, and my wife sewing under the fig tree while she watched him. But there was no one in the garden.

"They are at the noonday meal in the house, then, or perhaps the child is having his afternoon rest," I thought. "The house is very quiet."

I tiptoed into my home quite softly. Yes, there he lay in his crib – the darling. How still he was and how beautiful he looked, lying there so quietly! How white his little face appeared! I had forgotten he was so pale. Rachel must have him in the sun more when the days are warmer, I thought.

Softly, I tiptoed to the crib. Gently I placed the lamb in his arms. This was just as I had dreamed it many, many times.

Why, then, did I feel an unrest? Whence this vague knowledge that all was not well?

His little arm had seemed cold. I touched it again. It was very cold – as cold as death. Snatching the blanket from over the child I gazed with horror at a deep red gash across his heart.

How long I stood there I do not know. I could not tear my tormented eyes from the body of my son. Neither could I understand. Clearly this could have been no accident. Why had anyone wished to murder a child as innocent as the lamb in his arms?

I raised my eyes at last and Hannah was standing in the doorway, tears running down her cheeks.

I said, "Who?"

She answered, "The soldiers."

I said, "Why?"

She answered, "By order of the king."

I said, "Rachel?"

She shook her head sadly and looked at me with sorrowful eyes as she stood aside from the doorway, allowing me to pass into the bedroom where my young wife was lying. Rachel lay so quietly that at first I thought she, too, was dead. I fell upon my knees beside her, but she did not seem to know that I was there. I poured out my sorrow and my love, but she seemed not to hear. My sorrow gave place to wrath, and I stormed against the slayer of my son with wild and bitter words, speaking with more feeling than knowledge, for, in my haste to reach home, I had not stopped to talk with people by the way, and so had not learned of the king's decree that all boy babies should be killed.

Nothing I said seemed to arouse any feeling in Rachel. She lay quietly, gazing out of the window with dreamy eyes.

I thought, "This is grief and shock. She will recover as the days go by. Time heals all things."

Was I the one person on earth whom time completely failed, or were there others who trusted and were disappointed? Rachel did not grow better. She never wept, and she almost never spoke. She went about her household work dutifully but without interest. She would not be concerned with anything. The ever-changing beauty of the earth, the strange and unpredictable ways of the men and women who were our neighbors, the little words and gifts of love I brought her, all were apparently unnoticed.

As though in a fog she wandered through the days and nights, and every day she grew thinner. There was a clouded look in her eyes, and a hollowness in her voice that reminded me of old Bathsheba. Old Bathsheba had a devil, and wandered alone through the hills around Nazareth, howling and shrieking if anyone came near her. I would rather have seen Rachel dead than to see her become a second Bathsheba.

A year went by, and then another year. Month followed month, each filled with slow and hopeless days.

I said, "I will send Rachel back to her father's house. Beneath the roof where she once was so happy she may find happiness again. Wrapped in the warm protection of her parents' love, she may find peace. In the sunlit garden with her lighthearted young sisters, she may learn to laugh again."

So I took her back to her father's house, over roads that were filled with memories of a happier time. I left her with her parents and returned alone to my home, trying in vain to forget the shock and concern in the eyes of her loved ones when they beheld her.

I filled the lonely months of waiting with eager dreams of a healed and happy Rachel returning to be once more the peace and joy of my house. Six months had passed when the letter came from her father which ended all my hopes.

"There is nothing I – or any of us – can do," he wrote. "Come and take her if you want her. If you do not want her now, I shall understand. It may be better for you to dwell alone than with this child of sorrow. She will ever be welcome here. Leave her with us if it be your will."

Life for me had been no happier without Rachel. Besides, she was my wife. Sadly I returned to get her and bring her home. There was pity in her father's eyes, and in her mother's, as they made her ready and sent us on our way.

We set forth at sunrise and rode until night brought an end to safe journeying. In all that time, Rachel said no word of any kind. I talked of all the things I knew. She did not even seem to hear. We camped for the night. Perhaps Rachel slept. I do not know. I only know that it was well after midnight when I fell at last into an exhausted sleep.

We rose at dawn and began the second day's journey. With the coolness of the morning air, fresh courage rose within me and I began anew my attack on Rachel's indifference.

"Look at those lambs on the hillside," I exclaimed with enthusiasm. "The little black one runs around butting all the others. Is he not a frisky fellow?"

She gazed at the lamb without interest, then turned her eyes back to the winding road. I tried again.

"Those olive trees are growing very old. The owner should be replacing them soon. I have planted a new olive tree on the right side of our doorway. It is just a little tree, but already the sparrows have found it and are making a nest. The tree is so small it seems scarce able to bear the weight of the straw, but it stands up proudly as though it were glad to be the foundation of a home."

As I had expected, this was of no concern to Rachel. I rode on in silence.

Sometimes we met or passed other travelers on the road. I tried to interest Rachel in some of them.

"Look at that young bridegroom with his bride," I said once. "The bride must be twice as old as he. Will they be happy, do you think?" When Rachel did not answer, I continued, "If he chases her over these hillsides, he will not have so much difficulty catching her as I once had catching you, remember?"

Apparently she did not remember.

Suddenly, I saw a gruesome thing. A leper woman stood near the roadside, begging. She dared not come too near, but, from the distance at which the law held her, she begged food for herself and her son. The woman was ragged and disheveled. Her clothes were exceedingly dirty, but since her fingers had already been eaten away by the disease, she could scarcely have been blamed for that. Her matted, dirty hair hung down over a face fearfully marked by disease. Even a casual observer would know that she had few days remaining in this world.

In marked contrast to the aged, filthy, diseased woman, the boy stood fresh and young and fair. He was a little fellow, not more than five years old. When, with pleading tones, the woman begged food for herself and the child, the boy ran down to the roadside and brought back whatever compassionate wayfarers saw fit to toss him. I perceived that, in spite of all her protests, the lad placed the tastiest morsels between the lips of his mother.

In happier days I would have done all I could to spare Rachel such a sight as this. Now, I thought that the sorrows of others, in this case far greater than hers, might serve to take her mind away from her own troubles.

"Poor little boy," I said, "What will become of him when his mother dies? She surely cannot live much longer."

But the sorrows of others touched Rachel no more than their joys.

The roads were crowded with travelers at this time of year. Toward noon two men, large and coarse in appearance, rode up behind us. The road was narrow at this place. We rode between a steep cliff on the right and a sharp drop into a valley on the left. Passing was clearly impossible, and the men were annoyed at the slowness of our going. I urged my donkey to greater speed, but either the situation had made no impression upon Rachel's clouded mind, or else it made no difference to her. She continued her slow, unheeding pace. The men grumbled, then they grew mocking.

"Look you, Jacob," said the smaller one. "It is a pair of snails that have climbed out of the hillside and choose to make a little journey into town."

"I am thinking, Simon," answered Jacob, "that the town will be dead as Sodom and Gomorrah long ere they arrive."

Simon's laugh was long and loud. Encouraged by the appreciation of his friend and, no doubt, by the wine of which he must have partaken long and heartily, he drew forth his sword.

"A probe from this good blade might bring forth speed from even a snail," he grinned, as he prodded my wife firmly in the back.

Wild anger rushed through me. I had no sword, but I seized a bag of provisions from the back of my donkey and swung it at Simon fiercely. He dodged it, and in so doing rammed his donkey against the one my wife was riding, causing its hind feet to slip backward over the cliff.

For a second we stared breathlessly at the struggling animal. My wife held firmly to her mount, but the expression of her face did not change. Even when the panting little donkey succeeded in getting his four feet firmly planted once more upon the path, she gave no indication of any relief she may have felt. Weak as I was with fear, I still had the strength to marvel that any human being could be so indifferent to her own life or death.

Then Jacob was charging at me with drawn sword. Even as I leaped from my donkey and dodged the blow, I glanced at Rachel. Looking into her eyes I saw – and this was the thing that finally broke my heart – that she was as indifferent to my danger as she had been to her own. Her calm, uncaring expression had not changed.

There was no heart left in me for fighting. Truly, Jacob could have slain me there and I would not have opposed him. But his companion had become alarmed at the seriousness of the quarrel and had caught Jacob's arm. With some difficulty he succeeded in restraining Jacob, and, as soon as the path had widened, hurried him along his way. My wife and I rode on in silence.

Toward sunset we came to a little spring by the roadside. The water trickled down from a rock to make a little crystal pool at its base. Green grass, generously sprinkled with flowers, grew around the clearing. Several tall trees added beauty and peace to the scene. The sheer loveliness of the place startled me out of the dark brooding into which I had fallen. I glanced at Rachel, but her troubled eyes still rested on the road ahead.

"We might as well eat here," I said. "Truly, it seems a place good for rest and refreshment."

Apparently we were not the only ones who thought so. A man and his wife and their small son were also camping by the spring and were preparing for their evening meal. They seemed a friendly family of simple folk. Feeling the need of human companionship after the long and difficult journey, I went over to them and we began to talk. The child played quietly, dipping his tiny fingers into the spring and letting the water trickle off.

I learned that the strangers were on their way to Nazareth, and that the man, like me, was a carpenter. Soon we were deep in a discussion of the best way to fashion a yoke that would not hurt the neck of the animal that wore it. The woman spoke pleasantly to my wife, who was listlessly setting out our supper. When Rachel returned no answer, I explained that my wife was not well. The woman's eyes were gentle and sympathetic.

As she sliced a loaf of good, homemade brown bread the woman talked to me. They had been living in Egypt, she said, but now they were going home.

"You have a lovely little son," I said. In truth the boy was fairer than the lily of the valley. I could not seem to take my eyes from him. Somehow, watching the boy, I felt completely quiet and at peace – a feeling strange to me.

"Thank you," the woman said. She smiled. "He seems to make friends wherever he goes. Sharon, the woman in whose home we found lodging in Egypt, loved him very much. She was quite ill when we first came to live with her. Day by day, as she cared for the child in the garden while I was busy, she seemed to grow better. Sometimes I wonder if the sunshine and fresh air were what she had been needing."

"Perhaps it was the renewed interest in life a child can bring," I said, for Rachel was out of hearing.

The mother continued her story. "Sharon's heart was heavy when she knew that we would not be in Egypt today, for this is the child's birthday. She prepared for the lad a bottle of fresh juice from the grapes of her vine. That vine is the pride of her life. It is a special one, crossbred in a way that only she knows, and it produces grapes of an especially rare and delicate flavor. She is famed throughout all the region for the luscious fruit. She insisted on giving me this bottle of juice for the boy, and on baking him a little cake of honey and dates, so that he may celebrate his birthday even though we are neither in Egypt nor at home. The child has talked eagerly of the good things all day long. He loved Sharon, and I think the food and drink will taste even better because they came from her."

"I think they should taste quite good, no matter whence they came," I said, eyeing the rich red liquid the mother was pouring into a cup.

The little boy had run up eagerly and was watching with bright-eyed anticipation. With the utmost caution, he took the cup carefully in one hand and the golden brown honey cake in the other. He walked over toward the little spring where a few smooth stones made a suitable place for a small boy to sit down.

The clattering of hoofs diverted my attention to the road. Another party was stopping by the spring. I gave a groan, for it was Jacob and his friend Simon. They seemed not to notice me. The donkeys leaped thirstily for the water, sending up a cloud of dust that almost choked us.

"Ah, water!" shouted Jacob, jumping from his donkey

with haste. "Not so good as wine, perhaps, but truly my thirst is great. Out of my way, child."

He gave the little boy a shove that sent him sprawling into the dust. The precious honey cake flew in one direction, the cup in the other; and the rich red liquid spilled out and soaked like blood into the ground.

I watched the little boy get slowly to his feet. I waited for his howl of anger and frustration. There was only Jacob's boisterous laughter, followed by a great stillness. Not one of us moved, but Jacob's eyes turned uncertainly toward the father of the child who stood in the shadows not far away.

The child's soft voice broke the stillness. "Gone," he said, looking down at his empty cup. The word was not a reproach. He seemed, rather, to be trying to convince himself that this thing had really happened to him.

"Gone it is, and gone I must be," shouted Jacob, with another worried glance at the child's father, who had stepped forward from the shadows. Jacob hastily mounted his donkey and rode away, closely followed by Simon.

"Gone," the baby said again, this time with complete and full realization. He picked up his empty cup, washed it carefully in the spring, filled it to the brim with the clear cold water and drank long and deeply. I could not believe the depths of quietness in his eyes. I looked in vain for anger, frustration, bitterness – there was only infinite calm. Quietly, he took bread from the plate his mother had prepared. Sitting down upon the rock he began to eat and drink.

A gasp at my side made me turn. Rachel was looking at the boy and there were tears on her cheek. Then, over the rim of the cup, the child's clear eyes met hers, and a look passed between them that was not for me to understand.

From somewhere far off, a night bird called. The bright evening star appeared from behind a cloud. A feeling of peace came upon me so deep that I no longer struggled even to think. The rest of that evening I remember only dimly, as though it were a dream. I think that we ate our food. I know that later the child and his mother and father departed, for they said an extra hour of travel this day would make it possible for them to reach Nazareth on the morrow. Rachel and I spread out our blankets. I drew mine over me tightly and sank instantly into deep and dreamless sleep.

It was very early morning when I awakened. Sitting up and rubbing sleep-filled eyes, I perceived that the red sun was only beginning to rise beyond the hill. Then I saw that Rachel was not under the blanket beside me.

I looked toward the spring; but she was not there washing her face in the cool water, as I had hoped she might be. I looked across the clearing to the woods beyond, but she was nowhere to be seen. Panic seized me. Had her weary mind at last given way and was she wandering like old Bathsheba across the hills? Or had the little boy, the one being on earth with the power to attract her, so bewitched her that she had left all else to follow him?

I looked up the road in the direction from which we had come. I leaped to my feet, my heart beating wildly. For, lo, Rachel was coming! And a great joy filled my heart – for she sat upon the saddle tall and straight, riding like a queen. There was a smile upon her lips, and her eyes, clear and shining, met mine with the old look of loyalty and love.

And before her in the saddle, his curly head just reaching her heart, the leper's child came riding.

The Well of the Star

Elizabeth Goudge

On the road to Bethlehem there is a well called the Well of the Star. The legend goes that the three Wise Men, on their journey to the Manger, lost sight of the star that was guiding them. Pausing to water their camels at the well, they found that it again reflected in the water.

I

DAVID SAT CROSS-LEGGED by himself in a corner of the room, separated from the other children, clasping his curly toes in his lean brown hands, and wished he were a rich man, grown up and strong, with bags full of gold and thousands of camels and tens of thousands of sheep. But he was not rich; he was only a diminutive ragged shepherd boy who possessed nothing in the world except the shepherd's pipe slung around his neck, his little pipe upon which he played to himself or the sheep all day long, and that was as dear to him as life itself.

At the moment he was very miserable. Sighing, he lifted his hands and placed them on his stomach, pushing it inward and noting the deflation with considerable concern. How soon would he be dead of hunger? How soon would they all be dead of hunger, and safely at rest in Abraham's bosom? It was a very nice place, he had no doubt, and suitable to grandparents and people of that type who were tired by a long life and quite ready to be gathered to their fathers, but hardly the place for a little boy who had lived only for a few short years in this world, who had seen only a few springs painting the bare hills purple and scarlet with the anemone flowers, only a few high summer suns wheeling majestically through the burning heavens.

If only it were summer now, instead of a cold night in midwinter! If only mother would light a fire for them to warm themselves by, a bright fire that would paint the walls of the dark little one-roomed house orange and rose color, and chase away the frightening shadows. But there was no light in the room except the flickering, dying flame that came from a little lamp, fast burning up the last of their oil, set on the earth floor close to his mother, where she sat crouched beside her sick husband, swaying herself ceaselessly from side to side, abandoned to her grief and oblivious of the wails of four little cold and hungry children, younger than David, who lay altogether on their matting bed.

If only he were a rich man, thought David, then it would not matter that storms had destroyed the barley, that their vines had failed, or that their father, the carpenter of this tiny village on a hilltop, could no longer ply his trade. Nothing would matter if he were a rich man and could buy food and wine and oil and healing salves; they would be happy then, with food in their stomachs, their father well, and comforting light in this horrible darkness of midwinter.

How could he be a rich man?

Suddenly there came to David's mind the thought of the wishing well far down below on the road to Bethlehem. It was a well of clear sparkling water and it was said that those who stood by it at midnight, and prayed to the Lord God Jehovah from a pure heart, were given their heart's desire. The difficulty, of course, was to be pure in heart. They said that if you were, and your prayer had been accepted, you saw your heart's desire mirrored in the water of the well – the face of someone you loved, maybe, or the gold that would save your home from ruin, or even, so it was whispered, the face of God Himself. But no one of David's acquaintance had ever seen anything, though they had wished and prayed time and again.

Nevertheless he jumped up and crept noiselessly through the shadows to the door. He had no idea whether his heart was pure or not but he would give it the benefit of the doubt and go down to the well. He pulled open the door and slipped out into the great cold silent night.

And instantly he was terribly afraid. All around him the bare hills lay beneath the starlight in an awful waiting, attentive loneliness, and far down below, the terraces of olive trees were drowned in pitch-black shadow. But the sky was streaming with light, so jeweled with myriads of blazing stars that it seemed the weight of them would make the sky fall down and crush the waiting earth to atoms. The loneliness, the darkness, the cold, and that great sky above turned David's heart to water and made his knees shake under him. He had never been out by himself so late at night before and he had not got the courage, hungry and cold as he was, to go down over the lonely hills and through the darkness of the olive trees to the white road below where they said that robbers lurked, wild sheep-stealers and murderers who would cut your throat as soon as look at you, just for the fun of it.

Then he bethought him that just over the brow of a nearby hill a flock of sheep were folded, and their shepherds with them. His own cousin Eli, who was teaching David to be a shepherd, would be with them, and Eli would surely be willing to leave the sheep to the other shepherds for a short time and go with David to the well. At least David would ask him to.

He set off running, a little flitting shadow beneath the stars, and he ran hard because he was afraid. For surely, he thought, there was something very strange about this night. The earth lay so still, waiting for something, and overhead that great sky was palpitating and ablaze with triumph. Several times, as he ran, he could have sworn he heard triumphant voices crying, "Glory to God! Glory to God!" as though the hills themselves were singing, and a rushing sound as though great wings were beating over his head. Yet when he stopped to listen there was nothing; only the frail echo of a shepherd's pipe and a whisper of wind over the hills.

He was glad when he saw in front of him the rocky hillock behind which the sheep were folded. "Eli," he cried, giving a hop, skip, and a jump, "are you there? Jacob? Tobias? It's David."

But there was no answering call from the friendly shepherds, though there was a soft bleating from the sheep; only that strange stillness with its undercurrent of triumphant music that was heard and yet not heard. With a beating heart he bounded round the corner and came out in the little hollow in the hills that was the sheepfold, his eyes straining through the darkness to make out the figures of his friends.

But they were not there; no one was there except a tall, cloaked stranger who sat upon a rock among the sheep, leaning on a shepherd's crook. And the sheep, who knew their own shepherds and would fly in fear from a stranger whose voice they did not know, were gathered closely about him in confidence and love. David halted in blank astonishment.

"Good evening to you," said the stranger pleasantly. "It's a fine night."

David advanced with caution, rubbing his nose in perplexity. Who was this stranger? The sheep seemed to know him, and he seemed to know David, yet David knew no man with so straight a back and so grand a head or such a deep, ringing, beautiful voice. This was a very great man, without doubt; a soldier, perhaps, but no shepherd.

"Good evening," said David politely, edging a little closer. "'Tis a fine evening, but cold about the legs."

"Is it? Then come under my cloak," said the stranger, lifting it so that it suddenly seemed to spread about him like great wings, and David, all his fear suddenly evaporated, scuttled forward and found himself gathered in against the stranger's side, under the stranger's cloak, warm and protected and sublimely happy.

"But where are the others?" he asked. "Eli and Jacob and Tobias?"

"They've gone to Bethlehem," said the stranger. "They've gone to a birthday party."

"A birthday party, and didn't take me?" ejaculated David in powerful indignation. "The nasty, selfish brutes!"

"They were in rather a hurry," explained the stranger. "It was all rather unexpected."

"Then I suppose they had no presents to take?" asked David. "They'll feel awkward, turning up with no presents. Serve them right for not taking me."

"They took what they could," said the stranger. "A shepherd's crook, a cloak, and a loaf of bread."

David snorted with contempt, and then snorted again in indignation. "They shouldn't have gone," he said, and indeed it was a terrible crime for shepherds to leave their sheep, with those robbers prowling about in the shadows below and only too ready to pounce on them.

"They were quite right to go," said the stranger. "And I have taken their place."

"But you're only one man," objected David, "and it takes several to tackle robbers."

"I think I'm equal to any number of robbers," smiled the stranger. He was making a statement, not boasting, and David thrilled to the quiet confidence of his voice, and thrilled, too, to feel the strength of the arm that was round him and of the knee against which he leaned.

"Have you done a lot of fighting, great lord?" he whispered in awe.

"Quite a lot," said the stranger.

"Who did you fight?" breathed David. "Barbarians?"

"The devil and his angels," said the stranger nonchalantly.

David was momentarily deprived of the power of speech, but pressing closer he gazed upward at the face of this man for whom neither robbers nor devils seemed to hold any terrors, and once he began to look he could not take his eyes away, for never before had he seen a face like this man's, a face at once delicate and strong, full of power yet quick with tenderness, bright as the sky in early morning yet shadowed with mystery. It seemed an eternity before David could find his voice.

"Who are you, great lord?" he whispered at last. "You're no shepherd."

"I'm a soldier," said the stranger. "And my name is Michael. What's your name?"

"David," murmured the little boy, and suddenly he shut his eyes because he was dazzled by the face above him. If this was a soldier, he was a very king among soldiers.

"Tell me where you are going, David," said the stranger.

Now that they had told each other their names David felt that they were lifelong friends, and it was not hard to tell his story. He told it all – his father's illness, his mother's tears, the children's hunger, and the cold home where there was no fire and the oil was nearly finished, his longing to be a rich man that he might help them all, and the wishing well that gave their heart's desire to the pure in heart.

"But I hadn't meant to go down to the road alone, you see," he finished. "I thought Eli would have gone with me, and now Eli has gone to that birthday party."

"Then you'll have to go alone," said Michael.

"I suppose the sheep wouldn't be all right by themselves?" hinted David gently.

"They certainly would not," said Michael firmly.

"I'm not afraid, of course," boasted David, and shrank a little closer against that strong knee.

"Of course not," concurred Michael heartily. "I've noticed that Davids are always plucky. Look at King David fighting the lion and the bear when he was only a shepherd boy like you."

"But the Lord God Jehovah guided and protected him," said David.

"And the Lord God will protect you," said Michael.

"I don't feel as though He were protecting me," objected David.

"You haven't started out yet," said Michael, and laughed. "How can He protect you when there's nothing to protect you from? Or guide you when you don't take to the road? Go on now. Hurry up." And with a gentle but inexorable movement he withdrew his knee from beneath David's clinging hands, and lifted his cloak from David's shoulders so that it slid back with a soft rustling upward movement, as though great wings were folded against the sky. And the winter wind blew cold and chill about the little boy who stood ragged and barefoot in the night.

"Good-by," said Michael's deep voice; but it seemed to be drifting away as though Michael, too, were withdrawing himself. "Play your pipe to yourself if you are afraid, for music is the voice of man's trust in God's protection, even as the gift of courage is God's voice answering."

David took a few steps forward and again terror gripped him. Again he saw the bare lonely hills, and the shadows down below where the robbers lurked. He glanced back over his shoulder, ready to bolt back to the shelter of Michael's strong arm and the warmth of his cloak. But he could no longer see Michael very clearly, he could only see a dark shape that might have been a man but that might have been only a shadow. But yet the moment he glanced back he knew that Michael was watching him, Michael the soldier who was afraid neither of robbers nor of the devil and his angels, and with a heart suddenly turned valiant he turned and scuttled off down the hill towards the valley.

II

NEVERTHELESS he had the most uncomfortable journey. Going down the hill he cut his feet on the sharp stones, and fell down twice and barked his knees, and going through the olive grove below he saw robbers hiding behind every tree. There were times when he was so frightened that his knees doubled up beneath him and he came out in a clammy perspiration, but there were other times when he remembered Michael's advice and stopped a minute to play a few sweet notes on his precious pipe, and then he was suddenly brave again and rushed through the terrifying shadows whooping as though he were that other David going for the lion and the bear...But all the same it was a most uncomfortable journey and he was overwhelmingly thankful when with a final jump he landed in the road and saw the water of the well gleaming only a few feet away from him.

He leaned against the stone parapet and looked at it gravely. Water. In this land that in the summer months was parched with drought and scorched with heat, water was the most precious thing in the world, the source of all growth and all purification, the cure of sickness, the preserver of life itself. It was no wonder that men came to water to pray for their heart's desire – to water, the comforter and lord of all life. "Comfort ye, comfort ye, My people." It seemed to him that he heard voices singing in the wind among the olive trees, as though the trees themselves were singing, voices that sang not to the ear but to the soul. "He shall feed His flock like a shepherd: He shall gather the lambs with His arm, and carry them in His bosom. Wonderful! Counselor! The mighty God! The everlasting Father! The Prince of Peace!" Surely, he thought, if the Lord God Jehovah cared so for the little lambs, He would care also for David's sick father and weeping mother and the little hungry children; and covering his face with his brown fingers he prayed to the Lord God that he might have gold to buy food and wine and oil for that stricken house up above him on the hill. So hard did he pray that he forgot everything but his own longing, forgot his fears and the cold wind that nipped him through his rags, saw nothing but the darkness of his closed eyes and heard nothing but his own desperate whispering.

Then, sighing a little like a child awaking from sleep, he opened his eyes and peeped anxiously through his fingers at the water in the well. Would he have his heart's desire? Had he prayed from a pure heart? Was that something glittering in the well? He dropped his hands from his face and leaned closer, the blood pounding so in his ears that it sounded like drums beating. Yes, it was gold! Circles of gold lying upon the surface of the water, as though the stars had dropped down from heaven. With a cry of joy he leaned nearer, his face right over the water, as though he would have touched with his lips those visionary gold pieces that promised him his heart's desire. And then, in an instant of time, his cry of joy changed to a cry of terror, for framed in those twinkling golden points of light he saw the reflection of a man's face, a bearded, swarthy face with gleaming teeth and eyes, the face of a foreigner.

So the Lord God had not protected him. So the robbers had got him. He stared at the water for a long minute, stark with terror, and then swung round with a choking cry, both his thin hands at his throat to protect it from the robber's knife.

"Do not cry out, little son. I will not hurt you." The man stretched out a hand and gave David's shoulder a reassuring little shake. "I but looked over your shoulder to see what you stared at so intently."

The voice, deep toned, kindly, strangely attractive with its foreign inflection, chased away all David's fears. This was no robber. His breath came more evenly and he wiped the sweat of his terror off his forehead with his tattered sleeve while he looked up with bulging eyes at the splendid stranger standing in front of him.

He was tall, though not so tall as that other splendid stranger keeping the sheep up on the hill, and he wore a purple robe girdled at the waist with gold and a green turban to which were stitched gold ornaments that shook and trembled round his proud hawk-nosed face. David had one pang of agonized disappointment as he realized that it was only the refection of these gold ornaments he had seen in the water, and not God's answer to his prayer, and then amazement swept all other thoughts from his mind.

For the star-lit road to the well that a short while ago had been empty was now full. While David prayed, his ears closed to all sounds, a glittering cavalcade had come up out of the night. There were black men carrying torches, richly caparisoned camels, and two more splendid grave-faced men even more richly dressed than his friend. The torch-light gleamed on gold and scarlet, emerald green and rich night blue, and the scent of spices came fragrant on the wind. This cavalcade might have belonged to Solomon, thought David, to Solomon in all his glory. Surely these men were kings.

But the camels were thirsty and the first king drew David gently away from the well that they might drink. Yet he kept his hand upon his shoulder and looked down upon him with kindly liking.

"And for what were you looking so intently, little son?" he asked.

"For my heart's desire, great lord," whispered David, nervously pleating his ragged little tunic with fingers that still shook from the fright that he had had.

"So?" asked the stranger. "Is it a wishing well?"

"They say," said David, "that if you pray to God for your heart's desire from a pure heart, and if God has granted your prayer, you will see a vision of it in with water."

"And you saw yours?"

David shook his head. "You came, great lord," he explained. "I saw you."

One of the other kings, an old white-bearded man in a sea-green robe, was listening smiling to their talk.

"We three have lost a star, little son," he said to David. "Should we find it again in your well?"

David thought it must be a joke, for what could three great lords want with a star? But when he looked up into the fine old eyes gazing down into his he saw trouble and bewilderment in them.

"If your heart is pure, great lord."

A shadow passed over the old man's face and he turned back to the third king, a young man with a boy's smooth skin and eyes that were bright and gay.

"Gaspar," he said. "You are young and pure of heart; you look."

Gaspar laughed, his white teeth flashing in his brown face. "Only an old wives' tale," he mocked. "We've lost the star twenty times in the blaze of the night sky and twenty times we have found it again. Why should we look for it now in a well?"

"Yet pray," said the old man sternly. "Pray and look."

Obediently Gaspar stepped up to the well, his scarlet robe swirling about him and the curved sword that he wore slapping against his side, bowed his head in prayer, then bent over the well.

"I can see only a part of the sky," he murmured, "and each star is like another in glory – no – yes." He paused and suddenly gave a shout of triumph. "I have found it, Melchior! It shines in the center of the well, like the hub of a wheel or the boss of a shield."

He straightened himself and flung back his head, his arms stretched up toward the sky. "There! There!" he cried, and David and the elder kings, gazing, saw a great star blazing over their heads, a star that was mightier and more glorious than the sister stars that shone around it like cavaliers round the throne. And as they gazed it suddenly moved, streaking through the sky like a comet.

"Look! Look!" cried David. "A shooting star!" And he danced out into the middle of the road to follow its flight. "Look! It is shining over Bethlehem!"

The three kings stood behind him, gazing where he pointed, and saw at the end of the road, faintly visible in the starlight, slender cypress trees rising above the huddled roofs of a little white town upon a hill, and above them the blazing star.

Gaspar, young and excited, suddenly swung round and began shouting to the servants to bring up the camels, but the two older kings still stood and gazed.

"Praise be to the Lord God," said the old king tremulously, and he bowed his head and crossed his hands upon his breast.

"Bethlehem," said the king who was David's friend. "The end of our journey."

His voice was infinitely weary, and for the first time it occurred to David that these great lords had come from a long way off. Their beautiful clothes were travel-stained and their faces drawn with fatigue. They must, he decided suddenly, be lunatics; no sane men, he thought, would come from so far away to visit an unimportant little place like Bethlehem; nor be in such a taking because they had lost sight of a star. Nevertheless he liked them and had no wish to lose their company.

"I'll take you to Bethlehem," he announced, and flung back his head and straddled his legs as though it would be a matter of great difficulty and danger to guide them the short way along the straight road to a town that was visible to the naked eye.

"And so you shall," laughed his friend. "And you shall ride my camel in front of me and be the leader of the caravan."

David jigged excitedly from one foot to the other. He had never ridden a camel, for only well-to-do men had camels. He could not contain himself, and let out a shrill squeak of joy as a richly caparisoned beast was led up and made to kneel before them – a squeak that ended rather abruptly when the camel turned its head and gave him a slow disdainful look, lifting its upper lip and showing its teeth in a contempt so profound that David blushed hotly to the roots of his hair, and did not recover himself until he was seated on the golden saddle cloth before his friend, safe in the grip of his arm, rocking up toward the stars as the camel got upon its feet.

III

IT WAS ONE of the most wonderful moments of that wonderful night when David found himself swaying along toward the cypresses of Bethlehem, the leader of a caravan. Because he was so happy he put his pipe to his lips and began to play the gay little tune that shepherds have played among the hills since the dawn of the world, and so infectious was it that the men coming behind began to hum it as they swung along under the stars.

"It is right to sing upon a journey, great lord," said David, when a pause fell, "for music is the voice of man's trust in God's protection, even as the gift of courage is God's voice answering."

"That is a wise child you have got there, Balthasar," said old Melchior, who was riding just behind them.

"I didn't make that up for myself," David answered truthfully. "A man up in the hills told it to me. A man who came to mind the sheep so that Eli and the other shepherds could go with their presents to a birthday party in Bethlehem."

"Does all the world carry gifts to Bethlehem tonight?" questioned Balthasar softly. "Wise men from the desert with their mysteries, shepherds from the hills with their simplicities, and a little boy with the gift of music."

"Do you mean that we are all going to the same place?" asked David eagerly. "Are you going to the birthday party too? And am I going with you? Me too?"

"A King has been born," said Balthasar. "We go to worship Him."

A king? The world seemed full of kings tonight, and kings doing the most unsuitable things, too, keeping sheep on the hills and journeying along the highway, travel-stained and weary. On this wonderful topsy-turvy night nothing surprised him, not even the news that the birthday party was a King's; but desolation seized him as he realized that he wouldn't be able to go to it himself. For how could he go inside a grand palace when his clothes were torn and his feet were bare and dirty? They wouldn't let him in. They'd set the dogs on him…Disappointment surged over him in sickening waves. He gritted his teeth to keep himself from crying, but even with all his effort two fat tears escaped and plowed two clean but scalding furrows through the grime on his face.

They were at Bethlehem before he realized it, for he had been keeping his head bent for fear Balthasar should see his two tears. Looking up suddenly he saw the white walls of the little town close in front of him, the cypress trees like swords against the sky, and that star shining just ahead of them, so bright that it seemed like a great lamp let down out of heaven by a string. The gate of the town was standing wide open and they clattered through it without hindrance, which surprised David until he remembered that just at this time Bethlehem would be full of people who had come in from the country to be taxed. They would not be afraid of robbers tonight, when the walls held so many good strong countrymen with knives in their girdles and a quick way with their fists. The visitors were still up and about, too, for as they climbed the main street of the little hill town David could see lines of light shining under doors and hear laughter and voices behind them. And a good thing, too, he thought, for at any other time the arrival of this strange cavalcade in the dead of night might have caused a disturbance. The Lord God, he thought, had arranged things very conveniently for them.

"Which way are we going?" he whispered excitedly to his king.

"We follow the star," said Balthasar.

David looked up and saw that the star must have been up to its shooting tricks again, for it had now moved over to their right, and obediently they, too, swerved to their right and made their way up a narrow lane where houses had been built over caves in the limestone rock. Each house was the home of poor people, who kept their animals in the cave below and lived themselves in the one room above reached by its flight of stone steps.

"The king can't be here!" said David disgustedly, as the cavalcade, moving now in single file, picked its way over the heaps of refuse in the lane. "Only poor people live here."

"Look!" said Balthasar, and looking David saw that the star was hanging so low over a little house at the end of the lane that a bright beam of light caressed its roof.

"The star is making a mistake," said David firmly, "if it thinks a king could be born in a place like that."

But no one was taking any notice of him. A great awe seemed to have descended upon the three kings, and a thankfulness too deep for speech. In silence the cavalcade halted outside the house at the end of the lane, and in silence the servants gathered round to bring the camels to their knees and help their masters to the ground. David, picked up and set upon his feet by a sturdy Nubian whose black face gleamed in the torchlight like ebony, stood aside and watched, something of the awe that gripped the others communicating itself to him, so that the scene he saw stamped itself on his memory forever. The torchlight and starlight lighting up the rich colors of the kings' garments and illumining their dark, intent faces as though they were lit by an inner light; the stir among the servants as three of them came forward carrying three golden caskets, fragrant with spices and so richly jeweled that the light seemed to fall upon them in points of fire, and gave them reverently into their masters' hands. The birthday presents, thought David, the riches that Balthasar had spoken of, and he looked hastily up at the poor little house built above the stable, incredulous that such wealth could enter a door so humble.

But the door at the top of the stone steps was shut fast and no line of light showed beneath it or shone out in welcome from the window. The only light there was showed through the ill-fitting door that closed in the opening to the cave below, and it was toward this that Melchior turned, knocking softly on the rotten wood and standing with bent head to listen for the answer.

"But that's the stable!" whispered David. "He couldn't be there!"

But no one answered him, for the door opened and the three kings, their heads lowered and their long dark fingers

curved about their gifts, passed into the light beyond, the
door closing softly behind them, shutting David outside in
the night with the strange black servants and the supercil-
ious camels.

But his curiosity was too strong for him to feel afraid.
There was a hole quite low in the door and kneeling down
he pressed his dirty little face against the wood and squinted
eagerly through it.

Of course there was no king there; he had said there
wouldn't be and there wasn't; looking beyond the kings he
saw there was nothing there but the stable and the animals
and a few people, poor people like himself. The animals, a
little donkey with his ribs sticking through his skin, and an
old ox whose shoulders bore the marks of the yoke they
had carried through many hard years, were fastened to
iron rings in the wall of the cave, but both of them had
turned their sleepy heads toward the rough stone manger
filled with hay, and toward a gray-bearded man who held a
lighted lantern over the manger and a woman with a tired
white face, muffled in a blue cloak, who lay on the floor
leaning back against the wall. But though she was so tired
she was smiling at the men who were kneeling together on
the hard floor, and she had the loveliest and most welcom-
ing smile that David had ever seen.

And then he saw that the men she was smiling at were Eli,
Jacob, and Tobias, kneeling with heads bent and hands
clasped in the attitude of worship. And before them on the
hard floor, just in front of the manger, they had laid their
gifts; Eli's shepherd's crook that had been his father's,
Jacob's cloak lined with the lamb's wool that he had set such
store by, and Tobias's little loaf of bread that he always ate

all by himself in the middle of the night when he was guarding sheep, never giving a crumb to anyone else no matter how hard they begged. And beside these humble men knelt the kings in their glory, and beside the simple gifts were the three rich fragrant caskets, just as though there were no barrier between rich people and poor people, and no difference in value between wood and bread and gold and jewels.

But what could be in that manger that they were all so intent upon it? David had another peep through his hole and saw to his astonishment that there was a Baby in it, a tiny newborn Baby, wrapped in swaddling clothes. Normally David took no interest at all in babies, but at the sight of this one he was smitten with such awe that he shut his eyes and ducked his head, just as though he had been blinded by the sight of a king with eyes like flame sitting upon a rainbow-encircled throne.

So this was the King, this tiny Baby lying in a rough stone manger in a stable. It struck David that of all the extraordinary places where he had encountered kings this night, this was the most extraordinary of all. And then he gave a joyous exclamation. On the journey here he had cried because he had thought a barefoot dirty little boy would not be able to go to a king's birthday party, but surely even he could go to a birthday party in a stable. He leapt to his feet, dusted his knees, pulled down his rags, laid his hands on the latch of the door, and crept noiselessly in.

And then, standing by himself in the shadow by the door, he bethought him that he had no present to give. He had no possessions in the world at all except his beloved shepherd's pipe, and it was out of the question that he should give that for he loved it as his own life. Noiseless as

a mouse he turned to go out again, but suddenly the
mother in the blue cloak, who must have known all the
time that he was there, raised her face and smiled at him, a
radiant smile full of promise, and at the same time the
man with the gray beard lowered the lantern a little so that
it seemed as though the whole manger were enveloped
with light, with that Baby at the heart of the light like the
sun itself.

And suddenly David could not stay by himself in the shadows, any more than he could stay in a dark stuffy house when
the sun was shining. No sacrifice was too great, not even the
sacrifice of the little shepherd's pipe that was dear as life itself,
if he could be in that light. He ran forward, pushing rudely
between Balthasar and Tobias, and laid his shepherd's pipe
joyously down before the manger, between Balthasar's jeweled casket and Tobias's humble loaf of bread. He was too
little to realize as he knelt down and covered his face with his
hands, that the birthday gifts lying there in a row were sym-
bolic of all that a man could need for his life on earth – a cloak
for shelter, a loaf of bread for food, a shepherd's crook for
work, and a musical instrument to bring courage in the doing
of it, and those other gifts of gold and jewels and spices that
symbolized rich qualities of kingliness and priestliness and
wisdom that were beyond human understanding. "Wise men
from the desert with their mysteries," Balthasar had said.
"Shepherds from the hills with their simplicities, and a little
boy with the gift of music." But David, peeping through his
fingers at the Baby in the manger, did not think at all, he only
felt, and what his spirit experienced was exactly what his
body felt when he danced about on the hills in the first hot
sunshine of the year; warmth was poured into him, health

and strength and life itself. He took his hands away from his face and gazed and gazed at the Baby, his whole being poured out in adoration.

IV

AND THEN IT WAS all over and he found himself outside Bethlehem, trailing along in the dust behind Eli, Jacob, and Tobias, footsore and weary and as cross as two sticks.

"Where's my camel?" he asked petulantly. "When I went to Bethlehem I was the leader of a caravan, and I had three great lords with me, and servants and torches."

"Well, you haven't got them now," said Eli. "The great lords are still at Bethlehem. When Jacob and Tobias and I saw you there in the stable we made haste to take you home to your mother, young truant that you are."

"I don't want mother," grumbled David. "I want my camel."

Eli glanced back over his shoulder at the disagreeable little urchin dawdling at his heels. Was this the same child who had knelt in the stable rapt in adoration? How quick can be the fall from ecstasy! "You keep your mouth shut, little son," he adjured him, "and quicken your heels; for I must get back to those sheep."

"Baa!" said David nastily, and purposely lagged behind.

So determinedly did he lag that by the time he had reached the well he found himself alone again. The well! The sight of it brought home to him his desperate plight. From his night's adventure he had gained nothing. Up there on the hill was the little house that held his sick father, his weeping mother, and his hungry little brothers and sisters. And he must go home to them no richer than he went. Poorer, in fact, for now he had lost his shepherd's pipe, thrown away his greatest treasure in what seemed to him now a moment of madness. Now he had nothing, nothing in all the world.

He flung himself down in the grass beside the well and he cried as though his heart were breaking. The utter deadness of the hour before dawn weighed on him like a pall and the cold of it numbed him from head to foot. He felt himself sinking lower and lower, dropping down to the bottom of some black sea of misery, and it was not until he reached the bottom that comfort came to him.

His sobs ceased and he was conscious again of the feel of the earth beneath the grass where he lay, hard and cold yet bearing him up with a strength that was reassuring. He thought of the terraces of olive trees above him and of the great bare hills beyond, and then he thought of the voices he had heard singing in the wind up in the hills, and singing down below among the trees, and then suddenly he thought he heard voices in the grass, tiny voices that were like the voices of all growing things, corn and flowers and grasses. "They that sow in tears, shall reap in joy," they whispered. "He that goeth forth and weepeth, bearing precious seed, shall doubtless come again rejoicing, bringing his sheaves with him."

He got up, his courage restored, and stumbled over to the well, faintly silvered now with the first hint of dawn. He did not pray to be a rich man, he did not look in it for his heart's desire, he simply went to it to wash himself, for he did not intend to appear before his mother with dirty tear stains all over his face. If he could not arrive back home with bags full of gold and thousands of camel and tens of thousands of sheep he would at least arrive with a clean and cheerful face to comfort them.

Like all small boys David was a noisy washer and it must have been the sound of his splashings that prevented him hearing the feet of a trotting camel upon the road; nor could the surface of the well, much agitated by his ablutions, show him at first the reflection of the man standing behind him. It had to smooth itself out before he could see the swarthy face framed in the twinkling golden ornaments. When he did see it he blinked incredulously for a moment and then swung round with a cry of joy.

"So you thought I had forgotten you, did you, little son?" smiled Balthasar. "I would not forget so excellent a leader of a caravan. When you left the stable I followed after you as quickly as I could. See what I have for you."

He gave a bag to David and the little boy, opening it, saw by the first light of the dawn the shine of golden pieces. Lots of golden pieces, enough to buy medicines and healing salves for his father and food and warmth for all of them for a long time to come. He had no words to tell of his gratitude but the face that he tilted up to Bathasar, with eyes and mouth as round in wonder as the coins themselves, was in itself a paean of praise.

Balthasar laughed and patted his shoulder. "When I saw you give your shepherd's pipe to the little King," he said, "I vowed that you should not go home empty-handed. I think it was the little King Himself who put the thought into my head. Now I must go back to my country, and you to your home, but we will not forget each other. Fare you well, little son."

As he went up through the shadows of the olive trees David was no longer frightened of robbers, for he was far too happy. The trees were singing again, he thought, as the dawn wind rustled them. "Comfort ye, comfort ye, My people," they sang. And when he got out beyond the trees, and saw the great bare stretches of the hills flushed rose and lilac in the dawn, it seemed as though the hills themselves were shouting, "Glory to God!"

A Certain Small Shepherd

Rebecca Caudill

THIS IS A STORY of a strange and a marvelous thing. It happened on a Christmas morning at Hurricane Gap, and not so long ago at that.

But before you hear about Christmas morning, you must hear about Christmas Eve, for that is part of the story.

And before you hear about Christmas Eve, you must hear about Jamie, for without Jamie there would be no story.

Jamie was born on a freakish night in November. The cold that night moved down from the North and rested its heavy hand suddenly on Hurricane Gap. Within an hour's time, the naked earth turned brittle. Line Fork Creek froze solid in its winding bed and lay motionless, like a string dropped at the foot of Pine Mountain.

Nothing but the dark wind was abroad in the hollow. Wild creatures huddled in their dens. Cows stood hunched in their stalls. Housewives stuffed rags in the cracks underneath their doors against the needling cold, and men heaped oak and apple wood on their fires.

At the foot of the Gap, where Jamie's house stood, the wind doubled its fury. It battered the doors of the house. It rattled the windows. It wailed like a banshee in the chimney.

"For sure, it's bad luck trying to break in," moaned Jamie's mother, and turned her face to the pillow.

"Bad luck has no business here," Jamie's father said bravely.

He laid more logs on the fire. Flames licked at them and roared up the chimney. But through the roaring, the wind wailed on, thin and high.

Father took the newborn baby from the bed beside its mother and sat holding it on his knee.

"Saro," he called, "you and Honey come see Jamie!"

Two girls came from the shadows of the room. In the firelight they stood looking at the tiny wrinkled red face inside the blanket.

"He's such a little brother!" said Saro.

"Give him time, he'll grow," said Father proudly. "When he's three he'll be as big as Honey. When he's six he'll be as big as you. You want to hold him?"

Saro sat down on a stool and Father laid the bundle in her arms.

Honey stood beside Saro. She pulled back a corner of the blanket. She opened one of the tiny hands and laid one of her fingers in it. She smiled at the face in the blanket. She looked up, smiling at Father.

But Father did not see her. He was standing beside Mother, trying to comfort her.

That night Jamie's mother died.

Jamie ate and slept and grew.

Like other babies, he cut teeth. He learned to sit alone and to crawl. When he was a year old, he toddled about like other one-year-olds. At two, he carried around sticks and stones like other two-year-olds. He threw balls and built towers of blocks and knocked them down.

Everything that other two-year-olds could do, Jamie could do, except one thing. He could not talk.

The old women of Hurricane Gap sat in their chimney corners and shook their heads.

"His mother, poor soul, should have rubbed him with lard," said one.

"She ought to have brushed him with a rabbit's foot," said another.

"Wasn't that boy born on a Wednesday?" asked another. "'Wednesday's child is full of woe,'" she quoted from an old saying.

"Jamie gets everything he wants by pointing," explained Father. "Give him time. He'll learn to talk."

At three, Jamie could zip his shirt and tie his shoes.

At four, he followed Father to the stable at milking time. He milked the kittens' pan full of milk.

But even at four, Jamie could not talk like other children. He could only make strange grunting noises.

One day Jamie found a litter of new kittens in a box under the stairs. He ran to the cornfield to tell Father. He wanted to say he had been feeling around in the box for a ball he'd lost, and suddenly his fingers had felt something warm and squirmy, and here were all these kittens.

But how could you tell somebody something if, when you opened your mouth, you could only grunt?

Jamie started running. He ran till he reached the orchard. There, he threw himself face down in the tall grass and kicked his feet against the ground.

One day Honey's friends came to play hide-and-seek. Jamie played with them.

Because Clive was the oldest, he shut his eyes first and counted to fifty, while the other children scattered and hid behind trees in the yard and corners of the house. After he had counted to fifty, the hollow rang with cries.

"One, two, three for Milly!"
"One, two, three for Jamie!"
"One, two, three, I'm home free."

It came to Jamie's turn to shut his eyes. He sat on the porch step, covered his eyes with his hands, and began to count.

"Listen to Jamie!" Clive called to the other children.

The others listened. Then they all began to laugh.

Jamie got up. He ran after the children. He fought them with both fists and both feet. Honey helped him.

Then Jamie ran away to the orchard, and threw himself down on his face in the tall grass, and kicked the ground.

Later, when Father was walking through the orchard, he came across Jamie lying in the grass.

"Jamie," said Father, "there's a new calf in the pasture. I need you to help me bring it to the stable."

Jamie got up from the grass. He wiped his eyes. Out of the orchard and across the pasture he trudged at Father's heels. In a far corner of the pasture they found the cow. Beside her, on wobbly legs, stood the new calf.

Together, Father and Jamie drove the cow and the calf to the stable, into an empty stall.

Together, they brought nubbins from the corncrib to feed the cow.

Together, they made a bed of clean hay for the calf.

"Jamie," said Father the next morning, "I need you to help plow the corn."

Father harnessed the horse and lifted Jamie to the horse's back. Away to the cornfield they went, Father walking in front of the horse, Jamie riding, holding tight to the hames.

While Father plowed, Jamie walked in the furrow behind him. When Father lay on his back in the shade of the persimmon tree to rest, Jamie lay beside him. Father told Jamie the names of the birds flying overhead – the turkey vulture tilting its uplifted wings against the white clouds, the carrion crow flapping lazily and sailing, flapping and sailing, and the sharp-shinned hawk gliding to rest in the woodland.

The next day Jamie helped Father set out sweet potatoes. Other days he helped Father trim fencerows and mend fences.

Whatever Father did, Jamie helped him.

One day Father drove the car out of the shed and stopped in front of the house.

"Jamie!" he called. "Jump in. We're going across Pine Mountain."

"Can I go, too?" asked Honey.

"Not today," said Father. "I'm taking Jamie to see a doctor."

The doctor looked at Jamie's throat. He listened to Jamie grunt. He shook his head.

"You might see Dr. Jones," he said.

Father and Jamie got into the car and drove across Big Black Mountain to see Dr. Jones.

"Maybe Jamie could learn to talk," Dr. Jones said. "But he would have to be sent away to a special school. He would have to stay there several months. He might have to stay two or three years. Or four."

"It is a long time," said Dr. Jones.

"And the pocket is empty," said Father.

So Father and Jamie got into the car and started home.

Usually Father talked to Jamie as they drove along. Now they drove all the way, across Big Black and across Pine, without a word.

In August every year, school opened at Hurricane Gap.

On the first morning of school the year that Jamie was six, Father handed him a book, a tablet, a pencil, and a box of crayons – all shiny and new.

"You're going to school, Jamie," he said. "I'll go with you this morning."

The neighbors watched them walking down the road together, toward the little one-room schoolhouse.

"Poor foolish father!" they said, and shook their heads. "Trying to make somebody out of that no-account boy!"

Miss Creech, the teacher, shook her head too. With so many children, so many classes, so many grades, she hadn't time for a boy who couldn't talk, she told Father.

"What will Jamie do all day long?" she asked.

"He will listen," said Father.

So Jamie took his book and his tablet, his pencil and his box of crayons, and sat down in an empty seat in the front row.

Every day Jamie listened. He learned the words on the pages of his book. He learned how to count. He liked the reading and the counting.

But the part of school Jamie liked best was the big piece of paper Miss Creech gave him every day. On it he printed words in squares, like the other children. He wrote numbers. He drew pictures and colored them with his crayons. He could say things on paper.

One day Miss Creech said Jamie had the best paper in the first grade. She held it up for all the children to see.

On sunny days on the playground the children played ball games and three-deep and duck-on-a-rock – games a boy can play without talking. On rainy days they played indoors.

One rainy day they played a guessing game. Jamie knew the answer that no other child could guess. But he couldn't say the answer. He didn't know how to spell the answer. He could find nothing to point to that showed he knew the answer.

That evening at home he threw his book into a corner. He slammed the door. He pulled Honey's hair. He twisted the cat's tail. The cat yowled and leaped under the bed.

"Jamie," said Father, "cats have feelings, just like boys."

Every year the people of Hurricane Gap celebrated Christmas in the little white church that stood across the road from Jamie's house. On Christmas Eve the boys and girls gave a Christmas play. People came miles to see it – from the other side of Pine Mountain and from the head of every creek and hollow. Miss Creech directed the play.

Through the late fall, as the leaves fell from the trees and the days grew shorter and the air snapped with cold, Jamie wondered when Miss Creech would talk about the play. Finally, one afternoon in November, Miss Creech announced it was time to begin play practice.

Jamie laid his book inside his desk and listened carefully as Miss Creech assigned the parts of the play.

Miss Creech gave the part of Mary to Joan, who lived up Pine Mountain beyond the rock quarry. She asked Honey to bring her big doll to be the Baby. She gave the part of Joseph to Henry, who lived at the head of Little Laurelpatch. She asked Saro to be an angel; Clive the innkeeper. She chose three big boys to be Wise Men, four others to be shepherds. She named the boys and girls who were to be people living in Bethlehem. The rest of the boys and girls would sing carols, she said.

Jamie for a moment listened to the sound of the words he had last heard. Yes, Miss Creech expected him to sing carols.

Every day after school the boys and girls went with Miss Creech up the road to the church and practiced the Christmas play.

Every day Jamie stood in the front row of the carolers. The first day he stood quietly. The second day he shoved Milly, who was standing next to him. The third day he pulled Honey's hair. The fourth day when the carolers began singing, Jamie ran to the window, grabbed a ball from the sill, and bounced it across the floor.

"Wait a minute, children," Miss Creech said to the carolers.

She turned to Jamie.

"Jamie," she asked, "how would you like to be a shepherd?"

"He's too little," said one of the big shepherds.

"No, he isn't," said Saro. "If my father was a shepherd, Jamie would help him."

That afternoon Jamie became a small shepherd. He ran home after practice to tell Father.

Father couldn't understand what Jamie was telling him. But he knew that Jamie had been changed into somebody important.

One afternoon, at play practice, Miss Creech said to the boys and girls, "Forget you are Joan, and Henry, and Saro, and Clive, and Jamie. Remember that you are Mary, and Joseph, and an angel, and an innkeeper, and a shepherd, and that strange things are happening in the hollow where you live."

That night, at bedtime, Father took the big Bible off the table. Saro and Honey and Jamie gathered around the fire.

Over the room a hush fell as Father read:

And there were in the same country shepherds abiding in the field, keeping watch over their flock by night. And, lo, the angel of the Lord came upon them, and the glory of the Lord shone round about them: and they were sore afraid. And the angel said unto them, Fear not: for, behold, I bring you good tidings of great joy which shall be to all the people...And it came to pass, as the angels were gone away from them into heaven, the shepherds said to one another, Let us now go even unto Bethlehem, and see this thing which is come to pass, which the Lord hath made known unto us. And they came with haste, and found Mary, and Joseph, and the babe lying in a manger.

Christmas drew near. At home in the evenings, when they had finished studying their lessons, the boys and girls of Hurricane Gap made decorations for the Christmas tree that would stand in the church. They glued together strips of bright-colored paper in long chains. They whittled stars and baby lambs and camels out of wild cherry wood. They strung long strings of popcorn.

Jamie strung a string of popcorn. Every night, as Father read from the Bible, Jamie added more kernels to his string.

"Jamie, are you trying to make a string long enough to reach to the top of Pine Mountain?" asked Honey one night.

Jamie did not hear her. He was far away, on a hillside, tending sheep. And even though he was a small shepherd and could only grunt when he tried to talk, an angel wrapped around with dazzling light was singling him out to tell him a wonderful thing that had happened down in the hollow in a cow stall.

He fell asleep, stringing his popcorn, and listening.

In a corner of the room where the fire burned, Father pulled from under his bed the trundle bed in which Jamie slept. He turned back the covers, picked Jamie up from the floor, and laid him gently in the bed.

Next day Father went across Pine Mountain to the store. When he came home, he handed Saro a package. In it was cloth of four colors – green, gold, white, and red.

"Make Jamie a shepherd's coat, like the picture in the Bible," Father said to Saro.

Father went into the woods and found a crooked limb of a tree. He made it into a shepherd's crook for Jamie.

Jamie went to school the next morning carrying his shepherd's crook and his shepherd's coat on his arm. He would wear his coat and carry his crook when the boys and girls practiced the play.

All day Jamie waited patiently to practice the play. All day he sat listening.

But who could tell whose voice he heard? It might have been Miss Creech's. It might have been an angel's.

Two days before Christmas, Jamie's father and Clive's father drove in a pick-up truck along the Trace Branch road looking for a Christmas tree. On the mountainside they spotted a juniper growing broad and tall and free. With axes they cut it down. They snaked it down the mountainside and loaded it into the truck.

Father had to open the doors of the church wide to get the tree inside. It reached to the ceiling. Frost-blue berries shone on its feathery green branches. The air around it smelled of spice.

That afternoon the mothers of Hurricane Gap, and Miss Creech, and all the boys and girls gathered at the church to decorate the tree.

In the tiptop of the tree they fastened the biggest star. Among the branches they hung the other stars and the baby lambs and camels whittled out of wild cherry wood. They hung polished red apples on twigs of the tree. They looped paper chains from branch to branch. Last of all, they festooned the tree with strings of snowy popcorn.

"Ah!" they said, as they looked at the tree. "Ah!"

Beside the tree the boys and girls practiced the Christmas play for the last time. When they had finished, they started home. Midway down the aisle they turned and looked again at the tree.

"Ah!" they said.

Saro opened the door. "Look!" she called. "Look, everybody! It's snowing!"

Jamie, the next morning, looked out on a world such as he had never seen. Hidden were the roads and the fences, the woodpile, and the swing under the oak tree – all buried deep under a lumpy quilt of snow. And before a stinging wind, snowflakes still madly whirled and danced.

Saro and Honey joined Jamie at the window.

"You can't see across Line Fork Creek in this storm," said Saro. And where is Pine Mountain?"

"Where is the church?" asked Honey. "That's what I'd like to know."

Jamie turned to them with questions in his eyes.

"If it had been snowing hard that night in Bethlehem, Jamie," Honey told him, "the shepherds wouldn't have had their sheep out in the pasture. They would have had them in the stable, keeping them warm. Wouldn't they, Father? Then they wouldn't have heard what the angel said, all shut indoors like that."

"When angels have something to tell a shepherd," said Father, "they can find him in any place, in any sort of weather. If the shepherd is listening, he will hear."

At eleven o'clock the telephone rang.

"Hello!" said Father.

Saro and Honey and Jamie heard Miss Creech's voice. "I've just got the latest weather report. This storm is going on all day, and into the night. Do you think – "

The telephone, once it started ringing, wouldn't stop. No matter if it rang a long and a short, two longs and a short, a short and two longs, or whatever, everyone on the Hurricane Gap line listened. The news they heard was always bad. Drifts ten feet high were piled up along the Trace Branch road…The boys and girls on Little Laurelpatch couldn't get out. Joseph lived on Little Laurelpatch…The road up Pine Mountain through Hurricane Gap was closed, all the way to the rock quarry. Mary couldn't get down the mountain… And then the telephone went silent, dead in the storm.

Meanwhile, the snow kept up its crazy dance before the wind. It drifted in great white mounds across the roads and in the fencerows.

"Nobody but a foolish man would take to the road on a day like this," said Father.

At dinner Jamie sat at the table staring at his plate.

"Shepherds must eat, Jamie," said Father.

"Honey and I don't feel like eating either, Jamie," said Saro. "But see how Honey is eating!"

Still Jamie stared at his plate.

"Know what?" asked Saro. "Because we're all disappointed, we won't save the Christmas stack cake for tomorrow. We'll have a slice today. As soon as you eat your dinner, Jamie."

Still Jamie stared at his plate. He did not touch his food.

"You think that play was real, don't you, Jamie?" said Honey. "It wasn't real. It was just a play we were giving, like some story we'd made up."

Jamie could hold his sobs no longer. His body heaved as he ran to Father.

Father laid an arm about Jamie's shoulders.

"Sometimes, Jamie," he said, "angels say to shepherds, 'Be of good courage.'"

On through the short afternoon the storm raged.

Father heaped more wood on the fire. Saro sat in front of the fire reading a book. Honey cracked hickory nuts on the stone hearth. Jamie sat.

"Bring the popper, Jamie, and I'll pop some corn for you," said Father.

Jamie shook his head.

"Want me to read to you?" asked Saro.

Jamie shook his head.

"Why don't you help Honey crack hickory nuts?" asked Father.

Jamie shook his head.

"Jamie still thinks he's a shepherd," said Honey.

After a while Jamie left the fire and stood at the window, watching the wild storm. He squinted his eyes and stared. He motioned to Father to come and look. Saro and Honey, too, hurried to the window and looked.

Through the snowdrifts trudged a man, followed by a woman. They were bundled and buttoned from head to foot, and their faces were lowered against the wind and the flying snowflakes.

"Lord have mercy!" said Father, as he watched them turn in at the gate.

Around the house the man and the woman made their way to the back door. As Father opened the door to them, a gust of snow-laden wind whisked into the kitchen.

"Come in out of the cold," said Father.

The man and the woman stepped inside. They stamped their feet on the kitchen floor and brushed the snow from their clothes. They followed Father into the front room and sat down before the fire in the chairs Father told Saro to bring for them. Father, too, sat down.

Jamie stood beside Father. Saro and Honey stood behind his chair. The three of them stared at the man and the woman silently.

"Where did you come from?" asked Father.

"The other side of Pine Mountain," said the man.

"Why didn't you stop sooner?" asked father.

"We did stop," the man said. "At three houses. Nobody had room," he said.

Father was silent for a minute. He looked at his own bed and at Jamie's trundle bed underneath it. The man and the woman looked numbly into the fire.

"How far were you going?" asked Father.

"Down Straight Creek," said the man. He jerked his head toward the woman. "To her sister's."

"You'll never get there tonight," Father said.

"Maybe," said the man, "maybe there'd be a place in your stable."

"We could lay pallets on the kitchen floor," said Father.

The woman looked at the children. She shook her head. "The stable is better," she said.

"The stable is cold," said father.

"It will do," said the woman.

When the man and the woman had dried their clothes and warmed themselves, Father led the way to the stable. He carried an armload of quilts and on top of them an old buffalo skin. From his right arm swung a lantern and a milk bucket. "I'll milk while I'm there," he said to Saro. "Get supper ready."

Jamie and Saro and Honey watched from the kitchen window, as the three trudged through the snowdrifts to the stable.

It was dark when Father came back to the house.

"How long are the man and the woman going to stay?" asked Honey.

Father hung a tea kettle of water on the crane over the fire and went upstairs to find another lantern.

"All night tonight," he said, as he came down the stairs. "Maybe longer."

Father hurriedly ate the supper Saro put on the table. Then he took in one hand the lighted lantern and a tin bucket filled with supper for the man and the woman.

"I put some Christmas stack cake in the bucket," said Saro.

In his other hand Father took the tea kettle.

"It's cold in that stable," he said, as he started out the kitchen door. "Bitter cold."

On the doorstep he turned. "Don't wait up for me," he called back. "I may be gone a good while."

Over the earth darkness thickened. Still the wind blew and the snow whirled.

The clock on the mantel struck seven.

"I wish Father would come!" said Honey.

The clock struck eight. It ticked solemnly in the quiet house, where Saro and Honey and Jamie waited.

"Why doesn't Father come?" complained Honey.

"Why don't you hang up your stocking and go to bed?" asked Saro. "Jamie, it's time to hang up your stocking, too, and go to bed."

Jamie did not answer. He sat staring into the fire.

"That Jamie! He still thinks he's a shepherd!" said Honey, as she hung her stocking under the mantel.

"Jamie," said Saro, "aren't you going to hang up your stocking and go to bed?" She pulled the trundle bed from beneath Father's bed, and turned back the covers. She turned back the covers on Father's bed. She hung up her stocking and followed Honey upstairs.

"Jamie!" she called back.

Still Jamie stared into the fire. A strange feeling was growing inside him. This night was not like other nights, he knew. Something mysterious was going on. He felt afraid.

What was that he heard? The wind? Only the wind?

He lay down on his bed with his clothes on. He dropped off to sleep. A rattling at the door waked him.

He sat upright quickly. He looked around. His heart beat fast. But nothing in the room had changed. Everything was as it had been when he lay down – the fire was burning; two stockings, Saro's and Honey's, hung under the mantel; the clock was ticking solemnly.

He looked at Father's bed. The sheets were just as Saro had turned them back.

There! There it was! He heard it again! It sounded like singing. "Glory to God! On earth peace!"

Jamie breathed hard. Had he heard that? Or had he only said it to himself?

He lay down again and pulled the quilts over his head.

"Get up, Jamie," he heard Father saying. "Put your clothes on, quick."

Jamie opened his eyes. He saw daylight seeping into the room. He saw Father standing over him, bundled in warm clothes.

Wondering, Jamie flung the quilts back and rolled out of bed.

"Why, Jamie," said Father, "you're already dressed!"

Father went to the stairs. "Saro! Honey!" he called. "Come quick!"

"What's happened, Father?" asked Saro.

"What are we going to do?" asked Honey, as she fumbled sleepily with her shoelaces.

"Come with me," said Father.

"Where are we going?" asked Honey.

"To the stable?" asked Saro.

"The stable was no fit place," said Father. "Not on this bitter night. Not when the church was close by, and it with a stove in it and coal for burning."

Out into the cold, silent, white morning they went. The wind had laid. Snow no longer fell. The clouds were lifting. One star in the vast sky, its brilliance fading in the growing light, shone down on Hurricane Gap.

Father led the way through the drifted snow. The others followed, stepping in his tracks.

As Father pushed open the church door, the fragrance of the Christmas tree rushed out at them. The potbellied stove glowed red with the fire within.

Muffling his footsteps, Father walked quietly up the aisle. Wonderingly the others followed. There, beside the star-crowned Christmas tree, where the Christmas play was to have been given, they saw the woman. She lay on the old buffalo skin, covered with quilts. Beside her pallet sat the man.

The woman smiled at them. "You came to see?" she asked, and lifted the cover.

Saro went first and peeped under the cover. Honey went next.

"You look too, Jamie," said Saro.

For a second Jamie hesitated. He leaned forward and took one quick look. Then he turned, shot down the aisle and out of the church, slamming the door behind him.

Saro ran down the church aisle, calling after him.

"Wait, Saro," said Father, watching Jamie through the window.

To the house Jamie made his way, half running along the path Father's big boots had cut through the snowdrifts.

Inside the house he hurriedly pulled his shepherd's robe over his coat. He snatched up his crook from the chimney corner.

With his hand on the doorknob, he glanced toward the fireplace. There, under the mantel, hung Saro's and Honey's stockings. And there, beside them, hung his stocking! Now who had hung it there? It had in it the same bulge his stocking had had every Christmas morning since he could remember – a bulge made by an orange.

Jamie ran to the fireplace and felt the toe of his stocking. Yes, there was the dime, just as on other Christmas mornings.

Hurriedly he emptied his stocking. With the orange and the dime in one hand and the crook in the other, he made his way toward the church. Father and Saro, still watching, saw his shepherd's robe, a spot of glowing color in a great white world.

Father opened the church door.

Without looking to left or right, Jamie hurried up the aisle. Father and Saro followed him. Beside the pallet he dropped to his knees.

"Here's a Christmas gift for the Child," he said, clear and strong.

"Father!" gasped Saro. "Father, listen to Jamie!"

The woman turned back the covers from the baby's face. Jamie gently laid the orange beside the baby's tiny hand.

"And here's a Christmas gift for the Mother," Jamie said to the woman.

He put the dime in her hand.

Father, trembling with wonder and with joy, fell to his knees beside Jamie. Saro, too, knelt; and Honey, and the man.

"Surely," the woman spoke softly, "the Lord lives this day."

"Surely," said Father, "the Lord does live this day, and all days. And he is loving and merciful and good."

IN THE HUSH that followed, Christmas in all its joy and majesty came to Hurricane Gap. And it wasn't so long ago at that.

The Carpenter's Christmas

Peter K. Rosegger

A T LAST IT WAS OVER, this vigorous sweeping and scrubbing and chasing of dirt, this week-long turmoil during which nothing, not a piece of furniture, not a single wall decoration, remained in place, until every piece of wood had been cleaned, every stone whitewashed, every bit of metal polished. Now the house shone in purest cleanliness.

The calm after a storm has a solemn effect in any case, but particularly when the Christ Child is about to arrive. Somewhere in the house stands a readied cradle. Those who wear shoes must take them off; and those in their stocking feet must walk on tiptoe, for – He sleeps.

The goodwife bustled around in her rooms purposefully; she had to see that everything was right without marking the floor; check all the chests and closets and windows without touching anything, so that everything would retain its pristine beauty. The wind rattled the windowpanes, blowing snow into every nook and cranny, and the darkness of the skies almost turned the room into night. In the living room, on a table covered with white linen, were a crucifix, a burning blessed candle, and a crock holding a branch cut from the cherry tree three weeks ago on St. Barbara's Day, which was to bloom that night. Its buds glistened and swelled and would burst into flower any moment.

The woman ran to the door, opened it softly, raised her forefinger and hissed, "Pssst!" into the kitchen, where the servant girl wasn't quiet enough with the dishes. "Pssst! The Christ Child is asleep!"

The goodwife was in a deeply pious mood. Her graying hair was wound around her head in two braids; she had donned her red kerchief and her silk apron. With a rosary in her folded hands she sat in the armchair next to the table and could think of nothing except: Christmas Eve! The Christ Child!

Suddenly there was a noise in the corner. Her husband, the carpenter, who was lying on the bench against the wall, turned around and bumped his elbow so hard against the back rest of the chair that it crashed to the floor.

"Pssst!" she hissed, getting up. "My, but what a restless person you are!"

"I? Restless?" He brushed his hand over his face. "Can't a person sleep any more? Can't you leave me alone?"

"If you don't want to pray, you should at least be quiet, man. And you shouldn't sleep, either!"

"But, old lady, when a man sleeps he makes the least noise."

"So you think! That's when you make the most noise, when you sleep! If you're not upsetting a chair, beating about with your arms, you're poking a hole in the wall. Anyone would think there were at least two sawmills and a threshing machine in here."

"Yea, the sawmills and that threshing machine ought to be turned off on Christmas Eve," he answered calmly, sitting up.

"Oh, don't talk nonsense, please! Here, find yourself a nice Christmas prayer!"

She reached for the prayer book on the shelf, wiped the old, worn binding with her apron – yes, it was already dusty again! – and laid it on the table.

"What's the matter with you?" he asked tranquilly. "When they ring the bell, I'll pray all right. Just now I want to sleep some more."

"Stop arguing!" she cried impatiently, kicking at a footstool below the table.

He looked at her and grinned. "Woman," he said. "Not even old age helps you – you simply won't change!"

"You're the one to talk!" she answered. "A man ought to remember at least on a day like this, that he has holy water on him. Haven't you any piety in you at all? Don't you know that tomorrow is Christmas?"

"Am I doing anything wrong?"

"Nor are you doing anything right, either. Go on, find that Christmas prayer!"

"I've never let anyone order me to be pious. If it doesn't come by itself…"

"Come by itself? To you? Mary and Joseph, that'd be a long wait! All week long you are so unchristian that it's a scandal. Holidays are made for piety!"

"Oh, phht!" the carpenter replied crossly. "If a man works hard all week and does his duty in God's name and does nobody any wrong, he's supposed to be extra pious on Sundays, eh? Why, woman, how is a man to do that?"

"Pray, I said, and keep quiet! Holy Christ will be awakened soon enough when He comes to judge the quick and the dead…Jesus and Mary, what's that?"

For a moment it was quite dark in the room, as if a black cloth had been drawn across the window; then a heavy thud, and the wild whirling of the snow outside. The carpenter went to the window and looked out. The storm had broken off a heavy limb from the old fir tree standing in front of the house.

"Oh God, oh God, what a day!" the woman whined, wringing her hands. "That's a bad sign for a year without peace!"

"If the devil doesn't fetch you, it'll be just that," the carpenter growled amiably.

"Today I refuse to argue with you!" she answered with cold superiority. "But just you wait until the day is over. Then you'll see whom the devil will fetch!"

She took a little vessel of holy water from the door-jamb and sprinkled everything in the room, especially her husband. He stared at her grumpily and refused to stir.

"He doesn't even make the sign of the cross when he is sprinkled with holy water!"

She rushed to the kitchen, returned with a basin of glowing embers, sprinkled incense over it and carried it around, according to the old Christmas custom, close to the table, to the bed and, finally, to her husband, whose nostrils the incense attacked so vehemently that he began to curse and opened a window.

He opened the window just in time. From the road, over the whistling of the wind, came excited voices. The wind had done a good deal of damage in the village. The Widow Cenzi's roof had been torn off so that you could look from above into the crawling children's warren.

"That's because they don't pray, those people," the carpenter's wife sneered. "Mary and Joseph, that's how it is in this world. The entire Christmas Eve spoiled! And instead of saying his Christmas prayers now, he runs away! Who, I ask you, is to protect us, if not our dear Lord in heaven?"

The Widow Cenzi had three small children, the oldest of which was sick in bed with scarlet fever. She wasn't much liked in the village and it was said that in the fall she sometimes harvested potatoes where she hadn't planted any. Now the roof of her hut was torn down, with the shingles lying in the road, and the widow stumbled around with her children in the darkness trying to place them with friendly neighbors. Nobody wanted to harbor the child sick with scarlet fever until the teacher offered to take it in; but the teacher was ruled out because he might carry the infection into the school. The childless wife of the carpenter, too, was approached, but she didn't want her Christmas Eve spoiled by a sick child. Finally the village priest remembered that He who was expected that very night had said that whoever takes in a child, takes in Him – even though he wasn't quite certain how the quotation really ran. And so, with kindliness and the help of the quotation, he arranged with his housekeeper for the sick child to stay at the vicarage until the roof of the old home could be fixed, at least temporarily.

The carpenter had gone outside. His voice was louder than the wind as he called together his neighbors and his journeymen. They came with ladders, tools and boards. There was a hammering and sawing in the village that lasted all night under the light of the improvised torches – very much to the horror of the carpenter's goodwife , who esteemed the holy calm and heavenly peace of this night above all else. "How can the cherry branch bloom in all this turmoil? And how is the Christ Child to rest?"

When the bells in the church tower began to chime for Midnight Mass the men still shouted and hammered on the Widow Cenzi's roof. And while the parish sang in the church, the pounding and clanking of nails and tools still vied so with the noise of the storm that the women, thus cheated out of their Christmas humor, were positively horrified. At last, when all the bells tolled in unison and the organ jubilated at the high point of the Midnight Mass, the men who were helping to build the roof jumped down and strolled into the church too; and the carpenter found himself alone with two of his journeymen on the skeleton of the roof. The storm seemed to blow harder now, to tear down again what the hands of men had just put up.

The carpenter had expected to have the roof ready before morning. When he saw that most of the others had deserted him and that even the boys who had held the torches had thrown them in the snow and run to church, he began to curse mightily.

"To hell with the damn hypocrites! They practically chew off the toes of our good Lord; but in the meantime they let these poor wretches die of cold. They'll squat in the pews until they rot. But God in heaven can't really be proud of them. What a viper's brood! Hear them sing: 'Praise God in the highest!' And see how they kiss the waxen image of the Christ Child and cuddle it like a doll – while these poor little creatures are so cold they'll soon croak!"

When Midnight Mass was over and the people came out of the church, the carpenter was still up on his roof, working away, and cursing. One man said to the other, "Poor fellow, he'll go completely mad if we don't help him; and maybe we are a little to blame for his swearing, at that! Come on, let's pitch in. We can have that roof up in less than an hour."

Then another planted himself firmly in front of the speaker and said: "Do you really think, neighbor, that I would be so unchristian as to work on Holy Christmas Morn?" But his manner was so overbearing that the effect was far from what he intended.

"Did you hear that one?" someone asked. "In the face of such hypocrisy, I prefer the carpenter and all his cussing; and I, for one, am going to help him finish that roof!"

Others joined him. The torches were lit again and the sawing and hammering began once more with such renewed vigor that the carpenter's wife, in desperation, covered both her ears with her hands. "You can't sleep and you can't pray with all this noise going on. And that – that heathen husband of mine prefers this beggar woman to our Jesus Child, so that he won't even let Him rest in His cradle...God forgive him!"

On Christmas day when the sun rose, the icy wind still rushed over the rooftops, and over many a gable snow clouds still danced. But the roof of the Widow Cenzi's house was fixed and nailed down tight, a good fire crackled in her stove, and the woman with her children had returned to their home. The carpenter was lying on his bed, jacket and boots and all, snoring with a right good will. His wife stood in the doorway, staring at him in disgust.

She herself could not settle down. She was miserable. Even before the solemn High Mass she went over to the vicarage, but she could hardly say a single word between her sobs. What an unhappy woman she was, she finally managed to stammer, to have such a husband! True, he was

usually quiet and industrious, but he had simply no religion! Just no religion at all! And if she were to live to be a
hundred, she would never forget that night!

"Not a single Our Father did he say, nor did he welcome
the Christ Child with so much as a single short prayer!
What an end such a man will come to! Even this morning,
people are going from house to house telling each other
that they have never heard anyone curse as much as this
husband of mine on Holy Night! You must have heard it
yourself, Your Reverence, after Midnight Mass! I was
shivering in my soul!"

The priest sat with his hand folded in his lap and smiled
benevolently at the distracted woman. "To be sure, I heard
something," he said. "But I thought it was a prayer!"

"Prayer?" the woman moaned, raising her hands and
folding them high above her head, then letting them fall
again as if she had had a stroke.

"My dear woman," the priest replied. "Some people
have strange ways of praying. The Jews, for example, wind
their prayer-belts around their heads and arms when they
pray. Others just turn the leaves of their prayer books.
And still others pass the beads of their rosaries through
their fingers. Well, our carpenter simply hammers nails into
wooden shingles during his Our Father."

The woman again clasped her hands in despair. "Did
you say 'Our Father,' Your Reverence? Some Our Father
that would be! How he cursed and shouted during Holy
Mass! If our dear Lord weren't so kind, the earth would
have opened and swallowed him!"

"I admit," the priest replied, "that his words may have
been chosen somewhat – unfortunately. But his intentions
were certainly good. And that's really what counts. All the

while he was cursing and shouting, I'm sure he didn't have another thought in his head other than to provide a roof for the poor widow and her children and his conviction that other men ought to be helping him. We probably all prayed devoutly last night, but I have an idea that the carpenter's prayer with his saw and hammer pleased our Good Lord the most."

"And now," the woman cried, "when the others are on their way to High Mass, he lies sleeping like a...a donkey!"

"Let him sleep, my dear woman. Just as his work was his prayer, so is his rest."

As the carpenter's wife departed, she kept shaking her head. She could make neither head nor tail of all this. What was the world coming to? If cursing was praying, what then was praying? But she didn't get quite that far in her meditations.

What the Kings Brought

Ruth Sawyer

THIS IS A PERSONAL Christmas story. I spent a year in Spain some time ago. During the holiday season, by strange chance, I had a sharing in one of the oldest and loveliest of the Christmas legends. On Twelfth Night, or Epiphany, the Three Kings still ride from the East. To the children of the rich they bring *regalos,* or gifts; to the children of the poor they bring a *regalito,* a little gift.

I had spent *Nochebuena* – the Good Night – and Christmas Day in Spanish Morocco and I reached Seville five days before the Three Kings would ride. It was bitterly cold that winter; there were few tourists. The large hotels were nearly empty; the small family hotel where I stayed had only a scattering of guests. Everywhere one felt the suffering and poverty of the people. Yet I had been long enough in Spain to know that with a festival only five days off, everyone, in spite of the hunger and cold, would be ready to celebrate joyfully, even with little food and a little gift.

The first morning I walked out to the Parque Maria Luisa to see the *glorietas.* These are tributes to the most famous of the Spanish writers, little intimate patios with tile benches and bookcases. In the *glorieta* to Cervantes, where atop each bookcase rode delightful figurines of Don Quixote and his faithful Sancho Panza, I caught up with the park attendant bringing back the books to fill the bookcases. He was small and old and friendly. I found that his name was Alfredo and that he had packets of seed to sell that one might feed the birds. The birds were also friendly.

Before the morning was half over and all the books were back in the *glorietas,* Alfredo joined me and whistled the birds out of their trees, some to pick up seeds at our feet, some to take them out of our hands.

The next morning being sunny and warmer, I walked out again to the park and found Alfredo had a helper. He brought him up and introduced him with that courtesy I always found among the simple folk of Spain. "This is Pepe, *señora.* He has come a long way from a farm in the uplands. He hopes to earn enough money to buy a burro for his *papá.* So now you will please buy your seeds from Pepe."

He stood there close to Alfredo, a scrawny ill-fed little boy with eyes far too large for his face. He wore the thin black cotton knickers of the poor and a ragged jacket out at the elbows but neatly patched. His legs were bare; his feet, thrust into the *alpargatas,* the canvas, rope-soled shoes of the common folk, were blue with cold. As I looked at him, I wondered if he knew how many hundreds of seed-packets he must sell to buy a burro.

The three of us stood in silence for a little moment, and then pride and a deep love loosened Pepe's tongue: "I would have you know, *señora,* that the *papacito* is a good farmer. But he has been sick and there are many mouths to feed. When the autobus ran over our burro, the *papacito* had heavy loads to carry. This he must not do so I have come to buy a young, strong burro to help make him well again – the *papacito.*"

I looked down, more concerned now for the thin body, the pinched face and the courage that brooked no defeat. "I will take ten packets of seeds every morning, and perhaps you will tell me more about your family and the *papacito* who takes such good care of you all."

A smile broke through as money and packets changed hands. Courage spoke again in his last words: "I am right to help him – yes? You see I am the oldest and almost a man."

"You are indeed, *hombre.* I can see you already riding that burro the long distance home. *Buen' suerte.*" So did I wish him good luck and went back to the hotel.

That night, a young Jewish scholar, also staying at my hotel, asked if he might join me for dinner. He had come on a fellowship to do research work in history at the Archives in Seville. His grant barely covered his expenses and he was homesick after three months of hard work and little companionship. So I told him about Pepe and my morning in the park. I have always found the Jewish people quick and warm with their sympathy. Abraham was eager to know more; his questions came fast: "How old is this Pepe? Where is he living in the city? How much does a good burro cost? Why has Alfredo given the boy so much hope when he must know only too well he could never earn enough even to buy a goat?"

I could answer only one of the questions, but I defended Alfredo. The man had honesty and kindness. He had his reasons for encouraging the boy. As for the cost of burros, it had so happened that I had gone that afternoon to the market to price them. I had priced all kinds of burros –

young, old, starved and well-fed, and each burro had his own price. "In American money, a good burro would cost all of twenty dollars, probably more."

Abraham shook a sad head: "After paying for board and room and the many photostats I must have, there isn't enough left to pay for the hoof of one burro. How about you?"

I shook my head. "If I had enough it would never be the way to do it. Pepe has a great pride, first for himself – almost a man – then for the *papacito.* To hand out the money and say 'Go, buy that burro,' would hurt him terribly. We must find some other way."

We finished our dinner and sat in a long silence, thinking. Abraham spoke first. "Look. Suppose I play hookey from the Archives tomorrow and we go to the park together. How can I think of a plan to buy that burro until I see the boy and talk with him?"

And so we went. Abraham and Pepe gave each other a long, thorough looking over. Then the boy slipped a hand into Abraham's: "Come, *amigo,* I have something to show."

They left, fast friends, and I wasted no time with Alfredo. "Tell me more about Pepe, please. How did he come to Seville? Is he a relative? And does he really believe he can earn enough selling seeds to buy a burro?"

"He believes, I do not, *señora.* But how can I break that spirit, that pride? I must let him hope for a little while longer, until good fortune comes. Let us all pray it will come." His eyes had brimmed to overflowing and he wiped away many tears, I think, with his old woolen sleeve. Then he went on to tell how Pepe had come. It seemed that a relative of Alfredo's had a farm next to the one Pepe's father worked. Much ill fortune had come to that family – it was sad, and had nearly broken the *papacito*. The boy measured up to more than his years or his frail body. The relative thought in a big city like Seville there would be tourists and opportunity for Pepe to fulfill his great wish – to buy a burro so that the *papacito* might not have to work so hard.

"It is something to break one's heart. And the boy needs so much more than a burro, *señora* – warm clothes, new, stout shoes to keep his feet off the cold of the pavement. And before all, he needs food, much food to fill a stomach that has gone empty too long."

It was indeed something to break one's heart. But what to do! I still could not see our hurting Pepe's pride by offering him money. What I said to Alfredo was: "We must remember Pepe feels himself almost a man. Let us hope good fortune may come."

They returned, Pepe's hand still holding fast to Abraham's, his face turned upwards and almost radiant. It was as if he had suddenly found a friend and had shared a secret with him. When we started homeward, he was loath to let Abraham go.

As we walked we shared experiences, Abraham and I. Pepe had taken Abraham to a great fir tree whose branches almost swept the ground. They ducked under together and Abraham saw what the boy had done to make a home for himself in Seville. Under the tree had been spread an old mule-blanket. Between two tree roots had been scooped out a deep hole that now held the dead ashes of a last night's fire. With the true courtesy of a *caballero*, Pepe had swept a hand over his domain saying: "This is my *casa*. Now it is yours."

Abraham must have acknowledged this with equal courtesy, for Pepe had gone on with mounting delight: "Alfredo lets me gather all the faggots I need from under the other trees in the park. Every night he brings me my supper. *Café con leche* he brings in a small pot with much bread, sometimes a piece of sausage. It is good. You see, *amigo,* I am most comfortable."

As Abraham talked, I wondered was that coffee-with-milk and the bread all the lad had to eat throughout the day? Remembering the ample meals we had, my stomach as well as my heart was wrung with shame. What the boy had not told Abraham, for the good reason that he did not know it, was that if the city directors of the park found out that a small boy was camping out under one of the trees and building a fire every night, Alfredo would lose his job. To brush this distressing thought away, I told Abraham all Alfredo had told me. Then, remembering the look on Pepe's face when he and Abraham had joined us, I asked: "What was the secret Pepe shared with you?"

"How did you know there was a secret?"

"Surely he told you one," I said.

Abraham grinned. "He surely did. But how did you know?"

"His face. When you came back his face shone with a great happiness and a great expectancy that was all his own."

Abraham grinned. "There is a secret shared with thousands of children. In two days the Three Kings from the Orient will ride. Pepe has believed, ever since he heard the Kings rode through Seville, that they will bring him a burro for this *papacito* of his. He said it over and over: 'A present it will be, a *regalo* – a big one – because the *papacito* is such a good man.'"

And we had never thought of the Kings! So much could be done in their name. I could have shouted for joy. "Two days left and not a moment to waste. Two days!" And I hurried Abraham back to our hotel.

That night at dinner, after he had finished his soup, to my great surprise Abraham suddenly stood up on his chair to address the tourists in the dining room. In the few days I had known him I had thought of Abraham as a shy fellow, but I must have been mistaken. His voice was strong and urgent. "Many of you are strangers here. Many of you may not remember that on the day after tomorrow, which is Twelfth Night, the Three Kings will ride. Here in Spain the children believe he will bring them presents, at least one present. Now there is at this moment in Seville a very small, ill-fed little boy who has come from his father's farm in the uplands. That is a long journey for a small boy. He has come because he hopes to earn enough money to buy his much-loved *papacito* a burro. He thinks of himself as almost a man. He doesn't know – and no one has told him yet – that it will be months before he can earn enough to buy even an old and decrepit burro." Abraham stopped; his lips were dry. He seemed to be running out of those things he wanted to say. And so I said softly: "Keep on. Everyone is interested. You are doing splendidly."

I guess it was the encouragement Abraham needed. His usually solemn face broke into a smile: "I think you should know that this little one thinks – he thinks the Three Kings will bring him a burro to help this *papacito,* who is sick." Again came a silence. Abraham looked down at me and smiled again. Doggedly he went on: "Perhaps you are thinking just what we have been thinking all day – that because Pepe is a stranger in the city the Three Kings may not know he is here, and so they might not leave that burro that he is hoping for so much. After dinner I am going to pass my hat around. Anything you care to give to help the Three Kings remember this small boy we would greatly appreciate."

Around went the hat. Spanish *pesos,* English crowns and pound notes, American dollars went into it. Afterwards in my room we counted the money and knew that with my portion added there was enough to buy all that was needed.

All through the next day we shopped; stores would be closed on Twelfth Night. We found warm woolen knickers in all sizes and all black. I asked why only black? For a small boy navy or brown or even plaid would be so much gayer. The shopkeeper gave me a puzzled look, then answered: "The *señora* does not know, perhaps, that the poor are always losing some member of the family, always burying someone. In respect for the dead, they must wear black, so black they wear all the time."

So into the pile with the black knickers went warm stockings, strong sturdy shoes – allowing for growth – a heavy woolen blanket to serve as a burro-blanket when Pepe should ride proudly home to the *papacito,* and also as an extra covering at night under the fir tree. We spent some time choosing the jacket. It was the shopkeeper who helped us decide. "You are troubled about the black knickers. Here is a gay jacket, a kind of copy of the jackets the *matadores* wear in the bullring. I think it will please enormously that boy you are buying gifts for."

"These are gifts that the Three Kings bring. I think they would bring just such a jacket to Pepe," I said.

Our last purchase was the burro. Neither of us knew anything about horseflesh, or burro-flesh for that matter.

But we tried to act wisely. We felt legs and opened mouths and looked at teeth and found at last a good-tempered, well-fed little creature with every tooth sound in his head. By rare chance, one of the tourists from the hotel came along that moment and he knew a lot about ponies as well as horses. With skillful fingers, he tried legs, turned up hooves, opened the mouth and at last nodded his approval. "That burro is a good buy. He cannot be more than three, four years old." So we bought him and arranged with his former owner to add a bridle and deliver him at midnight the following night at the entrance to the Parque Maria Luisa.

The next day at early noon, the Three Kings rode along the street that bordered the plaza. The plaza filled as if by magic. One moment it held but a scattering of people, but before we knew it it was so crowded one could hardly move or even raise an elbow. Spanish crowds are good-natured and well-behaved. No one jostled or pushed. We had found a good vantage point at a far corner from where we could see the Kings approaching. I said a Spanish crowd does not jostle, but as we stood still and expectant, we felt a gentle pushing against our knees. Looking down, we saw Pepe. His relief showed as he clasped two eager arms about my knees.

"How did you ever do it?" I asked.

"It was the *señora's* shoes. There were not too many feet wearing American shoes."

"*Hombre*, you are clever. Wait with us and when the Kings come Abraham will lift you to his shoulders where you can see all." I gave a silent prayer that the Kings would come before Pepe smothered down there among everybody's shoes.

Soon we heard the music – haunting minor chords and cadences – played, I think, on old desert instruments. There were ancient viols, flutes and pipes that sounded like the pipes the shepherds play up in the Sierras. The music held an old-world quality. Then we saw the outriders. So closely were we packed that the only way Abraham could get the boy to his shoulders was by turning him about to face him – then, holding both hands, Pepe climbed upwards. With one leg on Abraham's shoulder, he slung the other around his neck. From this height, Pepe's voice rose in triumph: "Truly, I can see everything. And today I sold twenty packets of seeds!"

Each King had his standard-bearer who hailed the crowd with "Hola! Here comes the King." Caspar and Melchior rode white stallions, but Balthazar, the black King, rode a black stallion. The Kings' robes were gay with colors, heavy with gold lace and beadwork; their golden crowns were heavy with jewels. Following each King came a half-dozen burros with red tassels and bells on their harnesses. Their panniers were filled with toys. Following these came two two-wheeled carts drawn by bullocks. These were filled with toys and each bullock had a wreath gay with flowers and ribbons about its neck. As each King rode abreast of the crowd, he reached for a saddlebag and with a wide sweep of the hand scattered candies to everyone. There were chocolates, caramels and Turkish paste, all done up in silver and gold papers.

Pepe was quick with his catching. I could hear his happy, piping voice crying out: "I have caught two. I have caught many more." And so he had. But it was the burros that seemed to delight him most. "Just such a one – just such a burro would make the papacito very joyful." And above Pepe's voice came the shouting of the crowd: *"Magnifico! Más splendido que nada!"*

We waited for the crowd to scatter; then Abraham put Pepe back on his feet and gave the boy the most inviting invitation: "Look, *hombre!* This has given a man a big appetite. Let us find a restaurant with an empty table and fill our empty stomachs."

We had to search out three cafés before we found a table. We all had *café con leche* and *pan de gloria*, a delectable sweet bread; and Pepe had a generous length of hot sausage. There was a plentiful amount of butter and jam to eat with the bread and no one bothered to talk. I marveled at the boy's good manners. Pepe must have been very hungry, but not only did he take his food with grace, but he stopped suddenly, thrust his hand into the pocket of his knickers and brought out a fistful of candy: "For you. I want you to have some of the Three Kings' sweets." We thanked him but said we had no appetite left, and a half hour later we saw him off to the park. He turned twice to wave us a farewell. He did not know, but we knew we would not be seeing Pepe again.

Abraham gave him a last piece of advice. "Look here, *hombre.* Do you still believe the Kings will bring a burro for the *papacito?* For if you do, remember this. They are wise men as well as Kings and they do not leave even small gifts where boys stay awake watching for them to come."

"I will remember, *amigo.* I will sleep soundly because I believe and because I shall be very tired."

We picked up the burro at midnight outside the park. Abraham had his pocket full of oats, which he fed the burro while I tethered him to a tree just opposite the fir tree where Pepe slept. As quietly as we could, we ducked under that fir's low branches and found a bundle rolled up tightly in the old mule-blanket. Over the bundle we spread the new blanket; then we hung everything on low branches close to the trunk of the tree. Close beside Pepe we laid a cheap leather wallet with enough paper money inside to buy food for boy and burro on their way home. We stood there silently a moment and then, very softly, whispered the farewell all good friends say to those about to set forth on a journey: *"Vaya con Dios, amigo!"*

Two days later, when I went out to the Parque Maria Luisa to feed the birds, Alfredo told me of the boy's departure. Even Alfredo at the last believed that the Three Kings had come: "They brought him everything he needed as well as a fine burro. You should have seen him dressed for the journey. You should have seen him ride away on the burro with all the pride of a man. I shall miss that Pepe, *señora.*"

During the rest of my stay in Seville, I went often to the park to feed the birds with Alfredo, but I also missed that scrawny, ill-fed little boy with eyes far too large for his face.

The Christmas Rose

Selma Lagerlöf

ROBBER MOTHER, who lived in Robbers' Cave in Göinge Forest, went down to the village one day on a begging tour. Robber Father, who was an outlawed man, did not dare to leave the forest, but had to content himself with lying in wait for the wayfarers who ventured within its borders. But at that time travelers were not very plentiful in Southern Skåne. If it so happened that the man had had a few weeks of ill luck with his hunt, his wife would take to the road. She took with her five youngsters, and each youngster wore a ragged leathern suit and birch-bark shoes and bore a sack on his back as long as himself. When Robber Mother stepped inside the door of a cabin, no one dared refuse to give her whatever she demanded; for she was not above coming back the following night and setting fire to the house if she had not been well received. Robber Mother and her brood were worse than a pack of wolves, and many a man felt like running a spear through them; but it was never done, because they all knew that the man stayed up in the forest, and he would have known how to wreak vengeance if anything had happened to the children or the old woman.

Now that Robber Mother went from house to house and begged, she came one day to Övid, which at that time was a cloister. She rang the bell of the cloister gate and asked for food. The watchman let down a small wicket in the gate and handed her six round bread cakes – one for herself and one for each of the five children.

While the mother was standing quietly at the gate, her youngsters were running about. And now one of them came and pulled at her skirt, as a signal that he had discovered something which she ought to come and see, and Robber Mother followed him promptly.

The entire cloister was surrounded by a high and strong wall, but the youngster had managed to find a little back gate which stood ajar. When Robber Mother got there, she pushed the gate open and walked inside without asking leave, as it was her custom to do.

Övid Cloister was managed at that time by Abbot Hans, who knew all about herbs. Just within the cloister wall he had planted a little herb garden, and it was into this that the old woman had forced her way.

At first glance Robber Mother was so astonished that she paused at the gate. It was high summertide, and Abbot Hans's garden was so full of flowers that the eyes were fairly dazzled by the blues, reds, and yellows, as one looked into it. But presently an indulgent smile spread over her features, and she started to walk up a narrow path that lay between many flower-beds.

In the garden a lay brother walked about, pulling up weeds. It was he who had left the door in the wall open, that he might throw the weeds and tares on the rubbish heap outside.

When he saw Robber Mother coming in, with all five youngsters in tow, he ran toward her at once and ordered them away. But the beggar woman walked right on as before. She cast her eyes up and down, looking now at the stiff white lilies which spread near the ground, then on the ivy climbing high upon the cloister wall, and took no notice whatever of the lay brother.

He thought she had not understood him, and wanted to take her by the arm and turn her toward the gate. But when the robber woman saw his purpose, she gave him a look that sent him reeling backward. She had been walking with back bent under her beggar's pack, but now she straightened herself to her full height. "I am Robber Mother from Göinge Forest; so touch me if you dare!" And it was obvious that she was as certain she would be left in peace as if she had announced that she was the Queen of Denmark.

And yet the lay brother dared to oppose her, although now, when he knew who she was, he spoke reasonably to her, "You must know, Robber Mother, that this is a monks' cloister, and no woman in the land is allowed within these walls. If you do not go away, the monks will be angry with me because I forgot to close the gate, and perhaps they will drive me away from the cloister and the herb garden."

But such prayers were wasted on Robber Mother. She walked straight ahead among the little flower-beds and looked at the hyssop with its magenta blossoms, and at the honeysuckles, which were full of deep orange-colored flower clusters.

Then the lay brother knew of no other remedy than to run into the cloister and call for help.

He returned with two stalwart monks, and Robber Mother saw that now it meant business! With feet firmly planted she stood in the path and began shrieking in strident tones all the awful vengeance she would wreak on the cloister if she couldn't remain in the herb garden as long as she wished. But the monks did not see why they need fear her and thought only of driving her out. Then Robber Mother let out a perfect volley of shrieks, and, throwing herself upon the monks, clawed and bit at them; so did all the youngsters. The men soon learned that she could overpower them, and all they could do was to go back into the cloister for reinforcements.

As they ran through the passageway which led to the cloister, they met Abbot Hans, who came rushing out to learn what all this noise was about.

Then they had to confess that Robber Mother from Göinge Forest had come into the cloister and that they were unable to drive her out and must call for assistance.

But Abbot Hans upbraided them for using force and forbade their calling for help. He sent both monks back to their work, and although he was an old and fragile man, he took with him only the lay brother.

When Abbot Hans came out in the garden, Robber Mother was still wandering among the flower-beds. He regarded her with astonishment. He was certain that Robber Mother had never before seen an herb garden; yet she sauntered leisurely between all the small patches, each of which had been planted with its own species of rare flower, and looked at them as if they were old acquaintances. At some she smiled, at others she shook her head.

Abbot Hans loved his herb garden as much as it was possible for him to love anything earthly and perishable. Wild and terrible as the old woman looked, he couldn't help liking that she had fought with three monks for the privilege of viewing the garden in peace. He came up to her and asked in a mild tone if the garden pleased her.

Robber Mother turned defiantly toward Abbot Hans, for she expected only to be trapped and overpowered. But when she noticed his white hair and bent form, she answered peaceably, "First, when I saw this, I thought I had never seen a prettier garden; but now I see that it can't be compared with one I know of."

Abbot Hans had certainly expected a different answer. When he heard that Robber Mother had seen a garden more beautiful than his, a faint flush spread over his withered cheek. The lay brother, who was standing close by, immediately began to censure the old woman. "This is Abbot Hans," said he, "who with much care and diligence has gathered the flowers from far and near for his herb garden. We all know that there is not a more beautiful garden to be found in all Skåne, and it is not befitting that you, who live in the wild forest all the year around, should find fault with his work."

"I don't wish to make myself the judge of either him or you," said Robber Mother. "I'm only saying that if you could see the garden of which I am thinking you would uproot all the flowers planted here and cast them away like weeds."

But the Abbot's assistant was hardly less proud of the flowers than the Abbot himself, and after hearing her remarks he laughed derisively. "I can understand that you only talk like this to tease us. It must be a pretty garden that you have made for yourself amongst the pines in Göinge Forest! I'd be willing to wager my soul's salvation that you have never before been within the walls of an herb garden."

Robber Mother grew crimson with rage to think that her word was doubted, and she cried out: "It may be true that until today I had never been within the walls of an herb garden; but you monks, who are holy men, certainly must know that on every Christmas Eve the great Göinge Forest is transformed into a beautiful garden, to commemorate the hour of our Lord's birth. We who live in the forest have seen this happen every year. And in that garden I have seen flowers so lovely that I dared not lift my hand to pluck them."

The lay brother wanted to continue the argument, but Abbot Hans gave him a sign to be silent. For, ever since his childhood, Abbot Hans had heard it said that on every Christmas Eve the forest was dressed in holiday glory. He had often longed to see it, but he had never had the good fortune. Eagerly he begged and implored Robber Mother that he might come up to the Robbers' Cave on Christmas Eve. If she would only send one of her children to show him the way, he could ride up there alone, and he would never betray them – on the contrary, he would reward them, in so far as it lay in his power.

Robber Mother said no at first, for she was thinking of Robber Father and of the peril which might befall him should she permit Abbot Hans to ride up to their cave. At the same time the desire to prove to the monk that the garden which she knew was more beautiful than his got the better of her, and she gave in.

"But more than one follower you cannot take with you," said she, "and you are not to waylay us or trap us, as sure as you are a holy man."

This Abbot Hans promised, and then Robber Mother went her way. Abbot Hans commanded the lay brother not to reveal to a soul that which had been agreed upon. He feared that the monks, should they learn of his purpose, would not allow a man of his years to go up to the Robbers' Cave.

Nor did he himself intend to reveal his project to a human being. And then it happened that Archbishop Absalon from Lund came to Övid and remained through the night. When Abbot Hans was showing him the herb garden, he got to thinking of Robber Mother's visit, and the lay brother, who was at work in the garden, heard Abbot Hans telling the Bishop about Robber Father, who these many years had lived as an outlaw in the forest, and asking him for a letter of ransom for the man, that he might lead an honest life among respectable folk. "As things are now," said Abbot Hans, "his children are growing up into worse malefactors than himself, and you will soon have a whole gang of robbers to deal with up there in the forest."

But the Archbishop replied that he did not care to let the robber loose among honest folk in the villages. It would be best for all that he remain in the forest.

Then Abbot Hans grew zealous and told the Bishop all about Göinge Forest, which, every year at Yuletide, clothed itself in summer bloom around the Robbers' Cave. "If these bandits are not so bad but that God's glories can be made manifest to them, surely we cannot be too wicked to experience the same blessing."

The Archbishop knew how to answer Abbot Hans. "This much I will promise you, Abbot Hans," he said, smiling, "that any day you send me a blossom from the garden in Göinge Forest, I will give you letters of ransom for all the outlaws you may choose to plead for."

The lay brother apprehended that Bishop Absalon believed as little in this story of Robber Mother's as he himself; but Abbot Hans perceived nothing of the sort, but thanked Absalon for his good promise and said that he would surely send him the flower.

Abbot Hans had his way. And the following Christmas Eve he did not sit at home with his monks in Övid Cloister, but was on his way to Göinge Forest. One of Robber Mother's wild youngsters ran ahead of him, and close behind him was the lay brother who had talked with Robber Mother in the herb garden.

Abbot Hans had been longing to make this journey, and he was very happy now that it had come to pass. But it was a different matter with the lay brother who accompanied him. Abbot Hans was very dear to him, and he would not willingly have allowed another to attend him and watch over him; but he didn't believe that he should see any Christmas Eve garden. He thought the whole thing a snare which Robber Mother had, with great cunning, laid for Abbot Hans, that he might fall into her husband's clutches.

While Abbot Hans was riding toward the forest, he saw that everywhere they were preparing to celebrate Christmas. In every peasant settlement fires were lighted in the bathhouse to warm it for the afternoon bathing. Great hunks of meat and bread were being carried from the larders into the cabins, and from the barns came the men with big sheaves of straw to be strewn over the floors.

As he rode by the little country churches, he observed that each parson, with his sexton, was busily engaged in decorating his church; and when he came to the road which leads to Bösjö Cloister, he observed that all the poor of the parish were coming with armfuls of bread and long candles, which they had received at the cloister gate.

When Abbot Hans saw all these Christmas preparations, his haste increased. He was thinking of the festivities that awaited him, which were greater than any the others would be privileged to enjoy.

But the lay brother whined and fretted when he saw how they were preparing to celebrate Christmas in every humble cottage. He grew more and more anxious, and begged and implored Abbot Hans to turn back and not to throw himself deliberately into the robber's hands.

Abbot Hans went straight ahead, paying no heed to his lamentations. He left the plain behind him and came up into desolate and wild forest regions. Here the road was bad, almost like a stony and burr-strewn path, with neither bridge nor plank to help them over brooklet and rivulet. The farther they rode, the colder it grew, and after a while they came upon snow-covered ground.

It turned out to be a long and hazardous ride through the forest. They climbed steep and slippery side paths, crawled over swamp and marsh, and pushed through windfall and bramble. Just as daylight was waning, the robber boy guided them across a forest meadow, skirted by tall, naked leaf trees and green fir trees. Back of the meadow loomed a mountain wall, and in this wall they saw a door of thick boards. Now Abbot Hans understood that they had arrived, and dismounted. The child opened the heavy door for him, and he looked into a poor mountain grotto, with bare stone walls. Robber Mother was seated before a log fire that burned in the middle of the floor. Alongside the walls were beds of virgin pine and moss, and on one of these beds lay Robber Father asleep.

"Come in, you out there!" shouted Robber Mother without rising, "and fetch the horses in with you, so they won't be destroyed by the night cold."

Abbot Hans walked boldly into the cave, and the lay brother followed. Here were wretchedness and poverty! and nothing was done to celebrate Christmas. Robber Mother had neither brewed nor baked; she had neither washed nor scoured. The youngsters were lying on the floor around a kettle, eating; but no better food was provided for them than a watery gruel.

Robber Mother spoke in a tone as haughty and dictatorial as any well-to-do peasant woman. "Sit down by the fire and warm yourself, Abbot Hans," said she, "and if you have food with you, eat, for the food which we in the forest prepare you wouldn't care to taste. And if you are tired after the long journey, you can lie down on one of these beds to sleep. You needn't be afraid of oversleeping, for I'm sitting here by the fire keeping watch. I shall awaken you in time to see that which you have come up here to see."

Abbot Hans obeyed Robber Mother and brought forth his food sack; but he was so fatigued after the journey he was hardly able to eat, and as soon as he could stretch himself on the bed, he fell asleep.

The lay brother was also assigned a bed to rest upon, but he didn't dare sleep, as he thought he had better keep his eye on Robber Father to prevent his getting up and capturing Abbot Hans. But gradually fatigue got the better of him, too, and he dropped into a doze.

When he woke up, he saw that Abbot Hans had left his bed and was sitting by the fire talking with Robber Mother. The outlawed robber sat also by the fire. He was a tall, raw-boned man with a dull, sluggish appearance. His back was turned to Abbot Hans, as though he would have it appear that he was not listening to the conversation.

Abbot Hans was telling Robber Mother all about the Christmas preparations he had seen on the journey, reminding her of Christmas feasts and games which she must have known in her youth, when she lived at peace with mankind. "I'm sorry for your children, who can never run on the village street in holiday dress or tumble in the Christmas straw," said he.

At first Robber Mother answered in short, gruff sentences, but by degrees she became more subdued and listened more intently. Suddenly Robber Father turned toward Abbot Hans and shook his clenched fist in his face. "You miserable monk! Did you come here to coax from me my wife and children? Don't you know that I am an outlaw and may not leave the forest?"

Abbot Hans looked him fearlessly in the eyes. "It is my purpose to get a letter of ransom for you from Archbishop Absalon," said he. He had hardly finished speaking when the robber and his wife burst out laughing. They knew well enough the kind of mercy a forest robber could expect from Bishop Absalon!

"Oh, if I get a letter of ransom from Absalon," said Robber Father, "then I'll promise you that never again will I steal so much as a goose."

The lay brother was annoyed with the robber folk for daring to laugh at Abbot Hans, but on his own account he was well pleased. He had seldom seen the Abbot sitting more peaceful and meek with his monks at Övid than he now sat with this wild robber folk.

Suddenly Robber Mother rose. "You sit here and talk, Abbot Hans," she said, "so that we are forgetting to look at the forest. Now I can hear, even in this cave, how the Christmas bells are ringing."

The words were barely uttered when they all sprang up and rushed out. But in the forest it was still dark night and bleak winter. The only thing they marked was a distant clang borne on a light south wind.

"How can this bell ringing ever awaken the dead forest?" thought Abbot Hans. For now, as he stood out in the winter darkness, he thought it far more impossible that a summer garden could spring up here than it had seemed to him before.

When the bells had been ringing a few moments, a sudden illumination penetrated the forest; the next moment it was dark again, and then the light came back. It pushed its way forward between the stark trees, like a shimmering mist. This much it effected: The darkness merged into a faint daybreak. Then Abbot Hans saw that the snow had vanished from the ground, as if someone had removed a carpet, and the earth began to take on a green covering. Then the ferns shot up their fronds, rolled like a bishop's staff. The heather that grew on the stony hills and the bog-myrtle rooted in the ground moss dressed themselves quickly in new bloom. The moss-tufts thickened and raised themselves, and the spring blossoms shot upward their swelling buds, which already had a touch of color.

Abbot Hans's heart beat fast as he marked the first signs of the forest's awakening. "Old man that I am, shall I behold such a miracle?" thought he, and the tears wanted to spring to his eyes. Again it grew so hazy that he feared the darkness would once more cover the earth; but almost immediately there came a new wave of light. It brought with it the splash of rivulet and the rush of cataract. Then the leaves of the trees burst into bloom, as if a swarm of green butterflies came flying and clustered on the branches. It was not only trees and plants that awoke, but crossbeaks hopped from branch to branch, and the woodpeckers hammered on the limbs until the splinters fairly flew around them. A flock of starlings from up country lighted in a fir top to rest. They were paradise starlings. The tips of each tiny feather shone in brilliant reds, and, as the birds moved, they glittered like so many jewels.

Again, all was dark for an instant, but soon there came a new light wave. A fresh, warm south wind blew and scattered over the forest meadow all the little seeds that had been brought from southern lands by birds and ships and winds, and which could not thrive elsewhere because of this country's cruel cold. These took root and sprang up the instant they touched the ground.

When the next warm wind came along, the blueberries and lingon ripened. Cranes and wild geese shrieked in the air, the bullfinches built nests, and the baby squirrels began playing on the branches of the trees.

Everything came so fast now that Abbot Hans could not stop to reflect on how immeasurably great was the miracle that was taking place. He had time only to use his eyes and ears. The next light wave that came rushing in brought with it the scent of newly ploughed acres, and far off in the distance the milkmaids were heard coaxing the cows – and the tinkle of the sheep's bells. Pine and spruce trees were so thickly clothed with red cones that they shone like crimson mantles. The juniper berries changed color every second, and forest flowers covered the ground till it was all red, blue, and yellow.

Abbot Hans bent down to the earth and broke off a wild strawberry blossom, and, as he straightened up, the berry ripened in his hand.

The mother fox came out of her lair with a big litter of black-legged young. She went up to Robber Mother and scratched at her skirt, and Robber Mother bent down to her and praised her young. The horned owl, who had just begun his night chase, was astonished at the light and went back to his ravine to perch for the night. The male cuckoo crowed, and his mate stole up to the nests of the little birds with her egg in her mouth.

Robber Mother's youngsters let out perfect shrieks of delight. They stuffed themselves with wild strawberries that hung on the bushes, large as pinecones. One of them played with a litter of young hares; another ran a race with some young crows, which had hopped from their nest before they were really ready; a third caught up an adder from the ground and wound it around his neck and arm.

Robber Father was standing out on a marsh eating raspberries. When he glanced up, a big black bear stood beside him. Robber Father broke off an osier twig and struck the bear on the nose. "Keep to your own ground, you!" he said; "this is my turf." Then the huge bear turned around and lumbered off in another direction.

New waves of warmth and light kept coming, and now they brought with them seeds from the starflower. Golden

pollen from rye fields fairly flew in the air. Then came butterflies, so big that they looked like flying lilies. The bee-
hive in a hollow oak was already so full of honey that it
dripped down on the trunk of the tree. Then all the flowers
whose seed had been brought from foreign lands began to
blossom. The loveliest roses climbed up the mountain wall
in a race with the blackberry vines, and from the forest
meadow sprang flowers as large as human faces.

Abbot Hans thought of the flower he was to pluck for
Bishop Absalon; but each new flower that appeared was
more beautiful than the others, and he wanted to choose
the most beautiful of all.

Wave upon wave kept coming until the air was so filled
with light that it glittered. All the life and beauty and joy
of summer smiled on Abbot Hans. He felt that earth could
bring no greater happiness than that which welled up about
him, and he said to himself, "I do not know what new
beauties the next wave that comes can bring with it."

But the light kept streaming in, and now it seemed to
Abbot Hans that it carried with it something from an infinite distance. He felt a celestial atmosphere enfolding him,
and tremblingly he began to anticipate, now that earth's joys
had come, that the glories of heaven were approaching.

Then Abbot Hans marked how all grew still; the birds
hushed their songs, the flowers ceased growing, and the
young foxes played no more. The glory now nearing was
such that the heart wanted to stop beating; the eyes wept
without one's knowing it; the soul longed to soar away into
the Eternal. From far in the distance faint harp tones were
heard, and celestial song, like a soft murmur, reached him.

Abbot Hans clasped his hands and dropped to his knees.

His face was radiant with bliss. Never had he dreamed that even in this life it should be granted him to taste the joys of heaven, and to hear angels sing Christmas carols!

But beside Abbot Hans stood the lay brother who had accompanied him. In his mind there were dark thoughts. "This cannot be a true miracle," he thought, "since it is revealed to malefactors. This does not come from God, but has its origin in witchcraft and is sent hither by Satan. It is the Evil One's power that is tempting us and compelling us to see that which has no real existence."

From afar were heard the sound of angel harps and the tones of a Miserere. But the lay brother thought it was the evil spirits of hell coming closer. "They would enchant and seduce us," sighed he, "and we shall be sold into perdition."

The angel throng was so near now that Abbot Hans saw their bright forms through the forest branches. The lay brother saw them, too; but back of all this wondrous beauty he saw only some dread evil. For him it was the devil who performed these wonders on the anniversary of our Savior's birth. It was done simply for the purpose of more effectually deluding poor human beings.

All the while the birds had been circling around the head of Abbot Hans, and they let him take them in his hands. But all the animals were afraid of the lay brother; no bird perched on his shoulder, no snake played at his feet. Then there came a little forest dove. When she marked that the angels were nearing, she plucked up courage and flew down on the lay brother's shoulder and laid her head against his cheek.

Then it appeared to him as if sorcery were come right upon him, to tempt and corrupt him. He struck with his hand at the forest dove and cried in such a loud voice that it rang throughout the forest, "Go thou back to hell, whence thou art come!"

Just then the angels were so near that Abbot Hans felt the feathery touch of their great wings, and he bowed down to earth in reverent greeting.

But when the lay brother's words sounded, their song was hushed and the holy guests turned in flight. At the same time the light and the mild warmth vanished in un-speakable terror for the darkness and cold in a human heart. Darkness sank over the earth, like a coverlet; frost came, all the growths shriveled up; the animals and birds hastened away; the rushing of streams was hushed; the leaves dropped from the trees, rustling like rain.

Abbot Hans felt how his heart, which had but lately swelled with bliss, was now contracting with insufferable agony. "I can never outlive this," thought he, "that the an-gels from heaven had been so close to me and were driven away; that they wanted to sing Christmas carols for me and were driven to flight."

Then he remembered the flower he had promised Bishop Absalon, and at the last moment he fumbled among the leaves and moss to try and find a blossom. But he sensed how the ground under his fingers froze and how the white snow came gliding over the ground. Then his heart caused him even greater anguish. He could not rise, but fell pros-trate on the ground and lay there.

When the robber folk and the lay brother had groped their way back to the cave, they missed Abbot Hans. They took brands with them and went out to search for him. They found him dead upon the coverlet of snow.

Then the lay brother began weeping and lamenting, for he understood that it was he who had killed Abbot Hans because he had dashed from him the cup of happiness which he had been thirsting to drain to its last drop.

WHEN ABBOT HANS had been carried down to Övid, those who took charge of the dead saw that he held his right hand locked tight around something which he must have grasped at the moment of death. When they finally got his hand opened, they found that the thing which he had held in such an iron grip was a pair of white root bulbs, which he had torn from among the moss and leaves.

When the lay brother who had accompanied Abbot Hans saw the bulbs, he took them and planted them in Abbot Hans's herb garden.

He guarded them the whole year to see if any flower would spring from them. But in vain he waited through the spring, the summer, and the autumn. Finally, when winter had set in and all the leaves and the flowers were dead, he ceased caring for them.

But when Christmas Eve came again, he was so strongly reminded of Abbot Hans that he wandered out into the garden to think of him. And look! as he came to the spot where he had planted the bare root bulbs, he saw that from them had sprung flourishing green stalks, which bore beautiful flowers with silver white leaves.

He called out all the monks at Övid, and when they saw that this plant bloomed on Christmas Eve, when all the other growths were as if dead, they understood that this flower had in truth been plucked by Abbot Hans from the

Christmas garden in Göinge Forest. Then the lay brother asked the monks if he might take a few blossoms to Bishop Absalon.

And when he appeared before Bishop Absalon, he gave him the flowers and said: "Abbot Hans sends you these. They are the flowers he promised to pick for you from the garden in Göinge Forest."

When Bishop Absalon beheld the flowers, which had sprung from the earth in darkest winter, and heard the words, he turned as pale as if he had met a ghost. He sat in silence a moment; thereupon he said, "Abbot Hans has faithfully kept his word and I shall also keep mine." And he ordered that a letter of ransom be drawn up for the wild robber who was outlawed and had been forced to live in the forest ever since his youth.

He handed the letter to the lay brother, who departed at once for the robbers' cave. When he stepped in there on Christmas Day, the robber came toward him with axe uplifted. "I'd like to hack you monks into bits, as many as you are!" said he. "It must be your fault that Göinge Forest did not last night dress itself in Christmas bloom."

"The fault is mine alone," said the lay brother, "and I will gladly die for it; but first I must deliver a message from Abbot Hans." And he drew forth the Bishop's letter and told the man that he was free. "Hereafter you and your children shall play in the Christmas straw and celebrate your Christmas among people, just as Abbot Hans wished to have it," said he.

Then Robber Father stood there pale and speechless, but Robber Mother said in his name, "Abbot Hans has indeed kept his word, and Robber Father will keep his."

When the robber and his wife left the cave, the lay brother moved in and lived all alone in the forest, in constant meditation and prayer that his hard-heartedness might be forgiven him.

But Göinge Forest never again celebrated the hour of our Savior's birth; and of all its glory, there lives today only the plant which Abbot Hans had plucked. It has been named the Christmas Rose. And each year at Christmastide she sends forth from the earth her green stalks and white blossoms, as if she never could forget that she had once grown in the great Christmas garden at Göinge Forest.

Sources and Acknowledgments

Orbis Books has made every effort to identify the owner of each story in this book, and to obtain permission from the author, publisher, or agent in question. In the event of inadvertent errors, please notify us so that we can correct the next printing.

"Brother Robber" by Helene Christaller is reprinted from *Behold That Star: A Christmas Anthology* (Farmington, PA: Plough, 1966) and was originally published as "Bruder Räuber" in *Lichter im Strom*, by Helene Christaller, copyright by Friedrich Reinhardt AG Verlag, Basel. Reprinted by permission of Erdmann Nöeldeke.

"Three Young Kings" by George Sumner Albee is reprinted from *McCall's*, December 1955.

"Transfiguration" by Madeleine L'Engle (1992) is reprinted by permission of the author and Lescher and Lescher, Ltd., New York.

"Willibald's Trip to Heaven" by Reimmichl is a new translation of "The Cribmaker's Trip to Heaven," from *Behold That Star: A Christmas Anthology* (Farmington, PA: Plough, 1966). Originally published as "Der Krippenmachers Himmelgang" in *Weihnacht in Tirol*, by Reimmichl, copyright Verlagsanstalt Tyrolia, GMBH, Innsbruck. Used with permission of the publisher.

"The Guest" by Nikolai S. Lesskov is a translation of *Der Gast beim Bauern* (Paulus Verlag, Recklinghausen) and was first published in English in *The World's Christmas*, edited by Olive Wyon, copyright 1964 by SCM Press, Ltd.

"Christmas Day in the Morning" by Pearl S. Buck is reprinted by permission of Harold Ober Associates Incorporated, copyright © 1955 by Pearl S. Buck. Copyright renewed 1983.

"The Other Wise Man" by Henry van Dyke is reprinted from *The Other Wise Man* by Henry van Dyke (New York: Harper Brothers, 1899).

"The Miraculous Staircase" by Arthur Gordon is reprinted with permission from Guideposts. Copyright © 1966 by Guideposts, Carmel, NY 10512. All rights reserved.

"No Room in the Inn" by Katherine Paterson is reprinted from *A Midnight Clear: Stories for the Christmas Season* by Katherine Paterson, copyright © 1995 by Minna Murra, Inc. Used by permission of Lodestar Books, an affiliate of Dutton Children's Books, a Division of Penguin Young Readers Group, a Member of Penguin Group (USA) Inc., 345 Hudson Street, New York, NY 10014. All rights reserved.

More Classic Tales

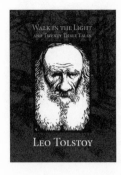

Walk in the Light
And Twenty-Three Tales
Leo Tolstoy

Uncluttered by the complexities of plot and character that daunt so many readers of the longer Russian masterpieces, Tolstoy's tales illumine eternal truths with forceful brevity. While inspired by a sense of spiritual certainty, their narrative quality, subtle humor, and visionary power lift them far above the common run of "religious" literature. Moralists purport to tell us what our lives should mean, and how we should live them. Tolstoy, on the other hand, has an uncanny gift for conveying what it means to be truly alive.

Contents: A Talk among Leisured People • Walk in the Light • God Sees the Truth, but Waits • A Prisoner in the Caucasus • The Bear-Hunt • What Men Live By • A Spark Neglected Burns the House • Two Old Men • Where Love Is, God Is • The Story of Ivan the Fool • Evil Allures, but Good Endures • Little Girls Wiser than Men • Ilyas • The Three Hermits • The Imp and the Crust • How Much Land Does a Man Need? • A Grain as Big as a Hen's Egg • The Godson • The Repentant Sinner • The Empty Drum • The Coffeehouse of Surat • Too Dear! • Esarhaddon, King of Assyria • Work, Death, and Sickness: a Legend • Three Questions

Please support your local bookstore, or call 1-800-258-5838.
For a free catalog, please write us at:
Orbis Books, Box 308
Maryknoll, NY 10454-0308
Or visit our website at www.orbisbooks.com

More Holiday Reading

Watch for the Light
Readings for Advent and Christmas

This collection of Advent meditations from favorite classic and contemporary spiritual writers provides inspiration for the most widely celebrated – and most maligned – holiday of the year. Ecumenical in scope, these fifty essays and poems celebrate the miracle of Christ's birth and infuse it with rich meaning for today. Authors include Arnold, Bonhoeffer, Day, Dillard, Eliot, Hopkins, Kierkegaard, C. S. Lewis, L'Engle, Manning, Merton, Norris, Nouwen, Romero, Yancey, and many others.

Bread and Wine
Readings for Lent and Easter

Containing selections grouped around such themes as temptation, crucifixion, resurrection, and new life, *Bread and Wine* can be dipped into at leisure or used as a guide to daily devotions – and returned to any time of year for spiritual revitalization. For breadth of scope and depth of insight, nothing rivals this collection. Authors include Arnold, Augustine, Berry, Chesterton, Day, Dostoevsky, Gibran, Kierkegaard, C. S. Lewis, Merton, Norris, Pascal, Tolstoy, Wilde, and many others.

Note: This title available from Orbis Books in 2006.

For more information on these and other titles, contact Orbis Books, Box 308, Maryknoll, NY 10454-0308, or visit our website at www.orbisbooks.com